✝

WARS I HAVE SEEN

BY GERTRUDE STEIN

RANDOM HOUSE · NEW YORK

THIS IS A RANDOM HOUSE WARTIME BOOK

IT IS MANUFACTURED UNDER
EMERGENCY CONDITIONS AND
COMPLIES WITH THE GOVERN-
MENT'S REQUEST TO CONSERVE
ESSENTIAL MATERIALS IN
EVERY POSSIBLE WAY.

Copyright, 1945, by Random House, Inc.

*Published simultaneously in Canada by
Random House of Canada Limited*

Manufactured in the U. S. A. by J. J. Little & Ives Co.

Designer: Ernst Reichl

WARS I HAVE SEEN

IDO NOT KNOW whether to put in the things I do not remember as well as the things I do remember. To begin with I was born, that I do not remember but I was told about it quite often, I was not born during the night but about eight o'clock in the morning and my father whenever I had anything the matter with me always reproached me by telling me that I had been born a perfect baby. I do not know whether the four living and the two dead older children had not been born equally perfect babies at any rate my father never reproached them with it when there was anything the matter with them. Anyway though I could not remember it from the beginning there was no doubt that I was the youngest of the children and as such naturally I had privileges the privilege of petting the privilege of being the youngest one. If that does happen it is not lost all the rest of one's life, there you are you are privileged, nobody can do anything but take care of you, that is the way I was and that is the way I still am, and any one who is like that necessarily liked it. I did and do.

The next thing I heard about myself was that I was eight months old. Of course I had been born in America, of course we were all of us born in America but all the same when I was eight months old we were not there. My uncle used to tell me about that. He was an art student in Germany, at that time, my mother's family who were not rich although all born in America and were not people who liked business, even if their father was a tanner, but tanning is not really a business at least it was not in those days, it was a trade and so my uncle after my mother married my father was helped by my father to go to Germany to study sculpture. In those far away days, Americans went to Germany to study art particularly sculpture and then after that they finished in Rome. That was the way it was and we were all in Europe and I was eight months old and they left me in the arms of my uncle, why was never explained, but anyway I cried and ladies he knew came along and he did not like it. He was young then but I was so much younger that he did not like it. He often told me about that many years after.

The next thing that happened was that I was a very little older and we were in Vienna, a nice place then. And now there was something I could remember as well as some things I could be helped to remember by hearing them told again and again, then and later.

Born that way there is no reason why I should have seen so many wars. I have seen three. The Spanish-American war, the first world war and now the second world war.

There were of course a number of others that did not particularly concern me. The Boer war I remembered that one, the Japanese-Chinese war, and the Russian-Japanese war I remember that one very well too. Each one of these wars I remember for another reason. I suppose it is not so remarkable that I should have seen so many wars having seen a good many countries when I was a baby and having a feeling about countries which I suppose sooner or later since wars are make you be one of those that see them.

And so we were in Vienna and I have never seen it again but it has always remained for me something very real. It was there that I first came to be and so of course it was real and then there were really things, there was a public garden, a formal garden and in a kind of a way a formal garden pleases a child's fancy more than a natural garden. It is more like a garden that you would make

yourself. And there was music and there was the old emperor who
was a natural figure to have in a formal garden and there was his
national anthem and then there were the salt caves and then there
were birds and butterflies and insects in the woods and there was
the catching of them and there was good eating and on my third
birthday a taste of Vienna beer. And there were my mother and
my brothers on horseback and there was a Czech tutor, one did not
realise how important all these nationalities were going to be to
every one then and a Hungarian governess, and there was the first
contact with books, picture books but books all the same since
pictures in picture books are narrative. I have just bought twenty
of them for the school children of Bilignin and they are narrative.

My mother so I heard them say at a later day did not like being
in Vienna all alone with five children. She had had a sister from
Baltimore with her, but she had gone away, my father had gone
back to America on business and my mother said she wanted to be
nearer America so she packed up and left the tutor and governess
behind her and with the five children she went to Paris. I continued
to be the youngest one. I was about four years old then and I do not
know whether I really remembered more about Paris but I think
I did. It always does make war because one of the things that
seemed to me in 1914 was that Paris was then the way I remembered it when I was four only then there was no war. But war
makes things go backward as well as forward and so 1914 was the
same as 1878 in a way.

Of course there are a good many times when there is no war
just as there are a good many times when there is a war. To be sure
when there is a war the years are longer that is to say the days are
longer the months are longer the years are much longer but the
weeks are shorter that is what makes a war. And when there is no
war, well just now I cannot remember just how it is when there is
no war.

And then my mother had enough even in Paris of being away
from America and all her family in Baltimore and my father going
back to America to do business and so we all packed up, after

having bought dozens of everything and we went to London and then to America. In London there was no war no war at all but the first theatre I ever saw, which was Pinafore and I do not remember it but I remember the hall of the theatre and I remember a glitter and I remember that one followed the other and that was all there was of London. The trip home on the boat I do not remember at all and I do not remember that any one ever said there was anything to remember. Up to that time such emotions as I had had expressed themselves in German and then in French and then in Baltimore although I do not think we stayed there very long emotions began to feel themselves in English. There was the one my mother told that there was one little Indian two little Indians three little Indian boys, four little five little six little seven little eight little Indian boys. And then also war obtruded itself, I do not quite know how but Baltimore was a place where when my mother was young there had been a war, and where she had seen the Yankee soldiers going from one station to another and they had been shot at and she remembered it and we remembered it and there was a mysterious uncle who went all through the war and came out with or without or only with or only without a pair of shoes and he was then in the shoe business and naturally there was a connection. It was only later when I was a passionate admirer of General Grant and the Northern army that I realised that the uncle had been in the Southern army.

After Baltimore we went to California and then I really did begin to remember. I naturally did remember, not all, but at least really some landscape as well as eating and moving. I do not remember that we saw Indians but I was told afterwards that we had, and now for almost a great number of years there was no war, there was history of course and there was the civil war which had been but otherwise there were no wars. Such wars as there were were inside in me, and naturally although I was a very happy child there were quite a number of such wars. Not many with anybody else because I was not quarrelsome and continuing being the youngest in the family continued being very well taken care of by everybody, also as being the youngest I had cajoling ways, one has when one continues to be the youngest.

In time of war you know much more what children feel than in time of peace, not that children feel more but you have to know more about what they feel. In time of peace what children feel concerns the lives of the children as children but in time of war there is a mingling there is not children's lives and grown up lives there is just lives and so quite naturally you have to know what children feel. And so it being now war and I seeing just incidentally but nevertheless inevitably seeing and knowing of the feeling of children of any age I do not now have to remember about my feeling but just feel the feeling of having been a certain age. And so there was life in California from about six to sixteen, and as each thing happened it did happen. So many things happened but really in remembering not more than one or two a year certainly not one every month certainly not one every week certainly not one every day. Well say two or three a year. Quite enough too to remember because the rest of the time was just the rest of the time.

During these years there was no war and if there was it was not any war of mine. But of course there was history, and there were novels historical novels and so there was in a way war all the time. Why not when there is always war and sometimes a nice war and sometimes an interesting war. And children do not take war seriously as war. War is soldiers and soldiers have not to be war but they have to be soldiers. Which is a nice thing. I remember that the only war that was not soldiers to me but war was the civil war. The other wars were soldiers emotion and something to see. They said things that sounded like soldiers not like war, but the civil war, not the other wars in America, not the revolutionary war or Indian wars they were soldiers not war. One of the first outside of English wars that I remember and after all that was an English war was the defeat of Braddock by the Indians because we had a story about that but this again was soldiers and not war but the American civil war was not soldiers it was war. And it is like the wars now they are not soldiers they are war. Veterans always feel that it is soldiers even though they know that it is war. Somehow General Grant was not a soldier he was war and that is the reason I liked him.

Well all this time I went to school and school in California meant knowing lots of nationalities. And if you went to school with them and knew about their hair and their ways and all you were bound later not to be surprised that Germans are as they are and French and Greeks and Chinamen and Japs. There is nothing afterward but confirmation confirmation of what you knew, because nobody changes, they may develop but they do not change and so if you went to school with them why should you not know them. Some one was just telling me that in German universities they had professors who studied the characteristics of races. Quite unnecessary if you went to school with them but naturally the Germans did not know that. General Grant did. He had been to school with all the Generals of the civil war so he always knew what they would do.

That was the thing that interested me the most in the memoirs that he wrote and that I read.

And so to go back to historical wars. I naturally liked history and Shakespeare's plays and historical novels and there was always war. Of course ancient history was full of wars and the Decline and Fall of the Roman Empire was full of war but these did not any of them interest me as wars. English wars interested me, some French wars and the American civil war. And I was right because the American civil war was the prototype of all the wars the two big wars that I have completely lived. Also the American civil war.

Naturally my mother being Baltimore there was the South, and naturally there was the north. My father I never took on in war although he was north.

Of course there were Indian wars naturally there was no cinema then but if there had been, Indian wars would have been like that, although one could know people who had been in them and could see them the real Indians on the stage and there was Fenimore Cooper they were not real wars, not as real as some English wars in history and certainly not as real as the American civil war. A very real war.

But naturally all my childhood was not taken up with enjoying past wars, although as an omnivorous reader naturally there was a great deal of war. There was one very funny thing about wars as a child sees it, although there are so many killed there being so many dead is not very real at all, my feeling about that was quite a separate thing and had nothing to do with wars. And that is natural enough. However near a war is it is always not very near. Even when it is here. It is very funny that but it is true. Perhaps if one were a boy it would be different but I do not think so. I think even when men are in a war actually in a war it is not very near, it is here but it is not very near. That is the way it seems to me from all I can hear and from all I can see. But the civil war was quite near. As near as a war can be. But as I say my childhood actual childhood had nothing to do with wars. As it really happened there were no wars just then none at all. There were just at the end of my adolescence but never before. From babyhood to the Boer war there was no war. No war at all.

So I had my childhood and my adolescence without outside of me there being any war.

What is there inside in one that makes one know all about war. You ask questions now why in Russia do not the Germans surrender when they are surrounded. And there is no answer except that perhaps they are afraid to. Perhaps. What is there inside one that makes one know all about war.

Death starts history and fears. And that begins very soon and dies out little by little or not at all or all.

A farmer on a hill said of the Germans, do not say that it had to do with their leaders, they are a people whose fate it is to always choose a man whom they force to lead them in a direction in which they do not want to go.

This same person on this same hill was saying, it was after a thunderstorm and we were talking about it together. Yes he said it is like them to call it a thunder and lightning war. Thunder and lightning a storm of thunder and lightning can cause a fair amount of damage and frightens you enormously but leaves nothing else behind it, no after-effect at all.

And so from the time I was little all through my adolescence although I read and read about wars, if you like history and historical novels you have to and historical plays, but there was no really outside war at least none that I noticed or that anybody around me noticed.

For a very long time I did not know what it was to be a child although I remembered it so well and I wrote as if I knew but actually there is a great difference between having it and remembering it, and there are so many children just now and as many ages as there are in a country school.

I went out in the moonlight, and it was so lovely and not cold although January and in the mountains and I took a walk and I met on the road a young gendarme who the French army having been demobilised had gone into the gendarmerie. He was not of the village that is to say he had married a girl in the village as he had been in garrison at Belley and they had had a simple wedding and had brought their own champagne and sausages and now they had a baby. And I said how goes it and he said I have just been appointed to the personal guard of the Marechal. Marechal Petain. Why that I said is a great promotion. Yes he said I do not know why, well I said you are rather better educated than your comrades, no he said just primary school, like they all have. And now he said I am going to Vichy and they are having my uniform made and I accompany him wherever he goes on my motorcycle. You know how to ride one I said. Oh yes he said I rode one in the war I was in the cavalry. Oh said I you were not then always in the Alpine troops, no he said after I escaped, I was a prisoner, I thought I would like a change. And said he now I am the personal guard of the Marechal and I am permanently attached to the government and if he dies whoever succeeds him, whether it is a dictator or something different I will be the personal guard of the government. He was only twenty-two and I wished him good luck and said perhaps we would meet in Paris and said he if the government goes there I will but I hope it will be free and I said I have good hope and he said I always have had and he said he was would say good-bye to me before he left and I said surely, and I went on walking with my white dog in the moonlight.

So as I say I know what it is to be any age now that there is a war and so remembering back is not only remembering but might be being.

It is funny about wars, they ought to be different but they are not.

In a way that is what makes it nice about France. In one war they upset the Germans by resisting unalterably steadily and patiently and valiantly for four years, in the next war they upset them just as much by not resisting at all and going under completely in six weeks. Well that is what makes them changeable enough to create styles.

So I was five years old when we came back to America having known Austrians Germans and French French, and now American English, a nice world if there is enough of it, and more or less there always is.

Back to America and Baltimore where my mother's people came from, I do not know why but one is always proud of the places your people come from, you may never see them or perhaps never see them again as a matter of fact I did but nevertheless, that is where your mother came from and I suppose there is more meaning to that than where you were born particularly if you never saw it again there where you were born that is where I was born. In Allegheny Pennsylvania. Anything can be a dream, and in war it is more a dream than anywhere. Just now they have sent forty thousand people out of their homes in Marseilles, it is so real to me that it is a dream, not that I know any of them, if I did it would not be a dream but we were in Marseilles so much during the last war and that makes it a dream and in San Francisco when I was a child along the water front, the women of the town all of them came from Marseilles, and when I saw them in Avignon and Arles along the river front and at Marseilles they all seemed to be wearing the same wrappers, that is the kind of dressing gowns that they wore in San Francisco not far from Chinatown and that we used to see when we went to San Francisco with our parents, so that is what war is it is the inhabitants in geography.

A very nice kind of war was the Indian mutiny the Sepoy revolt. I always liked reading about that from Jules Verne on, it was such a satisfactory sort of war for the young, it could not be more satisfactory, there were so few killed and even very few wounded and everybody was a hero, and there were no crowds, Hindoos of course but no other crowds to confuse you. In a modern war there are no crowds because everybody is in it, so much so that there are no individuals, well that is something else, it is a queer life one leads in a modern war, every day so much can happen and every day is just the same and is mostly food, food and in spite of all that is happening every day is food, I had a a friend who used to say Life dear Life, life is strife, life is a dear life in every way and life is strife in every way. The Germans say that war is natural peace is only an armistice that the natural thing is war, well that is natural enough because of course it is so, only when you have too much of it it is just as dull as peace, that is when you have had too much of it. And so I was a little girl in East Oakland California and of course one did have to find out that life although it was life there was death although there was death, and you had to find out that stars were worlds and moved around and that there were comets and that there was wind and rain, grass and flowers and birds and butterflies were less exciting in California, but most of all there were books and food, food and books, both excellent things. And then also and this is strange if you like but I was then already sceptical about Utopias, naturally so, I liked habits but I did not like that habits should be known as mine. Habits like dogs dogs have habits but they do not like to be told about their habits, and the only way to have a Utopia is not only to have habits but to be liked to be told about these habits, and this I did not like. I can remember very well not liking to be told that I had habits.

To come back to Shakespeare, Shakespeare which I read so much mostly the plays about wars, English kings and wars often said that nothing was anything that human beings had no meaning, that not anything had any meaning and everything was just like that. And it did worry me even when I was seven and eight not really worried me but it was there and then well not then but all the years I was grown up it was not like that and now when here in France when we all thought the young men were safe they are now all being taken away well it is like that, Shakespeare was right it is all just like that, even superstitions are all just like that, they mostly, said the very tall thirteen-year-old girl, they are always bad luck and then we all hope again, just like that, and although Shakespeare is right, we all do hope again.

Once upon a time the moon shone.

The visitors came.

The piano was struck that is the keys.

The ages although only differing between themselves and fifteen made them polite and complimentary, and no one is careless and if they are there is a loss.

War is never fatal but always lost. Always lost. And as they all said this, they knew that they meant what they said. Always lost.

And this brings me back to the time between eight and twelve when I read and read and in between I read all the historical plays of Shakespeare and all the other plays of Shakespeare and more and more this war of 1942-1943 makes it like that. The horrors the fears everybody's fears the helplessness of everybody's fears, so different from other wars makes this war like Shakespeare's plays. Rose d'Aiguy thirteen years old had just said that now having become superstitious because of course she has now become superstitious she notices that all the signs are bad signs, just like Macbeth just like Julius Caesar, the ides of March, and the general confusion, the general fear, the general helplessness, the general nervousness is just like all the kings, they are like that and they go on like that. The war 1914-1918 was not like Shakespeare but this war is the meaninglessness of why makes all the nothingness so real and when

I read Shakespeare between eight and twelve, I suppose I was drowned in all that but naturally did not believe it or did I. Certainly not later when there was more meaning and more dread. But in Shakespeare there is no meaning and no dread, there is confusion and fear, and that is what is now here.

It was when I was between twelve and seventeen that I went through the dark and dreadful days of adolescence, in which predominated the fear of death, not so much of death as of dissolution, and naturally is war like that. It is and it is not. One really can say that in war-time there is death death and death but is there dissolution. I wonder. May that not be one of the reasons among so many others why wars go on, and why particularly adolescents need it.

It was a very long time between twelve and seventeen, between Shakespeare and the Boer war which was the first war I knew to be a war, a real war where a country that was a natural country was at war.

And in between there was religion, which too had to do with adolescence and with war.

There is no love interest in these modern wars. I am speaking of the world wars but particularly of the 1939 war, there is no love interest, very little religion and no love interest. Religious people in these world wars are religious but otherwise they are like everybody in what they do and lovers the same way they may be in love but otherwise they are like everybody which was not at all as war was to me from babyhood to 1900, not at all.

From babyhood to fourteen which is the beginning of adolescence, life is mostly taken up with slowly knowing that stars are worlds, that words are ways and that force is strength and that wiles are ways as words are, in other words that one is one and that the others can come to be with that one. That is what is most occupying from babyhood to fourteen, and during that time there are things like having apples given one to take home one for you and the other four for the other four and slowly one by one they are eaten until there is none, and there is the reason for eating the last

one because since the other ones are eaten then of course there is
no sense in keeping the last one, because then the story has to be
told and why should it since after all all your life you can have it as
remorse that it has been done. War is like that, it goes on like that
it keeps going on like that and soon nobody has anything to eat
that is nobody who does not take what does not belong to them and
later although there is remorse the very last one has been eaten if
not there has to be an explanation and if there is an explanation
that does not help remorse nor does it help any one, remorse does
not and not eating it does not, and so as I was then so am I now,
and war, was not then but the feeling was just the same and eating
was just the same in so many ways. A fish bone can even be a worry
anything that can happen or has happened or has not happened
can be a worry and that is what war is, and so what is the difference
between life and war. There is none.

So then between babyhood and fourteen there are all these
things, and romantic war with them, not to believe in but to
dream.

Between babyhood and fourteen there was frequent change of
scene. Modern wars all wars are like that, they go places, where
they never heard of in many cases, and between babyhood and
fourteen there had been so many changes of scene. And different
ways of traveling about, and that also is like war. Just now all the
young men of France have to go, they do not know where, some of
them run away and when they run away they do not know where
and a great many of them are taken away they do not know where
and this is all as it was between babyhood and fourteen. Europe
and America and railroad and water and stage coach and walking
and horse back and in every there was no astonishment and that
is the way war is.

I remember being very worried in reading, if anybody in the
book died and did not have children because then nobody in that
family could be living yet, and if they were not living yet how
could they hear what was happening. This always bothered me
from that time on until just now and now well now it does seem

that the future is not important any more, the world has become so shrunken and it will never be different and so it does not mean much and there is no love interest, it is mostly parents who suffer, perhaps it was like that between babyhood and fourteen.

Dear Life life is strife Claribel used to say, but she did say dear life and in any way it is and she did say life is strife but is it.

It was all that between babyhood and fourteen, and it was the nineteenth century between babyhood and fourteen and the nineteenth century dies hard all centuries do that is why the last war to kill it is so long, it is still being killed now in 1942, the nineteenth century just as the eighteenth century took from the revolution to 1840 to kill, so the nineteenth century is taking from 1914 to 1943 to kill. It is hard to kill a century almost impossible, as was the old joke about mothers-in-law, and centuries get to be like that they get to be wearing like a mother-in-law. So as I was saying from babyhood to fourteen and of course longer much longer it was the nineteenth century and the wars civil domestic and foreign were nineteenth century wars, naturally enough.

Saint George and the Dragon, Siegfried and the dragon, anybody and the dragon, the dragon is always the century any century that anybody is trying to kill, and the worst of it all is that the one that says he is trying to kill the century that has to be killed is the last piece of the century that has to be killed and often the most long-lived, such as a Napoleon a Hitler or a Julius Cæsar the century has to be killed and they are the embodiment the most persistent end of it they are to live while really in its being killed they have to go, only nobody does tell them so, nobody and so they never do know, never do know.

However when I was a baby and then on to fourteen, the nineteenth century was full on.

In the nineteenth century, there was reading, there was evolution, there was war and antiwar which was the same thing, and there was eating. Even now I always resent when in a book they say they sat down to a hearty meal and they do not tell just what it was they ate. In the nineteenth century they often did. And in these days 1943 when eating well actually it is like prohibition one is so certain that one is never going to eat again that one is not greedy but one does eat everything well in these days you would imagine that you would not take pleasure in what the characters in a novel ate when they did eat, but one does enormously, well anyway the nineteenth century, liked to cry liked to try liked to eat liked to pursue evolution and liked war, war and peace peace and war and no more.

When I was then I liked revolutions I liked to eat I liked to eat I liked to cry not in real life but in books in real life there was nothing much to cry about but in books oh dear me, it was wonderful there was so much to cry about and then there was evolution. Evolution was all over my childhood, walks abroad with an evolutionist and the world was full of evolution, biological and botanical evolution, with music as a background for emotion and books as a reality, and a great deal of fresh air as a necessity, and a great deal of eating as an excitement and as an orgy, and now well just then there was no war no actual war anywhere.

In the nineteenth century there was nothing more exciting than climbing a high hill or a mountain and seeing the rain driving across a wide plain or valley with the sun following.

There was nothing more interesting in the nineteenth century than little by little realising the detail of natural selection in insects flowers and birds and butterflies and comparing things and animals and noticing protective coloring nothing more interesting, and this made the nineteenth century what it is, the white man's burden, the gradual domination of the globe as piece by piece it became known and became all of a piece, and the hope of Esperanto or a universal language. Now they can do the radio in so many languages that nobody any longer dreams of a single language, and there should not any longer be dreams of conquest because the globe is all one, anybody can hear everything and everybody can hear the same thing, so what is the use of conquering, and so the nineteenth century now in '43 is slowly coming to an end.

Between babyhood and fourteen years, it is hard to know

whether it takes a long time or whether it does not and if it does any part of it is interesting but very little of it is recollecting, very little and so emotion is remembered, a few dimensions, and what is seen and any day.

Some days there are coincidences and some days there are none and when there are coincidences as there are coincidences that does make superstition and at any age, there is the same astonishment and the same belief, and between babyhood and fourteen there were coincidences and astonishment. There are coincidences now yesterday and to-day and to-morrow and then for some time there are none, but any time they are astonishing when they come. It is a long time that there has been no correspondence with America and then some one offered to make one by cablegram and the next day a cablegram came, which is what makes superstition and when you are young very young superstitions are frightening and when you are old quite old superstitions are comforting.

War this war can neglect superstitions the war of 1943 because all the superstitions have been used up used up and passed away, and there is no feeling about having any new one or any old one. Some wars make everybody tired, not many of them, this one makes everybody more tired than most, I think the American civil war made everybody tired but it did not quite exhaust coincidence and superstition but this 1943 one, well in a way yes, and when I was in babyhood to fourteen little by little and all the time there was the excitement of coincidences, and of superstitions, coincidences were more exciting than superstitions in between superstitions were more exciting than coincidences and now again coincidences are not exciting but they are soothing now in 1943.

Everything begins again, now they denounce one another, why nobody knows, just perhaps to make coincidences now that there are no superstitions. Madame Chaboux just told me this one.

There is a woman living in the country, her husband was a farmer, there are more farmers than not. She was not well and she asked a neighbor to come and tend to her, she said she had pneumonia. The neighbor lived with another woman and the husband of each one of them was a prisoner a war prisoner. Well the one went to see the other, and she saw that the sheets were blood-stained and she said to the woman you have had a miscarriage have you not. And the other said how dare you denounce me. And she said but I did not I just asked to know. Well anyway she went home and about a week after a man in a uniform came and said the two women had to pay a thousand francs for having falsely denounced a neighbor and they said they had not and he said pay, and they paid. And they saw the other woman and she said she would take everything away from them and they all three had husbands who were prisoners and they were frightened and they told Madame Chaboux, her husband had been their doctor and Madame Chaboux told the mayor and he told her to go to the magistrate and she did and the police were pleased because they had always wanted a witness against the man and now they had two, and everybody was pleased and relieved even if they did not get their money back and their neighbor was still their neighbor and all the husbands were still prisoners.

Well between babyhood and fourteen no one could believe any such thing, not in the nineteenth century but now well 1943, what can stop anything since although there are still coincidences they are not, not really any superstitions because there are not. Everybody is too tired to have them even when they get one thousand francs which they do.

Such is war.

Between babyhood and fourteen there is if not everything a great deal there is the suspecting of life and death not being sure of the same but beginning to be doubtful that it might be the same. And there is nature and its evolution and then there is coming home before it is dark in the evening after playing and then there is the beginning of being a legend. One can become a legend any time between babyhood and fourteen and one can one does they do know how it can come to be true that they are a legend. It is easy to become a legend between babyhood and fourteen, and so ever afterwards books can be read, because books are

all about anybody who has become a legend, and I can remember
becoming a legend again and again between babyhood and fourteen, and seeing the others between babyhood and fourteen and
they can become a legend. They know they can they can become
a legend if they have a dog behind them on a bicycle in a basket,
they can become a legend, if they hold a flower in each hand, they
can become a legend if they had an accident and lost a finger,
they can become a legend, if they walk up and down hand in hand,
and one eye of one of them is always closed. They can become a
legend and they do because a legend any one between babyhood
and fourteen does become a legend, a pure legend. Later on the
legend is not so pure because you mix yourself up with it but
between babyhood and fourteen becoming a legend is just that
it is becoming a legend. I can remember becoming a legend, I will
tell several of them, several of those becoming legends and what
they have to do with war. This war 1943 is not very legendary,
that is one of its troubles, it is not like '14-'18 war and other wars
which naturally became legendary. This is more like the beginning of middle living when being legendary does not happen, but
as I say between babyhood and fourteen everybody is a legend
just anybody, and I was.

Coincidences come to be stronger and stronger between babyhood and fourteen, they replace faith, coincidences are the foundation of games, they are the foundation of faith, coincidences, in
between are not so important but from babyhood to fourteen and
then again much later, very much later when one is old coincidences are important, they are real, they recreate faith they are not
games, but they are the reality that makes a present and a future
when perhaps there could not really be any. Take war, in time of
war 1943, there have happened so many coincidences and they are
always happening little coincidences, nice little coincidences, later
on when I tell all about this coincidental war this meaningless
war, this war that put an end a real end an entire end to the nineteenth century there were so many coincidences and they were
the only reality in this time of unreality. The nineteenth century

called coincidences a law of chance and worked it out but now that the nineteenth century is dead, coincidences are real again, they recreate faith they make a future, and they will make the twentieth century. Everybody, wait and see.

But between babyhood and fourteen, coincidences were only really used as the really necessary basis of games, and what was real then were not coincidences but being a legend and I was, we were.

What makes the legend real between babyhood and fourteen is that there is then the first struggle not to die and the first struggle to help kill the century in which you are born.

It is a struggle not to die between babyhood and fourteen, not not to actually die, that is a matter for parents and nurses and guardians, but the not to know that death is there, and not to share, that is to be secret and not die, and not to not know why, that is what makes any one shy between babyhood and fourteen, and later on there are other things in between, there is eternity, there is or there is not being a king or a queen, but between babyhood and fourteen, beside reading writing and arithmetic, and counting, and games, and coincidences, and hot and cold, one is always either very hot or very cold between babyhood and fourteen.

There is no use in remembering between babyhood and fourteen, actually there was no war then, there might have been but actually there was no war then then when I was between babyhood and fourteen and I was a legend then, of course I was, to myself and to them and of course I was struggling not to be dying that is not to know that dying was dying and frightening was not only frightening but connected with any thing. Believe it or not, to-day they say, that children that anybody between babyhood and fourteen, does not live any life in between this which is not 1914 but 1943 and the nineteenth century is dead dead dead, and between babyhood and fourteen, I was there to begin to kill what was not dead, the nineteenth century which was so sure of evolution and prayers, and esperanto and their ideas. You might think

I mean that between babyhood and fourteen, I might mean to be doing what I was doing, and in a way I was, I see them now, between babyhood and fourteen and in a kind of a way I was.

What is a legend.

There are no legends now, because nobody can now can see how they have been not now, this is 1943.

From babyhood until fourteen, to play in a garden in the evening when it is darkening is a legend. It feels like that, it is like that, any evening when it is darkening.

Between babyhood and fourteen there comes a time when in reading you cannot help thinking what happened after and what happened to their children and their grandchildren and which one married which one and what war was going on when they were growing or grown up and were they after all the time it took to be born and grown were they killed in the war that was going on then. Now in 1943 when there are armies and armies and they come humming in and the air at night, when the moon is bright is full of them going over to Italy to do their bombing and the mountain makes a reverberation as a woman said to me like being inside a copper cooking utensil well then you keep on thinking how quickly anybody can get killed, just as quickly just as very quickly, more quickly even than in a book even much more quickly than in any book, those up there flying and bombing and those down below, with houses tumbling, and burning.

So between babyhood and fourteen you first begin to think of anything going on and going on, and at the same time stopping, but that is not reasonable no not at all reasonable between babyhood, and fourteen.

Between babyhood and fourteen their names might be Paul and Pauline and they might know how they learned the why and the when and the wherefore and how they learned excitement, hope and calm.

Imagine between the ages of babyhood and fourteen being either Paul or Pauline and living when there is no war or living when there is one.

Between babyhood and fourteen when I was living then there was no war and my name was neither Paul nor Pauline. I had an aunt named Pauline but I did not know of her then, and I did not know anybody by the name of Paul although I always did think it was a nice name and liked it when I saw it in a book.

How many books I read then, I am always reading books, there was of course Paul and Virginia under an umbrella, I do not know why but they always are under an umbrella and I thought the way the Negroes talked was very strange. Dialect in books was upsetting, even then and even now, then when there was no esperanto and now when there is no esperanto, no universal knowledge although everybody does know everything. You lose a stocking and it was the best one, it was lost in the stream when they were washing, there is no soap, this is 1943, and so they wash in running water and the stocking went down the stream and it was the very best woolen stocking, only one but of what use is only one stocking, and we neither of us slept very much that night, because the stocking was gone, her stocking, and yet in these days, what you keep you have that is you have while you keep it.

Between my babyhood and fourteen that was not true you had what you kept and kept what you had and you could wonder what the children and grandchildren were doing, particularly if it was already past. All very dreamy and exciting.

Then there was another thing, in Gulliver's Travels there was a description of the people that never die, and it is supposed to show that death is necessary, because those that do not die do not live then when they do not die. That is what some think and when I was between babyhood and fourteen I did think that it was not necessary to be old like that to never die, why could not one be young like that and never die, and if you do not cry and if you like never to die, why not go on being just like that. Why not. To be sure the time passes very slowly between babyhood and fourteen and if it did pass even slower really even slower then certainly there is no reason why any one should not live forever, no reason. It was many years later that I did think that if everybody did not die the earth would be all covered over and I, I as I, could not have come to be and try as much as I can try not to be I, neverthe-less, I would mind that so much, as much as anything, so then why not die, and yet and again not a thing, not a thing to be liking, not a thing.

But to come back to being between babyhood and fourteen and being a legend. Of course I was one. Any one is then one.

Roses and pansies, buttercups and daisies, this is what makes a legend, long before it makes poetry. And by a legend I mean that you do everything, just the way you should look as if you did, and you do. Any little girl and little boy between babyhood and four-teen, knows just how they seem, knows just exactly how they seem, and so it is natural enough that there was no war then, because really a war a really war is not quite legendary enough it is not exactly just the way it seems.

When my brother and I walked and walked up into the moun-tains on the dusty roads, and we left and we came and everything and nothing came in between, we were a legend then, just then. When we went camping and dragged a little wagon and slept closely huddled together and any little boy or any little girl could have been what any little girl or any little boy was, we were a legend then, we were legendary then. Any one is between baby-hood and fourteen. It is as if it were, and really any actual war is not like that, it really is not.

To-day, there was an airplane over our heads, and Victor, he is nineteen, said I am afraid. And we said and why are you afraid, well he said the reason I am afraid, of course they are not dropping bombs on us. Of course not we said even if they are boches because this is no place to drop bombs. Of course not said Victor, but I am afraid. Why we said, Because they are kids who are going up in those German planes now, and you know what kids are, they do not know what to do and they might fall down and so drop down upon us. Now that is not legendary. That is uncertain but between babyhood and fourteen, why you are afraid and why you are glad and why you are you, and why you play, and why you scream and then cry, all this however you think you can try, all this is legendary. There is nothing else but legend. Even if a little girl of six tells how she was sick and in bed and naturally they had fled, naturally in 1940, and when the doctor came to see he said three rooms in one bed or three beds in one room and nobody dead, and the little girl of six and a half could do nothing but laugh although she was not well, and they all had fled, and they were none of them dead.

This is what I mean when I say that between babyhood and fourteen it is a legend, anything and everything is what it can seem, and it does seem and there is nothing in between.

Eating and vomiting and war, the end of between being a baby and fourteen, makes this be a scene. Any day and in every way this can be seen, eating and vomiting and war. In any way that eating is something that is to be done with or without stealing makes vomiting and war. And the end of babyhood to fourteen, makes this not a dream, but an awakening. When a baby eats and vomits it is not war. But when fourteen eats and vomits then it is war.

There is one thing certain when there is no food or very little food, it is easy to digest, that food, much easier than when there is food, regular food. Now in 1943, well there is food of course there is food, and everybody well not everybody but quite a few find food. Every day they start to find food, and every day and in every way they find food. Some one said that it was like prohibition in America but it is not because then they finally found too much food, but here and now the only ones who find too much food are the farmers, and they do not find it, they grow it. They say and they mean it, it is what everybody wants, they wa~* food more than they want anything and we are the only ones that grow it and so we are the only ones who have the right to eat it, and eat it they do. Farmers used to be thin but now they are not. Nobody else used to be thin and now they are, men more than women, in general women can get along better with what is found to eat than men. But anyway even a little boy a very little boy a very fat little boy not yet four, when he sees on a strange lady's hat, three apples very little apples at that, says to the lady, I would like to have three apples like that and even when he knows that they are not real apples, he keeps on saying when he is awakening, I would like three little apples like that.

Anyway between babyhood and fourteen, anything they are saying, anything they are knowing, everything they are repeating is a legend, because it has to be a legend, to be learned, legs belong to them, feet to belong to them, hands and fingers come easier to belong to them and are not quite as legendary as legs and feet, not quite as legendary but still legendary enough.

And at the end of babyhood to fourteen, at the end there is nothing in between. What did she say when she was fourteen. She said she was not willing to be a queen. And he, he was not inter- ested in a king or a queen not when he was fourteen. Not at all. And in this way from fifteen to twenty-four began and it began with also ran.

Mediaeval means, that life and place and the crops you plant and your wife and children, all are uncertain. They can be driven away or taken away, or burned away, or left behind, that is what it is to be mediaeval. And being a pioneer has a little of the same not all the same but something of the same and when you are fifteen it is all very real, mediaeval and pioneer. And now and here 1943, it is just like that, you take a train, you disappear, you move away your house is gone, your children too, your crops are taken away, there is nothing to say, you are on the road, and where are they, if you go there is nobody to say so, anything can come and anything can go and they can say yes and no, and they can say, go, they never do say come, but yes they do now, they say come now, and they have to come and they have to go, everything is all the same what can happen here can happen there, and what can happen there can happen anywhere and it does, beside it does.

So at fifteen there comes to be a realisation of what living was in mediaeval times and as a pioneer. It is very near. And now in 1943 it is here.

It is disconcerting to know and it gives you a funny feeling, that any time not only that you can be told to go and you go but also that you can be taken. Nevertheless you stay, and if you stay you do not go away. That was true in mediaeval times too.

I have just been reading King John, when I was fifteen, King John was real, but now King John is realer, here and now it is all the same, that is the way they act and that is the way they are, the way they were in Shakespearean King John. It often makes me know that as a cousin of mine once said about money, money is always there but the pockets change, it is not in the same pockets after a change and that is all there is to say about money. Well power is the same thing, in King John it was the king and the church, and when I was young it was the middle class that is the middle class that had money, and now it is the lower middle class that is in power, and men can have and men will have money, if it is had it would not go on being the lower middle class, because that class has no legend and it has no love interest and it is not timely and it does not like to live, and move about and it does not care what it is all about, it knows what it is and it stays there, and that is what the lower middle class is and it is they that make the last there is of life in the nineteenth century because they have no hope and no adventure. Think of the dictators they are just like that. What did I say. I said it was just like that.

However fifteen is not just like that, not very likely although when it is the lower middle class it tries to be but fifteen is really mediaevel and pioneer and nothing is clear and nothing is sure, and nothing is safe and nothing is come and nothing is gone. But it all might be.

At fifteen they light a pack on their back. It makes them feel strong. At fifteen they conquer when they have a pack on their back. And now in 1943, everybody has a pack on their back, they go about just like that, they need anything and everything that can be put into a pack on their back. And so from fifteen to twenty-four and now from five to ninety everybody can have a pack on their back, in hope of finding something to put into that pack on their back.

From fifteen to twenty-four there was the Boer war, and it was the first time I knew about how many or how few should surrender and it was the first time I knew about khaki and all that, and it was the same with everybody, and now here khaki is over, at least right here, Germans and Italians wear sad green and grey, and any color can be dirty that way.

Between fifteen and twenty-five they all can be quite a good deal alive.

From fifteen on to twenty-five it is natural to think that every Sunday is good weather. And to hope that every day will be Sunday bye and bye. At fifteen walking and riding and coming and going is always a pleasure and everything else is an indecision, and everything else is better or more than that. And here and now in 1943, now that the war is coming to an end, everybody that is nobody knows whether there is or is not any future and at fifteen it is like that everybody and nobody knows whether there is or is not any future. Funny things happen, you milk a goat for the first time, you see a girl taller than yourself for the first time and you are not sure whether she is beautiful or not, you spend all day intending to go somewhere and nothing happens and you wonder if you will ever be revenged. That is what is now happening in 1943 and fifteen years old is like that. You think everything is funny and the moonlight is not clouded over and the wind blows and trees make a noise and people say funny things, they do not mean what they say, fifteen years old is like that and now in 1943 it is like that. There is a funny story about a goat.

A young woman came from Switzerland to Aix-les-Bains to work in an embroidery shop, and she went to live with a woman who always had one boarder. When she came the woman said to her I must tell you that I do not keep a cow I only keep a goat. Oh dear said the young Swiss, I come from the mountains where my people ever since I was a baby kept one cow just to nourish me. Oh dear I cannot drink goat's milk, never never. All right said the woman I will arrange with a neighbor and you shall have your cow's milk as you want it. The young woman stayed there for three years and lived happily ever after. She married and from time to time she went to see the woman who had been kind to her when she had come there a stranger. Many years later the older woman was sick and dying, and the younger woman went quite often to see her, and then one day a message was brought that the woman was dying and must see her. She went and the dying woman said, before I die I want to tell you, all those years you lived with me I deceived you, it was not true that I got you cow's milk from a neighbor, I just gave you goat's milk and you did not know and I did not tell you but now before I die I must tell you, I could not die deceiving you, and they cried together and she died and it was all over.

She told us this because we were all happy, this was in 1943, she had just gotten a cow for herself and her husband and her children and we had just gotten a goat, and we were all so happy and we were telling about it to each other. We said that we had never wanted to taste goat's milk and now we had and it was more delicate and sweeter and lighter and creamier than a cow, yes she said and she told us her story, and they had a cow now, that is to say that had bought one for a farmer who had just lost his horse which had died, and they did not buy him a new horse they bought him a cow so they could have milk of a cow. Nobody knows unless they have been in it what it is to eat only things cooked in water and now she had a cow and we had a goat a lovely white goat, whose name is Bizerte, because we got it the day of that victory in the morning. I love to walk the goat and now I let it loose a man told me to and I always do whatever they tell me to which is in a way the way it is between fifteen and twenty-four and no more. We laugh very much we are so pleased to have the goat.

Fifteen to twenty-four, yes there was a war there, the Boer war.

Fifteen the time does not pass slowly but a great deal of time there is nothing to do except stand around, in games and in the evening and in the day, stand around, not even get up and sit down but just stand around. And now, just now, everybody has to grow something to eat or run around to find something to eat now in 1943 so it is not like fifteen, but more like twenty-two, at twenty-two, everybody is very busy just to be you.

And that was the time there was the Boer war and it was a shock and a surprise to know that armies could surrender, not many killed and they could surrender and the war not be over. That was the new thing the Boer war told us, the English could surrender even when there was a smaller percent of them dead than there should have been according to statistics before they did surrender but they did not lose the war. And that was a new thing. When they had surrendered like that in our revolutionary war then the war was over, they lost it but in the Boer war when they did like that the war was not over and they had not lost it and that was a new thing. That went very well with my being twenty-two or something very well indeed.

But at fifteen there was no war when I was fifteen no war at all.

Between fifteen and twenty-two it is not natural that some one surrounded by enemies who would not speak to him ate the only piece of chocolate and they were men not boys and they all wanted it. Naturally enough in 1943. When you are fifteen it is rather wonderful that any one can do such a thing, have enemies who will not speak to him and eat the chocolate cake the only piece and all the enemies who would not speak to him wanting it. It is a funny thing about enemies. It does take such a long time to believe in them believe that they are enemies, and then after all nobody really does seem to believe in them believe that they are enemies. It is about when one is fifteen that one first begins to hear about enemies not in books of course books are full of enemies, but in life. What are enemies and what is war, and are there enemies in war or are they not. From fifteen on one can begin to wonder about such a thing, along with eternity and clouds and beauty and faith. Enemies are not important whether they are real or not, I can remember when I was sixteen seeing a play then modern in which a woman or was it a girl had so many enemies among the other women or girls and could I believe it, no I could not. But he who in 1943 ate the chocolate cake he always believed that he had enemies and that enemies were real even when one was fiften. But about war well he was not so sure that enemies are enemies during a war. And perhaps they are and perhaps they are not.

Our two servants, they are sisters, we are just in this house a nice big modern house alone against a mountain with a lovely park all full of bushes and big trees, and firs, and the two sisters one a good cook and the other a very perfect chamber maid, they know all about enemies, in war and in peace. Now in 1943 they have forgotten about peace, perhaps there is no such thing but they know all about enemies in war real enemies and enemies that are enemies. It sounds like the same thing but it is not.

There are so many enemies in Shakespeare.

Between fifteen and twenty-four there is so much time in which you do nothing but stand around and wait for it to happen. Now in 1942 in April 1942 there is no longer any standing around waiting for something to happen that is among those who are not fighting of course those who are fighting are like that, they are standing around waiting to do something but everybody else is now as is normal in adult life they are busy not necessarily with everything but they know from day to day that they will do something to-morrow. From fifteen to twenty-three or four nobody does know really know that they will do something to-morrow.

Between the ages of fifteen and twenty-three nobody ever can get back in time.

And now in 1943 at any age nobody can get back in time. And for the same reason, there is so much to do, there is nothing to do, there is no way for anybody to leave home and everybody is on the road and everybody talks to everybody and beside sometimes you know them all of which makes it impossible for anybody to get home in time. In time for what. Well just to get home in time or to get back in time and that is the way it usually is between fifteen and twenty-three. Nobody can get back in time.

War and enemies.

As I was saying there are so many enemies in Shakespeare.

We have now two sisters no longer young who run this house

which we have taken and where we are very comfortable and even rather magnificent and they know what enemies are.

They were born in the upper reaches of the river Rhone. We always like Thornton Wilder's story of the American tourist who said that there were two schools of thought about pronunciation, some said it should be pronounced Rhine and some said it should be pronounced Rhone. Well anyway they were born on the upper reaches of the river Rhone, a nice river that is always accompanied by a great deal of wind, a little wind or a big wind but it is always accompanied by wind. They were born and they had strange names given to them, they were not twins in fact one is definitely older and the other is definitely younger, and the strange names which were given to them were Clothilde and Olympe although to them they were natural names not strange names at all. The family around them died and then the younger one was quite young, seventeen she went to be a chamber-maid in Moravia where they talk a strange language but where life was pleasant, the older Clothilde had a son, this son was killed in the beginning of the war 1914-1918 and she never had another one. So every one was dead around them they had a little furniture, and in the meantime each one of the two of them separately were personal maids to different Italian countesses, they always like them to be noble and they lived 1914-1918 and a little later then with the Italians who were not enemies not to them then. Then they came back to the valley of the Rhone Clothilde a cook and her sister a maid and they did and they did not know what enemies were. Here they were very comfortable and relatively magnificent. And then many natural things happened and things changed the way they change and then came '39, and their mistress went away because bombardments might come that way and so they stayed on here alone that is sometimes two alone and sometimes one alone but always alone in a big house and park and alone. Then the war came to be a little more war that is soldiers were there and then soldiers came and soldiers went away and it was disturbing but they did not realise that enemies could be more of a bother than that but they can. And then the enemy came, it was here right here right here in the house and remaining in the house and they were enemies and nobody could deny that they were enemies certainly not Clothilde and Olympe. Olympe and Clothilde and they knew what enemies were enemies were like that.

Enemies being like that make enemies tremble. They made so much noise they said to them you are vanquished and they knew the enemies were there, but that was not what being vanquished was, being vanquished was a sadness and a sorrow and a weakness and a woe, but it was not a horror. The enemy there, here, that is a sorrow that they wished they could be spared but they were not. The enemies were there. They were all alone in the kitchen, they did not sleep there, they just could not do that, they could not sleep with the enemy there, they found a little room outside to which they went to sleep, but all day and each day they were in the kitchen and the enemy were living there, not in the kitchen but in the house. It was awful, they can never forget.

The day they won the enemy came in one by one to tell them so not only that they had won but that the others were done and that every one would be done one by one. Alas it was too true only two years after it was not so, that is to say if they had won the enemy had not finished everything it was only beginning and perhaps they were not winning.

But the enemy had come in one by one on the day they had won to tell them and they had not stolen what was in the house because that would be stealing but they had broken open the trunks of the two women and taken everything because as they were only servants and were then in the kitchen taking everything away from them was not stealing and so they broke open the trunks and took everything. There was a woman who used to wash the clothes for the enemy in a kind of a way she was an enemy herself, not an enemy who could frighten one but just an enemy and she said the enemies would win because they had wonderful weapons that no one had ever seen, all the enemies had wonderful weapons that no one had ever seen. And now say Clothilde and Olympe and now in 1943, perhaps it is true they the enemy feel the wonderful weapons that no one has ever seen, perhaps they do.

And so it is true that they are all kinds of enemies, some that frighten some that steal and some that like a fiend make you come to heel. That is what Olympe has to say. To-day it is a fiend that is a mistress who says come and she has to go who makes her so unhappy that she has to cry.

It is funny and when you are fifteen you begin to know that enemies are not what they seem, and then by twenty-four you know enemies are enemies and in between well and then later and now it is not certain that enemies are what they seem.

At fifteen man and animals fruit trees and flowers beginning not to be things to pick but to feel. In the year '43, milk was more and more difficult to have. There was no milk not even skimmed milk and so everybody who could had a goat. We had a goat. When I was fifteen I did not care for goats I like a wall and I had read about fruit trees growing on the sunny side of a wall and I always said when I was fifteen that when I was older and could have it I would have a wall and have fruit trees growing on the sunny side of a wall. I remember the first time I ever saw fruit trees arranged to grow on a wall. It was just after the Spanish American war and we were in Paris for the exposition and McKinley had just been shot and I saw fruit trees trained to grow on the sunny side of walls and it reminded me of when I was fifteen and I wanted to grow fruit trees on sunny sides of the wall and my brother said that he would keep a goat on the wall to eat the fruit trees. And now it is 1943 and there is no milk and we keep a goat and I walk the goat and I like the goat, goats are very willful and I have found out why we like flowers. Because goats pick flowers to eat, and children pick flowers because animals pick flowers to eat and children pick flowers like that.

At fifteen flowers commence to have other meanings, beauty is beauty and flowers are flowers and flowers are no longer flowers as the goat picks them.

Beauty is its own excuse for being, that begins at fifteen that

WARS I HAVE SEEN

and that enemies are not what they seem, that all belongs at fifteen. At fifteen overbearing that is the need to be the one that has to dominate the other one by not studying, by studying, by fighting, by not fighting, by war, red war, white war, green war and black war. Black war is fighting, red war is war, white war is exciting and green war is disappointing. And at fifteen war has begun, and every one knows that with the sun or without the sun war has begun.

What happened. She Lucy Lilly Lamont, wanted what she wanted and she was not stupid she was overbearing and crazy and not nervous but obstinate and she felt superior. That can make enemies even if nobody is your enemy. It is just like this but not in a way. In a war anybody can forget about Lucy Lilly Lamont. Why not when she is of no importance in a war. And this is what made us feel as we did about the Boer war, it was the first war that made us feel that wars were wars but that they were not important because nothing changed. We only know now that we felt that way then now in 1943, but we did we most certainly did begin to feel that way then.

Lucy Lilly Lamont was fifteen all her life, they have a way of saying it here, they say she never left the primary grades, it is that that makes her the other side of fifteen all her life, and it is very interesting, war is and is not like that, a good deal of war is like that and then when everybody is tired of war then it is not at all like that.

Fifteen.

Every time I watch them I ask them how old they are. They are usually younger than fifteen or older, it is not very often that they are just fifteen and when they are it is very special. Being fifteen is very special, being eleven or thirteen is not so special, being seventeen or nineteen is not so special. Being fifteen is very special.

And now it is June 1943 and two of the young men who are twenty-one have come to say good-bye, they hope they are not going to die right away but all who are twenty-one have to go to

Germany as hostages to be put in a pen, they say to work in factories but there is no work, and if they go into hiding well it would be all right if it were not for the winter but will it be over before the winter, they ask me to tell them but can any one tell them, do I know, well anyway I can say that they might amuse themselves by learning and reading German and they might amuse themselves by saying that they are going traveling as students, and say they, if we do not consider them as enemies will the Americans like it, will they, might it not displease them, but said I you can learn their language and read their literature and contemplate them as if you were travelers and still know them to be enemies. Why not. Well said they why not. Anyway they said you have cheered us, and I kissed them each one of them and wished them well, and one of them came back to shake hands again and I kissed him again and said be prudent and he said I will and they went away up the hill. Oh dear me one cannot sleep very well.

But from fifteen on you can think about enemies, quite certainly think about enemies.

The idea of enemies is awful it makes one stop remembering eternity and the fear of death. That is what enemies are. Possessions are the same as enemies only less so, they too make one forget eternity and the fear of death.

So many things begin around fifteen. Money, possessions eternity, enemies, the fear of death, disappointments begin a long time before and sorrow, but around fifteen you can begin to write them down, which makes the depth and consolation of disappointment and sorrow. All this can and does begin around fifteen and then a little later came the Boer war, and war as no longer something that belonged to others and to history and to stories but something that was going on now and was a disillusion and disappointing. I did not know anybody who was fighting or any of their relations, but it was the time when anglo-saxonism had come in America to be a very conscious feeling, Dooley had made fun of it and we all felt it and it was disappointing it was not what Kipling and the describers of the Mutiny had made one feel was

Anglo-Saxon it was something different it was only we did not
know it it was the beginning of the ending of the nineteenth
century which now in 1943, is dying quite quickly, but we who
were active then we felt it because we already had a beginning of
the twentieth century and so although we did not know it we felt
that the Boer war was the first shot fired at the nineteenth century,
and although we thought we were of it we knew inside that we
were not and we knew we should regret what the nineteenth
century was but we knew we did not regret it we wanted something else and we were to have it.

In Shakespeare's Henry VI I just found that he said that Joan
of Arc and she was not yet dead not in the play in fact she was just
beginning and Shakespeare said that she would be the great French
saint that she would replace Saint Denis, and she was only made a
saint very late, very late indeed, just in time for the war of 1914
but she undoubtedly and Shakespeare was right she undoubtedly
is the great French saint and has completely replaced Saint Denis.
It is funny this business of being right. Everybody wants to be
right, even the one who said he would rather be right than president. It is so natural to say and I was right was I not.

I am wondering if Laval and the rest of them think they are
right now in 1943, to be sure the Kiddie wrote to me in 1942 and
said that at the end of 1942 there would be good news and in the
spring of 1943 there would be more good news than bad news and
as the summer came on the summer of 1943 the good news would
be so good there would be no letters in the newspaper printing
presses big enough to make headlines to celebrate them, and now
the Italian islands are going one by one, one by one and there is
only one more water to cross, and everybody who knows what an
enemy was is now worried because and that is very strange, everybody knowing that everything is coming to an end every neighbor
is denouncing every neighbor, for black traffic, for theft, for this
and for that, and there are so many being put in prison, poor
Madame Berard said it was so sad to see her husband going off
between two policemen just as if he was a criminal and to know

that some of their neighbors were pleased to see it. To be sure he had been killing meat and did he sell it or not or only serve it in quantity in his restaurant and her boy has to go to Germany because he is twenty-one even though he is a great mathematician and is to be a great man in the university of Lyon and the family were always gentle and kindly and obliging and never charged too much even when they might have and indeed it was all true they never did.

It is hard to know about enemies at fifteen it all begins, knowing everything and never being happy again, excited yes but never happy again. And now Olympe has to go away and she knows what enemies are, they are Germans that is what enemies are and here there are none and she has to take a train and there she has to see them and the thought of it is making an old woman of her and she does not want to go, no no she does not want to go, but her mistress says the duty of a servant is to obey her mistress and not to follow her own changing fancy, but her fancy has never changed, she has always known what the enemy is what her enemies are, yes she has always known and more than ever since they have been in her home.

And so the Boer war was disagreeable but not really serious not even for the Boers, like all defeated people they got the best of it, it is better to be defeated and win than win and be defeated. Now here in 1943 it seems so strange to see the enemy weakening just slowly weakening, quickly weakening, not being defeated or anything but just weakening, the French do better, they get defeated but they do not weaken, while the Germans do not get defeated they weaken, and when they weaken enough to go out like a lamp with no oil, or with no wire, out, it does not die it just weakens to nothing. Until they weaken everybody says about them but they are still strong, and then they weaken. There you are, that is to say here we are 1943.

After the Spanish-American war there was the Boer war, and that was no longer fifteen that was older, I was in the medical school then the first year and I went out to San Francisco to see my brother Mike who had just been married.

The Spanish-American war was the first to me modern war. Modern is like realism, modern is always modern to some one as realism is always real to some one, not to some one but to a great many at one time. Modern, how nicely it is modern now then and when.

What was modern then was seeing all the middle western men, young men, boys too many, going out to San Francisco, and catching everything and then going off in boats to the Philippines. I was just reading Shakespeare's Henry the Fifth and I found it astonishing how easily they talked of transporting ten thousand, fifteen thousand even twenty thousand soldiers across the water from England to France. How when they had such comparatively little tonnage, did they get so many of them across, how did they, well anyway so they say they did. Call it modern if you like but soldiers any quantity of them at any time can be carried across the ocean, any quantity of them at any time and now here in June 1943, we are waiting for them, waiting for them, to bring us shoes and stockings and dental floss, here in the country we have plenty to eat although we would like more cake and sugar and butter but still here in the country having a goat and chickens we do have plenty to eat and fish, we do have plenty to eat. But one does get so tired of seeing everybody planting and growing vegetables you think how nice it will be to have those happy days come back when vegetables grew not in the ground but in tins. A vegetable garden in the beginning looks so promising and then after all little by little it grows nothing but vegetables, nothing, nothing but vegetables.

Well anyway the Spanish-American war was modern but it was completely nineteenth century, there was nothing but the question of sea power and whose sea power was it, we all read a book that told us it, but then we had known it anyway, because of Nelson, and now we were doing it again, and it was very exciting, we were all finding out about the difficulty of having to have two

fleets a Pacific one and an Atlantic one, and we were all getting to
feel that we were to be, well there it was still nineteenth century
completely nineteenth century and we were not thinking about a
twentieth century, and we were so excited that we were not realising
that the nineteenth century was beginning to be over, not the least
bit in the world. I was young then but I can still see those young
men in San Francisco, those middle-western young men of twenty
and twenty-one, with their undeveloped necks, their rather doughy
faces, I see why they call them dough-boys, they are like that
between twenty and twenty-one, they go to sleep anywhere sitting
or standing, their heads and their mouths and their eyes can go to
sleep anywhere, and open or not open, that is what it is to be
twenty or twenty-one, and now here and now, it is just the same,
the young of twenty-one, the young Frenchmen of twenty-one are
all being deported to Germany, two came to see me to say good-bye
to ask how I could encourage them and all I could say was try to
study them and learn their language and get to know their literature, think of yourselves as a tourist and not as a prisoner, and they
were worried and nervous and they said will the Americans like
it if we think of them like that, sure I said all the Americans want
is to make you free, and they said yes we know that. It makes me
feel very very much like that, I used to say to any Frenchman or
Frenchwoman who complained of anything, I said but every time
I go out in the village of Bilignin there I see all your young men
whatever is happening they are still there and that is everything
that they are not gone. But now they are gone and going. Some of
them betake themselves to the mountains others are conspiring,
the son of our dentist a boy of eighteen has just been taken because
he was helping and will he be shot or not. Oh dear. We all cry.
But there is nothing to do but wait for us to come nothing to do.
And they look so, I saw a train full of them, everybody was hand-
ing them up wine and bread, although nobody has much of it for
themselves or to give them, and there they were with the gendarmes, going away. And they were awake then and pretty soon

they will be tired out and go to sleep any way that it is possible to be sleeping, in a chair or standing or in any way.

It is funny but my memory of those middle-western boys going out to the Philippines was that they were just like these French boys twenty and twenty-one going off to Germany, as deported and held away from every one. Dear me.

So that was realism. Anything is realism but that certainly was realism.

And it all made me remember the impression I have when I read Wyandotte or The Hutted Knoll which was about then, the shock I had in reading that book because for the first time I realised what it meant not to know whether any one was loyal to you or not, did they or did they not believe in you, were they interested in your interests and how can you tell. I had read laments of great men and many novels but in some strange way Wyandotte or The Hutted Knoll made me understand that you could think that some one was devoted to you and loyal to you and really not at all they were opposed to you and would if such a thing were necessary denounce you. And now and again in June 1943 it is happening all around one.

Well in the first place Olympe who knows who her enemies are, and are they, could they become another thing or rather could those to whom she was loyal could she stop being loyal to them, could she want so much not to leave you and when she really did have it to leave you did she at the last hour turn against you so as to prepare her mind to be attuned to the other to whom she was going. Could she and did she. She did. Might she and would she denounce the first one the second one or any one or would she only prepare herself in case she had to do something and it might be that something and would any one she was leaving realise that she had not been very serviceable in fact that she had been rather useless although everything made any one think that she was perfection and almost saintly as a character. Dear me. It is like a detective story particularly as her sister Clothilde used a cheap enemy perfume to drown out the smell of onions and cooking on

her and does it came to be known that she slept in her mistress'
room. Dear me dear me.

How many mirrors there can be in a house when all the doors
and the doors are many and very wide and tall are filled with
mirrors and what a pleasure to see one's self in them. Expectedly
and unexpectedly what a pleasure.

And now in June 1943 something very strange is happening,
every day the feeling is strengthening that one or another has been
or will be a traitor to something and what do they do they send
them a little wooden coffin sometimes with a letter inside sometimes with a rope inside to tell them to hang themselves, and
sometimes it is sent by post or by railroad and sometimes it is hung
up in a tree and sometimes hung up in front of the front door. Oh
dear me. When this you see remember me is what they mean
because some of these people have told where young men of
twenty-one were hidden, and it was not necessary to tell they just
did tell and so somebody sent them a small wooden coffin. Of
course they had to find a reliable carpenter to make the coffins but
they did find him.

So the Spanish-American war and seeing all those middle-
western men in San Francisco, made me realise what realism is.

Just to-night June 1943 I was out walking in the twilight in
the mountain village of Culoz where I live now and my dog Basket
was running around and a young man in working clothes said he
is a nice dog but I have been whistling to him and he wont come.
Oh I said you have to do more than whistle, you have to talk
English and he said my father could and I could too once but I
now have forgotten. And I said but how is that not that you have
forgotten but that your father talked English, that he said is very
simple he is an American, ah I said yes, he came to France in the
last war as a soldier he married a Frenchwoman, he got a good job
at Chaumont and he stayed, and in '38 we intended to go away
but my mother fell ill and we did not leave. And she, I said, oh
she is dead, and he, oh he is in a concentration camp when America
came into the war they came and took him, and you, we are four

brothers and a sister, and the oldest is an actor in the Comedie Française and the second is a plumber and the third is head butcher in a camp of youth and here I am working for farmers and my name is Robert Nelson White and I looked as if I was not sure that all he said was so and he said here are my papers, they do not spell white right, but my name there is Robert White, I left out the Nelson all right. And it all made me feel a little funny anything these days these strange days can make you feel a little funny so I shook hands with him and we went up Basket and I up the hill and he Robert Nelson White went on down, down the hill.

Now all that made me feel all the more how different was that Spanish-American war. I asked Robert Nelson White if his father was a Frenchman by blood, if his grandfather or grandmother either one was French but no he said he was always American his people never had been anything but American and his little sister of fourteen was at school and he and his brother had crossed the lines at night to come into the free zone and here he was.

In the Spanish-American war romance was simple and realistic like the young Californians who went to the war and General King wrote novels about it and in one he said and I threw the bridle of my horse to my orderly Ned Hanford, and it was Ned Hanford and when he read these simple words, he had a thrill he always had a thrill. That was the way it was then in the Spanish-American war. It was then that they began to think about realism. The Red Badge of Courage by Crane, and any simple description of war as done by the Russians, later on a naval battle in the next war, the Russo-Japanese war, which described it just as it was not as it felt or looked. But anyway there they were they middle-western boys in San Francisco, and there was Chinatown and there was the French quarter, and there were the Lurline baths and there was everything that they never had seen before. It is always that way in war, always.

And now in June 1943, it is trying, there are so many sad things happening, so many in prison, so many going away, our dentist's son and he was only eighteen and he should have been taking his entrance university examinations and he with others in a camion took shoes and clothes and weapons to give to the young men who had taken themselves to the mountains, to avoid being sent away and what has happened to him and to them. I have just met a very charming woman courageous and lives in an old castle and has five children and the youngest one is twenty-one and he has gone, she has never lost any money but life is always dearer and she and her children have worked very hard to keep their castle sheared their own sheep, and everything, and now she said, of course she would not mind Christian's going away, that is to say not to mind if it were not the times are so uncertain and so troubling, and he is very sweet and he is big and tall and very winning and since he was born there have never been three months without their seeing him, never and now, well I said he hopes to come back for the vintage and she had clear eyes very wide open and she said yes.

And all that makes one think more and more of the strangeness and the unreality of those middle-western boys who were naturally called dough-boys, being in San Francisco, and then going to the Philippines, when they got to the Philippines and back again I never saw them so I do not really know what happened to them, by that time we were all interested in realism in literature, and that kind of went on until 1938, when it was all over, there was an end of the nineteenth century and realism was the last thing the nineteenth century did completely. Anybody can understand that there is no point in being realistic about here and now, no use at all not any, and so it is not the nineteenth but the twentieth century, there is no realism now, life is not real it is not earnest, it is strange which is an entirely different matter.

During the Spanish-American war there were food scandals, and in the Boer war there were concentration camps where they had nothing to eat, and all that is natural enough. The concentration camps for the Boers excited us all, nobody knew then how everybody was finally that is everybody in Europe was finally not going to have anything to eat. There was famine in China even in

Russia and there was famine in India and every one then in the time of the Boer war and before and after was very much excited about it but now here in 1943 not having anything to eat enough to eat, having what you can eat, buying eating black, that is black traffic, thinking about eating, everybody on the road bicycling or walking with a pack on their back or a basket in the hand, or a big bundle on the bicycle, hoping for provisions, somewhere in the country there would be an egg or something or something, and perhaps you will get that something. One day I was out walking, well naturally I had a basket and big prospects and hopes and I met a nice gentle little bourgeoise from Belley, and it was spring time and she had a very charming and quite large bouquet of flowers very beautifully arranged in her hand and I said what a charming bouquet of flowers, yes she said eyeing the bouquet carefully, yes, I have been in the country to visit some relations, and I had hoped, I had hoped perhaps for an egg, perhaps even perhaps for a chicken, and she heaved a little breath they gave me these flowers. They are very charming flowers I said, yes she said, and we said good-bye and went each one on our way. There are so many people in prison because they sell what they should not sell, and yet, well and yet, I met Roselyn I said you are looking very well, the restrictions do not seem to have had any effect on you, well said Roselyn, one finds things. Roselyn, I said, you indulging in black traffic, mais non, she said of course I would not, to find something is one thing, to indulge in black traffic is quite another thing. Explain the difference to me I said Well said Roselyn, to find is when you find a small amount any day at a reasonable price which will just augment your diet and keep you healthy. Black traffic is when you pay a very large sum for a large amount of food, that is the difference. And she is right that is a difference and we all all day and every day go about and in every way we do or do not find something that helps the day along. As Madame Pierlot said, you do not buy now-a-days only with money you buy with your personality. Jo Davidson used to say that you always had to sell your personality, but now it is not a question of selling it is a question

of buying by personality. Nothing is sadder these days than people
who never make friends, they poor dears have nothing to eat,
neither do the indiscreet, and yet almost everybody does eat.
Almost everybody, almost, it comes hardest on middle aged men,
not women they resist better but middle aged men, without wine
and cheese, they get thinner and thinner and thinner. We women
of a certain age, we reduce to a certain place and then we seem to
get along all right, but the middle aged men get thin, and thinner
and thinner. Naturally those that had been fat. Oh dear me.

So the Boer war was the first time we really realized that war
made them thin that is the civilian population, it must have been
true in the civil war, but at that time, there were so many pioneers
and pioneers are always thin, and Boers were fat, and the Boer
war made them thin just like that.

I just heard a nice story about a farmer's wife. She complained
that her cow could not live because she had no hay. Some one who
had a large house and a lot of land heard her and said I will give
you two thousand pounds of hay that is a load of hay as a present
if you will sell me every day a litre of milk. And said the farmer's
wife what will I do having so much less butter. No not at all said
the farmer's wife. The Boer war might be like that just like that
and so is 1943.

And so there was the Spanish-American war. So much happened
in the Spanish-American war, to us and to me to the United States
and to us, something to Spain too and to any Spaniard but then
that was a habit, they always had these things happen in Europe.
But with us although in a kind of a way in our short history it
had very frequently happened still it was not a habit.

To-day we were at Aix-les-Bains, end of June 1943 when this
you see remember me, and in a kind of way it was different but in
a kind of way it was the middle western dough boys in San Francisco. We were at the station it was the first of July and there were
many trains and many people, on one track where our train should
have been it was not. And then a train came along, all trains go
very slowly now, the engineers are used up the track is used up and

the coal is bad so therefore there are a fair number of trains moving they move at a walk. This train that came along and kept moving and did not stop had on it tanks and trucks which did not look very strong, as they were not armored and seated on them and seated in the open cars placed on trucks and seated anywhere were Germans all naked except a little trouser nothing on their heads and sitting there and the train went on slowly and all the French people were as if they were at a theatre that was not interesting and the train went on slowly and then our train came in and I got on it with my white dog Basket and the French people were pleased, Basket was the real circus, he was a theatre that they found interesting and they were interested and they said so, and nobody had noticed the train full of Germans except four young Frenchmen from the camp de Jeunesse and they like all young fellows of that age laughed, which reminded me of the dough boys in San Francisco, in the midst of the San Francisco public. Which ones. Those Germans.

It is funny funny in the sense of strange and peculiar and unrealisable, the fact that so many are prisoners, prisoners, prisoners every where, and now Berard where we used to lunch is in prison, for black traffic, and an Alsatian and his wife and his son, because of the younger son who went to the funeral of his fiancée and on his way he was taken and he escaped and they were in prison and now they are out and he is in safety but where. Anywhere. And whole countries in prison and now we have a feeling that they who put everybody in prison are now in prison they feel themselves in prison, they feel imprisoned. They have just told us that our friends the American consul and vice-consul although in prison and are very free and amusing themselves and have flowers in their rooms and play tennis and send messages and make excursions. Oh dear me, when this you see, but after all, when this you see, and after all you would imagine that with all that I would not any longer want to read mystery stories and spy stories and all that but not at all I want to read them more than ever, to change one reality for another, one unreality for another and so the Spanish-American war made us Americans conscious of being a world power, conscious of the school of realism, conscious of England being nineteenth century, with Kipling and the white man's burden, was in a way for me the beginning of killing the nineteenth century, which is now not any longer dying but dead and the little coffins that are being sent to all pro-Germans are part of the funeral. French people like New Englanders like funerals, they are a peaceful occupation, nice and quiet, and certain. Ah say the French before all this we were so happy but we did not appreciate our good fortune.

Realism.

After all there has to be realism realism in romance and in novels and the reason why is this. Novels have to resemble something and in order that they do there must be realism. Of course all writers had had realism, writers and readers always have a realism, after all living is in a way always real, that is to say what one hears and sees, even what one feels is in a way always real, but the realism of the present seems new because the realism of the past is no longer real.

And so just at the time of the Spanish-American war, there commenced the difference between Kipling's realism, which was romanticism, but real enough, and the French and Russian realism, which was so real that it was real enough. Was it real as anybody could know realism, or was it not. Just at the time of the Spanish-American war and later the Russo-Japanese war this question of realism was becoming the vital question for Americans who having a land with a clear light manufacturing light and resistant steel, their life needed a clean and resistant realism but at the same time they needed to move around and you cannot keep moving around without feeling romantic. The nineteenth century was then in its full strength and everybody knew it, and everybody knew that when a thing is like that you have to begin to try to forget it, and they all began to they all began to begin to forget it.

It is funny about things being real. Something happened a few months ago like that, in February 1943.

We had been in Bilignin all these years of the war and now our lease had run out and our landlord and his wife wanted their home back, not that they needed it just then, but they did want it back. And so for the first time in my life, I had a lawyer and a law-suit, and we lost but nevertheless, they gave us longer, and the authorities said as long as they did not consent that we should be put out the others in spite of what the law said could do nothing about it. And then the situation changed, the French army was disbanded, and our landlord who was a captain did have more reason in asking to have his house back again and so finally some one offered us this house in Culoz, and it is quite wonderful even though modern, but after you have been living in an old house for so long a new house has pleasant things about it, windows that fit and light and air, well anyway we told the lawyer it was all right, and the new law-suit we were about to start did not go on, and we had made all our arrangements for moving including our electric water heater and our bathtub and our electric kitchen stove and our refrigerator, and we had made all preparations, and our late landlords had decided to behave nicely at last and I went down to say good-bye to everybody in Belley and first of all to my lawyer. I had always been so much taken with the way all English people I knew always were going to see their lawyer. Even if they have no income and do not earn anything they always have a lawyer and now for the first time in my life I had a lawyer, and so I went down to say good-bye to my lawyer.

We had recently quite a number of difficult moments. America had come into the war, our consul and vice-consul in Lyon with whom we had gotten very friendly because they had taken a summer home right near us and kept a white goat called Gene-vieve, and there we first found out that you could have goat's milk that did not taste of goat, had been interned first at Lourdes and then taken to Germany and now I went to Belley to say good-bye as we were moving. My lawyer said that everything was nicely arranged and we thanked each other and said what a pleasure it had all been, and then he said and now I have something rather serious to tell you. I was in Vichy yesterday, and I saw Maurice Sivain, Sivain had been sous-prefet at Belley and had been most kind and helpful in extending our privileges and our occupation of our house, and Maurice Sivain said to me, tell these ladies that they must leave at once for Switzerland, to-morrow if possible otherwise they will be put into a concentration camp. But I said we are just moving. I know he said. I felt very funny, quite completely funny. But how can we go, as the frontier is closed, I said. That he said could be arranged, I think that could be arranged. You mean pass by fraud I said, Yes he said, it could be arranged. I felt very funny. I said I think I will go home and will you telephone Madame d'Aiguy to meet me. He said shall I walk home with you, I did feel very funny, and I said no I will go home and Madame d'Aiguy will come down to see you and arrange and I went home. I came in, I felt a little less funny but I still did feel funny, and Alice Toklas and Madame d'Aiguy were there, and I said we are not moving to-morrow we are going to Switzerland. They did not understand that and I explained and then they did understand, and Madame d'Aiguy left to go and see the lawyer and arrange and Alice Toklas and I sat down to supper. We both felt funny and then I said. No, I am not going we are not going, it is better to go regularly wherever we are sent than to go irregularly where nobody can help us if we are in trouble, no I said, they are always trying to get us to leave France but here we are and here we stay. What do you think, I said, and we thought and I said we will walk down to Belley and see the lawyer and tell him no. We walked down to Belley it was night it was dark but I am always out walking at night, I like it, and I took Alice Toklas by the arm because she has not the habit of walking at night and we got to Belley, and climbed up the funny steps to the lawyer, and I said I have decided not to go. Madame d'Aiguy was still there and she said perhaps it was better so, and the lawyer said perhaps we had better go and then he said he had a house way up in the mountains and there nobody would know, and I said well perhaps later but now I said to-morrow we are going to move to Culoz, with our large comfortable new house with two good servants and a nice big park with trees, and we all went home, and we did move the next day. It took us some weeks to get over it but we finally did.

But what was so curious in the whole affair was its unreality, like things are unreal when you are a child and before you know about realism as we did in the Spanish-American war and the Russo-Japanese war just that.

And also the strange quality of government employees, I know a great deal now that and Russian literature about that same time of the Russo-Japanese war taught us about that.

It was around those days that three things happened that made me know about those kind of things. There was my eldest brother coming home from the East as a member of the G. A. R., he had to grow a beard to look old enough, of course he did not belong but there were privileges in traveling and other things so he came along with them. It was then I first knew about officialdom and what one did by bribing. Of course that has to do with war, because the ordinary person that is one leading a peaceful life particularly men comes in contact with officials but in war-time, sooner or later everybody does. The second thing was the famous Oscar Wilde trial and the question of public opinion and the third thing was the Dreyfus case and anti-semitism.

Anybody can ask a question and anybody can answer a question, and during war-time they ask questions more than ever particularly in war-time like this one of 1943. Who said Christine aged six of her mother who is the Italians, Italians being in occupation it was a natural question, why the Germans said her mother, and who are friends of the Germans, why the Italians said her mother, and who are friends of the English said Christine, why the Americans said her mother, and is Stalin friends with Germans said Christine, no with the English said her mother, and who are the French friends of, said Christine, why no one said the mother.

So if you ask questions and there is an answer it is not nevertheless any less illuminating, but anybody can ask questions in the year 1943, in July.

Nevertheless there are more public servants than ever, more police, more regulations, more avoidance of the law, more prisoners, more coming and going and everybody sooner or later has to know a great many public servants a very great many, and certainly very certainly they do not ask or answer questions, and if they do they do not mean to they ask them because that is what they are told to do. We have an acquaintance, she was taken by the Germans because well there was a reason, there usually is a reason one might say there always is a reason. And they asked questions and she kept answering saying she did not know the answer to the questions. Nobody does know whether she does know the answer to the questions they asked her. And all the time all around her, there was opening and closing of revolvers and police dogs coming and going and lying down and getting up and suddenly she laughed, quite pleasantly and the man asking her questions said do not laugh at me and she said I am laughing pleasantly that is to say I am laughing at the absurdity of my being here not able to answer the questions you are asking and so she was in prison for two months and then once more they called her to ask questions and as she did not know the answers any more than she had before the man asking said now you can go, and she said where and he said wherever you like and she said you mean I am free and he said yes you are free, and she said but I have no money left, it all went in prison and I have none left for car-fare, and my friends live quite a way off, could you give me twenty soux for car-fare, and he said yes he could and she said do, and he gave it to her and she went away and she was free.

The thing that is most interesting about government servants is that they believe what they are supposed to believe, they really do believe what they are supposed to believe, which has a great deal to do with wars and wars being what they are. It really has.

I once asked some one who should know why public servants in the army in every branch of government service did not seem to have the kind of judgment that the man in the street any man or any woman has about what is happening. Oh he answered the reason is simple, they are specialists, and to a specialist his specialty is the whole of everything and if his specialty is in good order and it generally is then everything must be succeeding. In the German army they call these specialists the bees, because in their cells they are supposed to make honey, not money honey. And so this is what makes war, and then makes the failure of war. I have said so often between 1939 and 1943, I cannot understand why men have so little common sense why they cannot understand when there is no possibility of their winning that they will win, why they cannot remember that two and two makes four and no more. And now everybody knows except the public servants they are still believing what they are supposed to believe nobody else believes it, not even all their families believe it but believe it or not, they do still believe it, believe what they are supposed to believe. And so naturally they believing what they are supposed to believe make it possible for the country to think they can win a war that they cannot possibly win, and so they go to war, and all because the public servants really believe what they are supposed to believe they really do. Of course most people in peace time do not realise this because the public servants who are like that practically never come in contact with them, and as nobody believes what they are supposed to believe, really one might say nobody believes that is nobody in ordinary life believes what they are supposed to believe because they are too busy making a living to have time to believe what they are supposed to believe, but public servants not having the necessity of making a living because their present past and future are secure, and practically unchangeable, they have all the time and strength to put into believing what they are supposed to believe and the result of this is war, the wars, that they are sure to lose, I suppose even the wars they are sure to win, well anyhow. It was Lee in the civil war, who was such a typical public servant, and who believes what he was supposed to believe, and at that time when my brother who did not belong came out to California with them all he had to do was to wear a beard to look old enough I vaguely began to know that public servants have nothing to do

with the business of living because they do believe what they are
supposed to believe, it makes a certain kind of clergyman, and
school teacher as well as army, and government employees. Oh
dear me, and will we have more to eat to-morrow, we always worry
but as yet we always have had, in spite of the government servants
believing what they are supposed to believe.

The next thing that impressed me at that time, was the Oscar
Wilde story, and that largely because of the poem he wrote about
his imprisonment, up to that time I had never conceived the possibility of anybody being in prison, anybody whose business it was
not naturally because of natural or accidental crime to be in
prison, and in California in those days of course even natural or
accidental crime did not mean prison. And now in 1943 the large
part of the men of a whole nation are in prison. Prisoners, prison,
of course we did know about Andersonville and Libby prison,
but that was romantic, but now there are too many for romance,
many many too many. Anybody can be a prisoner now, even those
who are only in a training camp feel themselves to be prisoners.
We have just had a letter from Victor the baker's son twenty years
old who has been our gardener. He is the only son with four sisters
and is much loved by his family. He says,

Life has completely changed since I have been here, I never
stop thinking of my former life, in those days when I wanted to
go out, I went out, I remained out as long as I wanted to stay out,
I came in when I wanted to, but alas that life is over, for the eight
months that I am to stay in this isolated camp where we never see
any civilian, the whole round of the week. Sunday we go out but
in a group and with our chief, so we are not free. And then to-day
too a letter from a real prisoner in Germany, and he says, I always
liked you and your country and I have not changed my mind, far
from it.

Well he is free to say what he will but that is very difficult to
stop, very very difficult, even in prison.

Another friend a political prisoner told us, that they never
have as much information real information about everything as in

prison. And a hotel keeper whom we liked, well there is black traffic, and there is this and there is that, and they all are in prison, and now the Germans and the Italians in July 1943 as the pressure is commencing all around them, they feel imprisoned. There is no doubt that every one really wants to be free, at least to feel free, they may like to give orders or even to take them, but they like to feel free, oh yes they do they do like to feel free, and so Oscar Wilde and the Ballad of Reading Gaol was the first thing that made me realise that it could happen, being in prison.

And then the next thing was the Dreyfus affair, that is anti-semitism, and that is a very strange thing in connection with mediaevalism and nineteenth century and how a century is so hard to kill, anything is so hard to kill, thank heaven.

He can read acasias, hands and faces. Acasias are for the goat, and the goat gives milk, very necessary these days and hands and faces are hands and faces, and dreams when one is dancing and falls asleep are real, and all this has this to do with anti-semitism that it is true and not real and real and not true.

Through and through.

There is a strange delusion.

Before industrialism Jews were international bankers and be-fore that international money-lenders, but since industrialism, all the Jewish money in the world is only a drop in the bucket and all of it together could never buy anybody to make war or make peace, not a bit. The Rothschilds in the Napoleonic wars and just after, were the end of the Jewish financial houses. After that began industrialism and in that the Jews have never been an economical power as anybody knows who knows and as everybody knows who knows. But the European particularly the countries who like to delude their people do not want to know it, they must know it of course, anybody must know it, and the Jews do not want anybody to know it, although they know it perfectly well they must know it because it would make themselves to themselves feel less important and as they always as the chosen people have felt themselves to themselves to be important they do not want anybody to know it.

But of course everybody must know it, the big names in industrialism and in the financing of industrialism are not in any modern country Jewish and everybody must know it but nobody wants to know it, because everybody likes it to be as it was supposed to be and not as it was because nobody likes anything to disappear, and as for so many hundreds of years it was so and of course religion does get mixed up with it but as it is not any longer possible to keep it strictly a religious question, and complicate life with Christianity, so it is inevitable that they all want to go on believing what they know is not so, and it was first made real for me by the Dreyfus trial and now from Germany who is so desperately clinging to any past century, any past century is a hope and a force any past century even any present century, they to cling to a century and what that century stood for, they have thus to keep themselves together, and so anti-semitism which has been with us quite a few centuries is still something to cling to. When the star is red they will fight in France and the star is red to-night the twenty-third of July, it is red. Red white and blue all out but you. Anyway financially there is no sense in anti-semitism. That is what I say.

From the Russian-Japanese war on I became for purposes of daily living a European and so not only were wars different but also the century was different the twentieth century had begun. Science was over, because believe it or not the twentieth century is not interested in science it really is not.

In these days we have to have animals around us because we have to have milk and eggs and there is no way to buy them so we have chickens and a goat, and I take care of them August 1943. And I have been struck by the fact that do what you like that is what they like and what they are but they always must have five toes, chickens and goats, and dogs and everything. Now there is no reason for it it is just what you might say a mystic number, a number that pleases but having been made it is there, five is there everywhere when there are toes. And this has a great deal to do with that, that the nineteenth century believed in science but the twentieth century does not. Not.

Saint Odile, oh yes Saint Odile.

I said once that the farmers of Bilignin just before this war said that if they had to thrash the wheat with flails the way it used to be done none of them would grow wheat, they would only grow wheat if the thrashing machine came around to thrash it, and now 1943, they are all thrashing their wheat with flails, and they fish eels so that they can take the skin, there is no leather left, and the eel skin replaces the leather in the flail, and they do it, not because there are no machines, there are indeed electric ones which they never had before, but if their wheat is thrashed by machine the government can control it, and if it is thrashed by flail, each man when and where he likes, instead of all together with a machine why of course some of it can get kept, can get hidden can get eaten, oh dear, of course beating wheat with a flail is as much science as doing it with an electric machine, but it does not make people feel the triumph of science, not at all it just makes it middle ages and secret, and that is why the twentieth century is not interested in science, so called, not at all, while the nineteenth century had nothing if not that nothing at all.

And now about Saint Odile.

Our young servant when she came this morning and I asked her was there any news said I can tell you very little, it is always the same some one is winning and some one is losing. It is always the same.

And that is what made the prophecies of Saint Odile seem different, the final winning was so tremendous. This is the story.

In 1940 when we were all filled with sorrow and despair and a little hope and a complete certainty that after all, the Germans were not going to win. To my great surprise a prisoner a young musician who said the worst of being a prisoner was that you were all day and all night always together with seventy other men, men alone always together, just like Cummings described it in The Enormous Room. Well anyway he said in spite of everything every morning all of the roomful took it simply and completely for granted that the Germans were not going to win. They all greeted each other good-morning and how long before the Germans are going to be defeated. But said I how did you keep that faith. We do not keep it he said we had it, we just naturally did not have any other feeling. Well we the civilian population did not have it so simply, we had to have the prophecies of Saint Odile but they did help a lot.

To-day August 1943 I saw another returned prisoner, he was pale and his eyes glowed and as I came into the grocery store I heard some one say the pigs the rascals. And the grocer said to me do not be startled he is only talking about the Boches. Yes said the man I do not understand how anybody cannot realise that we are still at war with the Germans. An armistice is a pause but it is not an end, and as long as there is no peace we are at war, and as long as we are at war any one helping the enemy is a traitor to his country, that is the way I see it he said and his eyes glowed and he said they say that the Americans are slow but I dont know, Roosevelt said that in 1943 they would be here, and now it is 1943 and here they are. I dont know what anybody wants that satisfies me, they said they would be here and here they are. And I said I as an American I want to thank you and we shook hands and he said thank you and I said thank you.

This is what a prediction is. Just that, but of course that was near, it was said in '42, and then there is the unconditional surrender, which they are demanding from the enemy. When I was a child and later and always I admired General Grant, and I knew that they used his initials Ulysses Simpson to mean Unconditional Surrender Grant. It was reasonable very reasonable very logical I thought so then and I said it just today, if the winner wins, then the vanquished should give in, and why ask for terms beforehand, if the winner is going to be generous he is going to be generous and if he is not going to be generous he is not going to be generous so what is the use of making terms. Unconditional surrender and then let them be generous or not. That is reasonable, because any way the ones beaten are beaten. That is the difference between European logic and American logic just that. So in a way my always quoting Unconditional Surrender Grant was a prediction. In a way yes it was. It is strange just as strange as it can be. Since yesterday or day before yesterday it seems but it was only yesterday, we have a German officer a major and his orderly stationed in the house and now August 1943, they are very meek, just as meek as that. The cook said to him that it was the Germans who had stolen the gardener's radio, and that the gardener was a prisoner. He will be coming home now very soon, said the major.

Saint Odile predicted much further away that is what any one can say, does it make it more interesting, yes it does and no it does not and yes it does.

If you try to kill five hundred years or a thousand years is it more interesting than just killing one hundred years is it. And is there any hope that the hundred years or the thousand years which have been killed to make room for another thousand years or five hundred years will make that difference. Saint Odile thought so and thinking so she was a comfort to all of us. That is what makes predictions. Knowing what is going to happen to-day or to-morrow, or next week, that is some people's predictions, and other people's predictions is what some one person or kind of person will do at any time, and other people's predictions is what some country will do and what will happen when any one or any body of them do do it. I have always loved to read Shakespeare's Henry VI in three parts and now just now August 1943, I find it more so than ever much more even so much more so than ever which I always did find it fun when I was eight years old until now. Saint Odile.

Saint Odile said that the world would go on and there would come the worst war of all and the fire would be thrown down from the heavens and there would be freezing and heating and rivers running and at last there would be winning by the enemy and everybody would say and how can they be so strong, and everybody would say and give us peace and then little by little there would come the battle of the mountain and that was certainly Moscow, because even in the time of Saint Odile Moscow because of its many religious houses was called the Holy Mountain, and indeed it was there that the enemy received its first check, and then she said much later there would be fighting in the streets of the eternal city and indeed there it is, we did sometimes think it might be Constantinople or even possibly Jerusalem but no it certainly was Rome and now they are fighting in the streets of Rome, now in 1943 in August in the evening and that would not yet be the end but would be the beginning of the end, which it is, and then there would for the first time in the history of the world there would be peace, east and west, west and east and all together.

And this was a comfort so often a comfort and it is a comfort again, like a road you find on the map and then see in real life or a road you see in real life and then see on a map. So that is the difference between the nineteenth and the twentieth century just that.

This is my scientific history. Not Saint Odile, but this, that I am about to tell.

August 1943. Here we can see every night when the moon is bright and even when it is not, we cannot see them but we hear them, they hum and then from time to time they drop a light and they give us all a very great deal of delight. And why. Because they are going to drop bombs on the Italians. Anybody can like an Italian but just the same we can have a great deal of pleasure in hearing all these airplanes hum and see them drop lights on their way to bomb Italians. Why we all say do they not give in. Not so exciting perhaps but more useful, useful that is if you want to go on living in a country that has not been overwhelmed by destruction. Last night just before the airplanes came there was a complete eclipse of the moon, the shadow of the earth fell on the moon, none too soon and then slowly it passed away, it was very nice, but none of the newspapers and none of the radios mentioned it. Eclipses are an amusement for peace time and yet all the same said my neighbor, she is a country-woman, it makes one think of all those worlds turning around and around. Yes I said it is more terrifying even than war. Yes she said. And it was twelve o'clock at night and the moon was shining bright again and we went to bed and a little after we heard the airplanes humming and we saw the lights dropping and then we shut out the moonlight and then we were sleeping. All this is an introduction to the nineteenth century feeling about science.

To believe in progress and in science you had to know what science was and what progress might be. Having been born in the nineteenth century it was natural enough to know what science was. Darwin was still alive and Huxley and Agassiz and after all they all made the difference of before and after. And now in 1943 none of it means more than it did. Not so much more as not more. Not more at all.

And I began with evolution. Most pleasant and exciting and decisive. It justified peace and justified war. It also justified life and it also justified death and it also justified life. Evolution did all that. And now. Evolution is no longer interesting. It is historical now and no longer actual. Not even pleasant or exciting, not at all. To those of us who were interested in science then it had to do tremendously with the history of the world, the history of all animals, the history of death and life, and all that had to do with the round world. Evolution was as exciting as the discovery of America, by Columbus quite as exciting, and quite as much an opening up and a limiting, quite as much. By that I mean that discovering America, by reasoning and then finding, opened up a new world and at the same time closed the circle, there was no longer any beyond. Evolution did the same thing, it opened up the history of all animals vegetables and minerals, and man, and at the same time it made them all confined, confined within a circle, no excitement of creation any more. It is funny all this and this was my childhood and youth and beginning of existence. War oh yes war but logical and incessant war, and peace oh yes, peace because if war is completely understood then peace was the ideal. It was just like that.

Stars are not really more than just what they look like. If they are then are they really realer than war. It is just that that makes the twentieth century, know what science teaches and whether it is or whether it is not what science teaches, since war is really and therefore it is what it is, that is everybody gets to meet anybody friends and enemies we have then now enemies in the house and in the barn, and it does not make any difference about the stars and it does not make any difference about war, only really it does make a difference about war seeing the trains pass with the enemy on them yes it does, but the stars whether they are what they look like or what science teaches, does it make any difference and anybody can answer that it does not.

I did live in the nineteenth century and the difference was that then the answer was that it did make a difference, that the stars were what science teaches and now in August 1943 it does not.

Naturally if you were born in the nineteenth century when evolution first began to be known, and everything was being understood, really understood everybody knew that if everything was really being and going to be understood, and if everything was understood then there would be progress and if there was going to be progress there would not be any wars, and if there were not any wars then everything could be and would be understood, and even if death and life were not understood and eternity and beginning was not understood well that is to say if they were not understood more than science understood them better after all except in the unhappiness of adolescence better not think about that. That was what the nineteenth century knew to be true, and they wanted it to be like that. To be sure there were a great many wars, but on the other hand there was a great deal of civilising going on so much so that by the time the twentieth century began almost any one could read and write, and now in the twentieth century anybody can listen to the radio, in any language and everybody is civilised enough to do that, but wars are more than ever and now everybody knows that although everybody is civilised there is no progress and everybody knows even though anybody flies higher and higher they cannot explain eternity any more than before, and everybody can persecute anybody just as much if not more than ever, it is rather ridiculous so much science, so much civilisation that is so much reading and writing and listening to the radio, and they persecute anybody, and put books on the index, that and ban them publicly just like that. It is funny.

Just now we have just been hearing about prisoners escaping from prison, it is very interesting. There is a nice story about a compass.

As some of them escape on foot and keep on on foot until they get home, it is better to have a compass. Two of them had with the compass gotten as far as the Swiss frontier and there they were caught by the Germans before they could cross it. They were questioned and they found the compass it was a lovely compass and the questioner put it on the table in front of him, the two while they were being questioned one of them leaned forward and took the compass and slipped it into his pocket. When the questioner missed the compass from the table he said search him and while they searched the one he slipped the compass to the other one and then while he was searched he slipped it back again, and then the examiner said search them both at the same time and the compass was found and was again put on the table in front of them. Then while the questioner went on one of them took the compass again and slipped it to the other one who put it into his shoe and then in making a movement it fell out on the floor and it was once more taken from them and put back on the table in front of them. The questioner went on and finally it was done and finished and they all stood up and they all left and one of the Frenchmen as he was leaving put his hand out in back of him took the compass and put it in his pocket and nobody noticed him or that it was gone as they all had left the room with them. They were sent away that evening and so nobody noticed the compass and nobody took it away from them, and so the two of them escaping for the third time with the help of the compass came into France and home and just the other day we saw them in August 1943 and they told us that and many other stories of prisoners escaping. We like that one perhaps the best.

William James was of the strongest scientific influences that I had and he said he always said there is the will to live without the will to live there is destruction, but there is also the will to destroy, and the two like everything are in opposition, like wanting to be alone and when you are alone wanting to have company and when you have company wanting to be alone and liking wanting eternity and wanting a beginning and middle and ending and now in 1943 the thing that we know most about is the opposition between the will to live and the will to destroy, and when like with the Germans it is almost fifty fifty they do not mind they commit suicide. There was a farmer who once said to me he said it in 1941, he said they say it is Hitler, but it is not Hitler. I fought all the other war and I know what Germans are. They are a funny people. They are always choosing some one to lead them in a direction which they do not want to go. They cannot help themselves they are not led, it is not the Kaiser, it is not Hitler, who leads them, it is they themselves who choose the man and really force him to lead them in a direction which they do not want to go. That is because the will to live and the will to destroy is fifty fifty which is what it ought not to be. And that is why French people do not have to say as the English do are we down hearted, no. They are so completely filled with the will to live that they never heard of down-heartedness. The other day here when the Germans came and occupied us again, here in Culoz, August 1943 one of the women said, well of course it is disagreeable, very disagreeable, but nothing as it would have been if we had been beaten. And she was quite right. They were not beaten, the Germans being beaten even if they did not beat them they themselves were not beaten and she was right.

The Chinese-Japanese war and the Russo-Japanese war completed the work of Christopher Columbus, it made the world all one, it made the East no longer a mysterious something, not so much later any American woman could make a home for a year in Pekin and then go home again to America just as she might go to Paris or to California, and so the work of Christopher Columbus was finished, the North Pole was found and the South Pole was found, and the work of Christopher Columbus was over, and so the nineteenth century which had undertaken to make science more important than anything by having finished the work of Christopher Columbus and reduced the world to a place where there was only that, forced the world into world wars to give everybody a new thing to do as discoveries being over science not being interesting because so limiting there was nothing else to do to keep everybody from doing everything in the same way but a world war particularly this present one where everybody had to stay at home and could not even write letters to friends not most of the time, as some one said not long ago, any public character can talk and talk all day long over the radio and any radio speaker but any of us who just want to send a post card to somebody well we just cannot, we have to stay at home and not meet anybody. Such is the result of the world war after the work of Christopher Columbus was all over, and science was not interesting any longer, and evolution was so completely confined to the earth and the earth was all there, and so the nineteenth century is over, killed at last, by the twentieth century.

But now not now we are still at the Russo-Japanese war and the first Balkan wars.

Now in September 1943 I am beginning to like trains again. For thirty years I never went into a train, automobiles were the means of transport including airplanes but no trains. When in America I did once or twice have to get into trains I was struck with the fact that there had been no progress in train travel, trains were just as dirty and just as much like themselves, night trains and day trains as when I knew them in the days of the Russo-Japanese war, or any other time. I once mentioned this to a French engineer and he said naturally enough, trains could not improve could not get more comfortable because cars had to keep the same shape. All the tracks having been made that is the road bed of a certain width cars could not be made wider nothing could really change there was too much to do to change anything, no~~~~ automobiles or airplanes which can constantly ~~~~ and their shapes. And then t~~~~ They spend so much more ~~~~

which made for thirty years made one feel that trains were far away, and now there being only walking bicycling and trains we take trains and all the old delight in trains comes back. The making of so many acquaintances. There being so many people in a compartment and in the corridors, there being so many things happening, there being eating and drinking and very strange eating and drinking these days in a train, everybody carrying something and some quite openly eating what they are not supposed to be having and others not eating anything at all at least it might just as well not be anything, and in a station having a long conversation with a very nice refugee she in one train and I in another one, and telling each other all about what we were and where we came from. It also is very amusing. The German army was a motorised army so everybody said and so everybody thought and so everybody knew and now their automobiles travel on the trains, there are none of them on the road. Here where we see the trains pass, continuously the German army moves with all its automobiles but all of them on the train. No automobile on the road. Not one, not one solitary one. All of them on flat baggage cars with soldiers sitting around them and this must be a pleasure to every one. To be sure in a way trains are more romantic than automobiles but even though Germans love the romantic, it cannot really be a comfort to them. I realised some years ago that trains were really more romantic than automobiles, and it was in this way. They were having their annual fair in Belley and they had as one of the attractions, a little tunnel and a train going in and coming out of it and going around and around. Almost everybody in Belley had been in automobiles some even in airplanes but quite a number had never been in a train, and it excited them going in and out of the little tunnel and around and around. There are two things that are exciting going around and around and around and going ___ght ahead on rails. Rails are in a way more romantic than a ___ ___turesque and it can even be endless and straight, ___ ___marked on it to separate one piece ___ ___done in modern highways,

So a few weeks ago we had here in the house first the German officers and then later on the Italians. It is funny to be Americans and to be here in France and to have that.

I like a thing they say if they say it every time they feel it. They say it of my dog Basket, every time they see him and they see him any time and they always say look at him you would take him for a sheep. And so all this time everybody in talking speaks of the Germans, they always were saying, but they are still strong, they are still powerful, just as Saint Odile said they would say and they have been saying it any day and every day and in every way whenever the Germans were mentioned by them and naturally with the war going on and the Germans being in occupation they were mentioned every day and any day and they always said well until a month ago, they always said with meditation or conviction depending upon the person speaking they said they are still powerful, they are still strong. To-day and every day they go on mentioning the Germans, and now any one of them and every one of them as they speak of them they say in the same way, they are pretty sick, and nobody says anything when the Germans are mentioned except that the Germans are pretty sick now, quite sick now, and that is what I like that they repeat every day what they feel each day and that is not repetition that is saying each day what they are knowing, that Basket the poodle you would think he was a sheep, that the Germans until September 1943 were still very strong, that the Germans in September 1943 are sick, pretty sick, quite sick.

So Saint Odile did prophesy.

We had the Germans and then the Italians in the house in the months of August and of September.

When the Germans were here it was very different from '40, then every one was frightened of them and now it was unpleasant as one of the women said of course it was unpleasant but not unpleasant as if we had been conquered.

And she was right, the Germans not being conquerors any more nobody feels conquered.

It is full of excitement to know that Shakespeare and everybody is right about how people are. By this I mean, anybody can mean, that when you are in a country that is being occupied by an enemy, by two enemies in a manner of speaking, everybody is funny, that is they feel and they act in such different ways at any time. You think they think one thing and they act another. One country priest who outrages his congregation by preaching against the Americans, is delighted to meet me and makes a special effort to love my dog and love me. Others who are said to be one thing say other things and under conditions distinctly unfavorable for them, oh it is all so complicated and every day and in every way I like the complications being so complicated. The 1914-1918 war was a simple war with simple feelings and all the veterans of that war are confused with this war, they do not understand, and they cannot find themselves, everything is so opposed to anything that is straightforward, I must say I like it, I like things that look as if they were there when they are elsewhere. I do like it. I do not like to fish in troubled waters but I do like to see the troubled water and the fish and the fishermen. I suppose I do not like to fish in troubled waters because I do not care about fishing at all, but that is another matter.

After the Germans left we had Italians in the house. They were rather attaching, foolish and could not keep away from the young servant, they went in one door and came out another and then they were still there, but otherwise they were sad, and they hated the Germans and they liked everybody else, and they were sad, they said if this went on they would have no country, they hoped some of them would still have a family but would they, oh said they holding their heads. Milan, and Turin, and Genoa and Cremona, oh dear. And we were sorry for them and they said they hoped they would stay here until the end of the war and the next day they had to go away, and they went around saying good-bye to the village where they had only been for eight days as if they were saying good-bye to the village in which they had been born.

The Balkans, first came to be something for me, from Tolstoi,

and our Slav brothers and then freeing them, it is extraordinary
how Bulgaria, which is the most Slav of all the Balkan peoples is
the one that has most passionately been ungrateful to the Russians
who freed them, but that makes it all like Shakespeare too which
is very exciting, and so from that time through the two Balkan
wars, and hearing lots of Serbs in 1914-1918 war, and visiting the
sick Serb men in France and the children to now when we have a
Servian dentist and his son is in prison for having ammunition
stored in his room to give to the young men who have escaped into
the mountains to avoid going to Germany as forced labor, and
they were so frightened that he was going to be shot, but fortunately he was in the hands of the Italians and they do not shoot
any one if they can avoid it and they can always avoid it. We have
a young maid working for us and she is Italian, that is French-
Italian and I tease her because she spends her Sundays visiting her
relations in prison. There is an uncle who was a restaurant keeper
and he is in prison for having given and sold food, which is known
as black traffic, and yesterday she went to Chambery to see a
cousin who was in the Italian army and now September '43, the
Italians have been put in prison by the Germans but this cousin
seems to have escaped in a truck, which he was driving but where
to nobody knows. It is a strange confusion nobody knows. Some
one was just telling of trying to find somebody who was in prison,
and so they took a bundle of clothes, and they went to all the
prisons in Lyon and in Paris and at each one they said they wanted
to give this bundle to such and such and they always said there is
no such name here until finally they found there was such a name
there and they found him.

The Balkans have always been confused like that from all
accounts, but now everybody and everything is confused like that,
peas and beans and barley grows, you nor I nor nobody knows,
where peas and beans and barley grows. I never did think that
everything and everybody would be naturally like that.

The prisons are all so crowded, there are so many things that
happen, there was one chronic thief in Bilignin who always stole

a turkey or grapes or something, and the last time when he was condemned to two months' imprisonment he had to wait three months before there was room in the prison to serve his two months. In between they let him stay at home. At the Hopkins' hospital when I was a medical student, when we asked some Negro where another one was, the frequent answer was oh he is in jail, but Miss, that is no disgrace. And it is like that now, what with black traffic, and this and that and politics, and this and that it is no disgrace.

And so there was the first Balkan war and the second Balkan war and then there was the first world war. It is extraordinary how having done a thing once you have to do it again, there is the pleasure of coincidence and there is the pleasure of repetition, and so there is the second world war, and in between there was the Abyssinian war and the Spanish civil war.

The French like variety, that is what makes them pleasant to live with. I like to think of all the forms of government they have had since the revolution until now, in very little over a hundred years I like to tease them about it, when they go solemn about their future. I tell them why worry when they have had such a record.

This is it.

In a little over a hundred years, they have had three different republics, two kinds of kingdoms, a commune, a dictatorship, and this present government of 1943, and yet they worry about what the next government is going to be. I say why worry, it can be anything and if it is it can change to anything else and after all what difference does it make except to the people in power. It certainly does not make any difference to anybody else ever, certainly not.

So after the Balkan wars, and as we had a Serb in the court, who was sensitive to noise, and a great patriot, and we knew a Bulgarian but that was later that was after the 1914-1918 war and he took care of my Ford car and we still know him, so after the two Balkan wars, and there will naturally be plenty more of them, our dentist is a Serb and he wears his linen blouse with extraordinary elegance, the Serbs are like that, and so as I say the world war 1914-1918 began and the nineteenth century a very resistant strong obstinate and convinced of its service to humanity and progress was trying to be killed that is to say they were trying to kill it but could they. No. Not even by the 1914-1918 war, they could not and they did not and now it is dead Hitler killed it, and like a very Samson he fell down with it and was killed in its ruins. It is rather nice that, no wonder there are predictions that come out right like Saint Odile no wonder when everything is the same with such an intense variety. Including goats and chickens including Saint Odile said that there would be fighting in the streets of the eternal city and that would not be the end but the beginning of the end and after that all the countries that had been invaded would invade the Germans and the countries would then get back all that had been lost and a little more.

I liked that a little more, it was a woman's thought, that they would need that consolation and that they would have it which they will. They will.

In the nineteenth century of course there were predictions but not important ones and if they were they did not make it be certain that there might be peace and no progress, peace and no progress that is what the twentieth century might do. Peace and no progress.

In the nineteenth century, there is the feeling that one is justified in being angry, in being right, in being justified. In the twentieth century it is not that it is right but that what happens truly happens.

Now in September 1943, just as the vintage is coming and grape juice is intensely sweet and pleasant, they can prepare for the beginning of the end and they do, the beginning of the end and they do.

But before that there is still the nineteenth century and the first world war, 1914-1918, and the witnesses of that war still can remember that war. I remember how amused we were when that war was not yet over that in an American newspaper they once said, for those of us who can remember the beginning of the war. It is difficult to remember the beginning of the war when the war is beginning to end. That is the reason why really although everybody says that they are going to hang everybody who was not patriotic during the war actually the war being over everybody forgets. Kipling made a song about lest we forget, and the French clandestine press says that the French should be taught to hate. But if they could hate how could they make fashions, you cannot make fashions if you are always remembering and how can you hate if you cannot remember. Etta Cone said that she could forgive but not forget and Alice Toklas answered, I cannot forgive but I do forget, Well anyway, there undoubtedly was the first world war and we and many many other veterans went through it and some of us have a veteran mentality and some of us have not.

Incontestably the 1914-1918 war was a nineteenth century war just as the 1939-19— war incontestably is not. And the hopes and the fears, and the relation to finite and infinity of this war and the method of belief and unbelief, and the hope of progress and reform all these things are not nineteenth century not at all not now.

It is interesting. We have Basket II. He is a pedigreed dog, twenty generations are behind him and all of them German. The other Basket was unpedigreed and entirely French. And Basket II, we have a cat, the peasants who gave it to us had called it by a name Hitler because of his mustache and Basket had not been friendly with him but no matter. But now suddenly he chases him chases him away. Is it an omen. Some things can be an omen but is it.

And just as some thing can be an omen but is it, so now in 1943, there is nothing that is nineteenth century, not here in France, except what is here that does not belong here. Believe it or not it is true. But now to return to the nineteenth century, to the 1914-1918 war, and the way veterans feel. They feel disappointed, not about the 1914-1918 war but about this war. They liked that war, it was a nice war, a real war a regular war, a commenced war and an ended war. It was a war, and veterans like a war to be a war. They do.

September 1943 they are harvesting their grapes to make their wine, it will be they all say a victory wine, and it is good in quantity and quality. They do not think of the future they only think of being free.

There is one thing that is certain, and nobody really realised it in the 1914-1918 war, they talked about it but they did not realise it but now everybody knows it everybody that the one thing that everybody wants is to be free, to talk to eat to drink to walk to think, to please, to wish, and to do it now if now is what they want, and everybody knows it they know it anybody knows it, they want to be free, they do not want to feel imprisoned they want to feel free, even if they are not free they want to feel free, and they want to feel free now, let the future take care of itself all they want is to be free, not to be managed, threatened, directed, restrained, obliged, fearful, administered, they want none of these things they all want to feel free, the word discipline, and forbidden and investigated and imprisoned brings horror and fear into all hearts, they do not want to be afraid not more than is necessary in the ordinary business of living where one has to earn one's living and has to fear want and disease and death. There are enough things to be afraid of, nobody wants to be afraid, just afraid, afraid of things people should not be afraid, they do not. This is true in October 1943, it is true. In 1914-1918, it was still the nineteenth century, and one might still think that something that would happen might lead one to higher and other things but now, the only thing that any one wants now is to be free, to be let alone, to live their life as they can, but not to be watched, controlled, and scared, no no, not.

Some one has just told me that in 1918, two little children had a vision that they saw the Virgin and she told them that the world was going to have a much worse war than the one they had just had, and when that came and the roads would be full of fleeing

people the Pope would be imprisoned in his house, the square of
Saint Peter's would be filled with a fighting multitude and the
Pope all alone in his home would be sitting and weeping. That is
what the Virgin told them.

I suppose in a kind of way what the nineteenth century really
meant was that they believed in free will, they did not believe in
the inevitable, and this 1939-1943 war makes people know that
the inevitable is inevitable and that everybody wants to be free,
and needs to be free, which really makes the present life an
absolute realisation of the old scholastic arguments about free will,
and necessity. The nineteenth century did not understand this,
not even in the 1914-1918 war which tried to end the nineteenth
century but since it itself did not understand it, it could not end
the nineteenth century, but now now we all realise, the inevitable
and the thirst for freedom, we all do.

It is all right, and a funny story. Everything is so logical, in
this war, it was much more confused in the 1914-1918 one, and
therefore the things one predicts are truer for this war than they
were for that one. A German whom we know, and have known all
this time, calls me the general, because I have been right about
what has been happening, but that is only because this war is
logical, more so than most wars, and I will tell you why.

As I said the grapes are being gathered to make the victory
wine. It is funny anything is funny. The 1914-1918 war made
everybody drink. There was never so much drunkenness in France
as there was then, soldiers all learned to drink, everybody drank,
and after war, and now in this 1939-1943 war, nobody drinks not
here anyway not in France, the wine is all taken away and there is
only enough even for the wine growers to have a bottle a day, they
who used to drink anything from four to nine bottles a day, and
those who are on the regular supply only have four bottles a
month, and oh dear me, after all is it better or is it worse. It is
pleasanter for the women and the children when men drink less
undoubtedly pleasanter, and the men's health is in general better,
that is if they could have a little more meat and fats, well anyway

are they healthier or are they not anyway they want to be free, and not have the wine taken away from them. They want to be free.

Undoubtedly this war is more logical that is more inevitable than any other war. They say there have been surprises but actually there have not been surprises. It all has been inevitable so much more so than the 1914-1918 war so much more so.

The 1914-1918 war was just like our civil war, it was that kind of a war and that made it possible for Elmer Harden to make Pierre Caous admit that it was a nice war. A nice war is a war where everybody who is heroic is a hero, and everybody more or less is a hero in a nice war. Now this war is not at all a nice war. The English are still feeling that there are nice modest heroes in this war but actually this war which is an interesting war is not a nice war, people are sacrificed and imprisoned, so many of them so very very many of them and in such very different ways, and there are so many that hide in the heather as it is called which may be anywhere, or not at all and the police who want not to arrest them get killed because they have to arrest them, and some are called one thing and some are called another thing, and everybody can change about what they call them and everybody does, and there is nothing to hope for, and yet it will end because it is inevitable that it should but nobody really can call it a nice war, not really, not really a nice war. The children play being taken to prison, and the children play the commandos in the heather, and anywhere from two years old they sit behind some one who is on a bicycle, and nobody pays any attention to them but they do not fall off not any of them, they hold on to whoever is in front of them and they go miles and miles like that because everybody has to go miles and miles in the hope of getting something to eat miles and miles, on foot or on bicycles. It is only the French who could make the bicycles last so long. They make noises all of them but they keep going that is somebody makes them keep on going and always with a very little child on behind the seat and holding on to the person in front of them. In 1914-1918 they did not do that.

To-day October 1943, I was very pleased to hear about somebody's troubles that had nothing to do with the war. It was like in 1916, when our servant was so proud of her brother who was dead having had a civil and not a military funeral. Our young servant was telling us to-day that in a working-class family it was better to have more daughters than sons. The son when he is little is not a help and when he gets older he is apprenticed to a trade and earns very little and then for a little while he contributes to the family purse and then he gets engaged to be married and he has to save for the marriage and then he gets married and that is the end, so if there are three or four boys and only two girls the mother has to go out working to help support the family and then has to come home and do all the house work and not get to bed until two o'clock in the morning, while if there are four girls and two boys it makes out very much better. The mother can stay at home and do the housework in the daytime which she does. It was pleasant listening to this which had nothing to do with war nothing at all to do with war.

Sometime and every one is hoping it is going to be pretty soon now there will be everything happening and nothing at all to do with war.

It is the story that they all told last fall. They were talking people in a position to know and one of them said it was going to be over now, and they all said eagerly how do you know and he said very easily, my wife has had enough of it.

Yes everybody has had enough of it everybody's wife and everybody's husband and everybody's mother and everybody's father and everybody's daughter and everybody's son, they all have had enough of it.

In 1918 they did not all feel like that, there had been a great deal of it, a great deal of war but not everybody was fully simply naturally and uninterestedly tired of it, they all have had enough of it. That is all.

That shows the complete difference between the 1914-1918 war and this war, both world wars, but one did not end the nineteenth century it tried to but it did not succeed but this one did or does. It does end the nineteenth century, kills it dead, dead dead.

There is another nice story that always pleases me, in a bus in Paris, there were on the back platform a German soldier and some Frenchmen and the soldier accidentally stepped on the foot of the Frenchman and he having sensitive feet hit out and hit the German, before anything more could happen a very little Frenchman at the completely other end of the bus came rushing and he too hit the soldier. They were all three taken to the police station, and the first Frenchman explained about his sensitive feet and how sorry he was he had made this instinctive action and he apologised and the soldier accepted the apology, and then the second and little Frenchman was asked why he had rushed out and hit the soldier. Well he said it was like this, I suddenly saw a Frenchman hit out and strike a German soldier and I said hello the war must be over let me go to it and I rushed forward and hit him. And now he said it was a mistake the war is not over.

Sometime it will not be a mistake the war will be over at any rate France will be free. And we. Nobody felt like that in the last war. It is like that other joke, in the 1914-1918 war everybody always used to say, we'll get them yet, and they did they got the best of them and somebody said in this war, they used to say in the last war we'll get 'em yet, and now he added we have them. It is nice to say in French very nice. But now everybody has had enough enough. That is the difference between the 1914-1918 war and the 1939-1943 war everybody has had enough.

Eating too much meat gives you indigestion and evil thoughts make you eat too much meat.

The funny thing about the '39-'43 is that anybody can feel anything can think anything. In '14-'18 everybody well if not everybody the great majority knew who was an enemy and who was a friend, if they did not know they were pretty sure, and they mostly were not mistaken an enemy was an enemy and a friend was a friend more or less. Life in the nineteenth century and '14-'18 was just going on with that although there was Clemenceau who said that nobody was what they were supposed to be the English who were supposed to be so calm tended to be hysterical, the French who were supposed to be so light-minded were terribly serious and sober, and the Americans who were supposed to be so quick were so slow. But even so almost everybody continued to feel simply, an enemy was an enemy and a friend was a friend and war was war and peace was peace, to be sure there was Trotsky who said to the Germans he wanted to make a treaty that was neither peace nor war, all these things showed that the nineteenth century had been pretty nearly killed but still it was very much alive, it believed in peace and in war, it believed in a possible Esperanto, and in progress, it believed in humanity and the white man's burden, it believed in a nation in arms, it believed in a future and a past it believed in veterans, in short it really was the nineteenth century. And now, except Germany there is really nothing left of the nineteenth century and when that will be exterminated then the nineteenth century is over, and the twentieth century has come to stay. I belong to the generation who born in the nineteenth century spent all the early part of my life in escaping from it, and the rest of it in being the twentieth century yes of course.

Wilson spoke of himself as having a single track mind, Americans are like that, they see what they see and it bothers the European. They see in this war that the only thing necessary to do is to destroy the German material at its base, nothing else is worth while doing or being killed in doing, there is no use fighting until the German material is destroyed at its base and then it is only necessary to do enough fighting to make them know that they have no material and then the war is over. Europeans do not understand that, they believe in fighting first and then destroying material as the completion of fighting not as prevention, and so the American has a single track mind and it all seems so slow to the European because nothing happens until nothing has to happen. Enough said that is not the way the French mind works.

In the last war 1914-'18, it was not so evident that they could take six different roads at once because after all it was a nineteenth

century war, and the way was a comparatively simple way and the
way to go had some variation, but on the whole they were fairly
united, they did want to win the war and that was quite simply
that, but the '39-'43 war not at all, not, at, all.

After the armistice in '40 I was surprised, I can always be
surprised but I was decidedly surprised, so many of them were not
sure that they did not want the Germans to win. And I said why, I
do not understand, how can any Frenchman feel that way, why,
I said why, and I said it pretty violently and pretty often. The man
at the bank explained something. He said there are a great many
different points of view and one single man can have quite a great
number of them.

Is it worse to be scared than to be bored, that is the question.

Any one man, so said the man at the bank, could want the
English to win, because as he was in business he wants business to
be secure, and if the Germans win business would not be secure
not for him, at the same time he has a son who is a prisoner, his
only son, and he wants the Germans to win because his son would
come home to him, and if the English were to win the war would
be long and his son might die before he came home to him, then at
that time Germany was allied to Russia and might that mean
communism and then he would want the English to win, and then
there is another point of view, the French love to talk about
discipline, they always think their country is very disorderly as a
matter of fact they are so traditional, and they love so passionately
to grow vegetables that they can really only be orderly, and never
anything else but they like to think there is no order and that there
should be. That is Petain's point of view, that was the point of
view of a crazy man at the end of the last war in 1918, who one day
started to ask everybody to show him their papers at the station,
and everybody did, naturally one does when asked to do so
authoritatively and finally there was a big crowd waiting to show
him their papers, military and otherwise, and a policeman came
up seeing the crowd and said what is all this, and everybody said
he asked us to show him our papers, and the man when he had

been taken to the police court and had been asked why he had gone on like that answered, because I want to put a little order into my country. The other day, when everybody was growing potatoes and everybody was putting on all they could in the way of disinfectant and hard at it they were and one day I was out walking on a little road and a nice elderly, retired civil servant came along and he had a blower in his hand, and I said pleasantly and you are disinfecting your potato plants, and he said yes, but it would be more useful if everybody did, but I said they all do as much as they can, not as much he answered as they would if there was more order in the country. That said he is what we French suffer from a lack of order. I was polite but I wanted to say oh Hell, you all feel you are in prison because you are always being ordered, and it is funny, if anybody is alone they want company and if they have company they want to be alone. Human beings are like that, finite and infinite, when they have peace they want war and when they have war they want peace, Well anyway. Then gradually things changed the Russians became Germany's enemy, and the French were having more points of view in one man than ever. The middle classes were once more torn, if the Russians win, would there be communism, if the Germans win would there be misery and oppression, if the English win would they lose all their colonies. Shall we, said the people of Lyon, shall we lose our land or our pocket books, which will we mind less. They even began to make jokes about it although it was very real, it is very real. The most astonishing people, astonishing to me, that they should feel like that, said they would if they were younger go and fight the Russians, what I said with the Germans well not exactly, against the English well not exactly, well what then I said, and they said well what, and that conversation ended. Conversations were leading very strangely in those days, in the days after the armistice. And then there was Petain. So many points of view about him, so very many. I had lots of them, I was almost French in having so many. This was what happened to me about him.

When the farmers heard that the Russians had come in to fight

the Germans, they were single minded about it, they all got drunk
with joy quite simply drunk with joy, and later when the Germans
did not get to Moscow, just the same they said the French army
under Napoleon, did take Moscow they could not hold it of course
but they did get there, they were on foot, on foot you understand
and on foot they got there and these others with all their automobiles they cannot get there. We got there they said we were on
foot but we did get there. The French all this time were making
jokes very funny jokes they still are but there was this nice one
about Napoleon. They said this was in '41, they said that Hitler
went to visit Napoleon in his tomb that time he was in Paris, and
Napoleon reluctantly came out of his tomb to speak to him. Hitler
said I am a great conqueror, perhaps not quite so great a conqueror
as you were, this he said politely, but pretty nearly as great a
conqueror, I too have conquered all Europe. And England, said
Napoleon, not yet, said Hitler, Napoleon sighed I didn't either,
and Russia said Napoleon, not yet said the other. I did not either
said Napoleon, go away, said Napoleon, and he went back to his
tomb, and shut himself in. It was pretty good for the Parisians to
have invented that story in the winter of '40 '41, pretty good. They
tell so many funny stories, and the Parisians are funny, that is what
bothers the Germans so, the jokes are never what they expect, no
never.

But to tell about Petain and all the things one could I could
think about him.

It's funny about honey, you always eat honey during a war, so
much honey, there is no sugar, there never is sugar during a war,
the first thing to disappear is sugar, after that butter, but butter
can always be had but not sugar, no not sugar so during a war you
always eat honey quantities of honey, really more honey than you
used to eat sugar, and you find honey so much better than sugar,
better in itself and better in apple sauce, in all desserts so much
better and then peace is upon us and no one eats honey any more,
they find it too sweet and too cloying and too heavy, it was like this

in the last war '14-'18 and it is like this in this war, wars are like
that, it is funny but wars are like that.

And just now there is also what happens in this war, not in the
last war, but in this war, as it happened in Napoleon's wars and
the wars before that, any war before that but not in the nineteenth
century wars not in '14-'18 war.

Anybody can be taken away from where he belongs and put
somewhere else to work, or to live, far away from where it is
natural to be. That is the way it was in the history of baronial wars
and all that, in all the historical novels that was what was so awful
anybody can be taken away, taken up in the street, taken at any
time and carried away to work in a far away country and perhaps
never to come home again at any age and in any place.

Victor is the son of a baker, a nice boy, and fond of children
and a kind of easy coming and going, he has four sisters and a
father and a mother and they all love Victor, he is the one each one
loves the best, each and every one. And Victor, is strong and well-
fed and at twenty he went to the Camp de Jeunesse, which replaces
military training in France, and he caught a bad cold and he was
in the hospital and then he was given convalescence leave and he
came home and he was not as well fed as he had been but that was
no matter it was easy to feed him up again, particularly as he was
to have ten more days of leave. This evening going up the mountain I met his father and another man. We stopped and talked,
but not as much about the war and Victor, but about the weather
and the moon and the mountain and my being fond of walking
and then I left them and they went on up the mountain, and I
made a round and I came in front of the bakery and there Victor's
mother was fumbling at the door not going in but not not going
in, and I said good-evening how is Victor, and she said he is not to
have any more leave, but I said he is really not well yet, and she
said yes he was to go to-morrow to Lyon for an examination, and
she said no, no he will not leave, not leave and she went in and I
went on, and he has not gone, oh dear me, we like Victor, if it all
will finish fast enough it is all right but if not, you cannot stay on

the mountain all night not in the cold but anyway they always come home at night why not if nobody wants to find them, why not.

And then I was walking along and a woman and I were talking, we were talking about apples and grapes and that money did not count, it was only food, that was important, for the first time in the history of France peasants do not care about money, food and food is what they want but said the woman there is my grandson my André, I call him the little Didie, he is in Germany, he is only twenty, he was very ill when he was twelve, and the doctor said he would have to go to a sanatorium and I said no let me try, and I took him, his voice was gone, and the doctor said no lessons and no work, nothing but out of doors and no talking nothing but out of doors, and so I made him a little suit that left most of him exposed to the sun and in some months he was better but the doctor said not better enough and so I kept him and then he was all cured and never sick again and he went on studying until he was nineteen and now he is in Germany and when he was examined to go his mother told the Germans he had not been strong and the first visit they said no he did not need to go and the second visit they said no he did not need to go and the third visit they said go and his mother said but no and the German said do you think we do not have better doctors there than here and he went and he can get the grippe and indeed they did take very good care of him but he has so little to eat, he writes, grandmother send me anything raw or cooked it makes no matter, and I have sent him five packages and he has only so far received one and it is hard to find things to send, and he writes anyway writes me letters long letters pages of letters, and I said do write him all the details of your daily life just the way we have been talking and how you remember him as a little boy that will comfort him, and is he the only grandson I said no she said he has a brother just eighteen and now his mother is afraid he will have to go it says so in the papers or at least everybody says so and he did not study like his brother he was apprenticed to a trade, well I said I really think it will be over soon and I hope said she you are right I do so hope so, with the bombardments of the factories the boys, they do not even say oh dear, it is just like the middle ages, they are carried off from them in their midst, and that is what is happening.

Marechal Petain, was the hero of Verdun in the 1914-1918 war everybody knows that, but many do not know that it was he who saved the French army from mutiny. This is the story. The French army in '17, was about through, they had had more than enough and they did not like what was happening to them, too many commanders-in-chief in quick succession and they were tired of the way they were being handled and when Petain was put in command, he said he and they needed a change, he said all officers should explain to their men what they wanted them to do and why before they ordered them to do anything, he arranged that everybody should have regular leave, every four months and that they should have ten days, a week in which they went back to the work they used to to steady down and then a couple of days to eat with all their relatives which is the French way and thus cheered by a regular civilian life they would go back to the front with a better strength and they did and the mutiny was over. Then after he retired he thought and wrote a great deal about how France was getting slack and how they could not win the next war, there being neither enough men enough material or enough allies and he also thought and wrote a great deal about a new political scheme which should consist of government by specialists and selected men, a sort of heroic rotarianism in every walk of life. I used to hear Bernard Fay talk about this and mixed up with it all was a desire to have back a king, they thought that kings suit France, most Frenchmen prefer a republic but everybody has to think as they like about that. And France is so traditional and it does so like novelties, and a king would be both a novelty and a tradition. There would be that. After that Petain was ambassador to Spain and he hoped Franco would do what he thought should be done but did he does he, and there was Portugal and they too were perhaps doing so, all this very much excited Petain and then came the war the 1939-'43 war, and of course that had begun. Petain was not very cheerful about it, he said over and over again without sufficient armament without a sufficiently well organized army and without enough allies, France was bound to be defeated. He had been a young officer in 1870 when the French had been defeated he had lived to see them victorious in 1914-1918 and now he was to see them again defeated, and they were. He was undoubtedly right, they were.

Petain had been a colonel before 1914 and once at an officer's mess he was listening to all the young officers talking war drinking to war laughing about war and then in a silence they heard Colonel Petain say, And do you think that war is always gay, toujours drole.

Well anyway there was the armistice Petain made it and we were all glad in a way and completely sad in a way and we had so many opinions. I did not like his way of saying I Philippe Petain, that bothered me and we were in the unoccupied area and that was a comfort. Many months later somebody wrote to me and said that in America everybody said that there was no difference between the occupied and unoccupied zone but we who lived in the unoccupied we knew there was a difference all right. One might not be very free in the unoccupied but we were pretty free and in the occupied they were not free, the difference between being pretty free and not free at all is considerable. A great many people complained that France was divided in two but it really was not it was for a very little while and then it gradually began to grow together again, others said there should not have been an armistice at all they should have gone to Africa and continued the fight but that was foolishness there were no industries no anything in Africa except a little food and a very small army, no Petain was right to stay in France and he was right to make the armistice and little by little I understood it. I always thought he was right to make the armistice, in the first place it was more comfortable for us who were here and in the second place it was an important element in the ultimate defeat of the Germans. To me it remained a miracle and I was always asking everybody why did the Germans grant it, why, it would have been so easy for them to take the whole why did they only take the half, it would have been easier for them to attack England from Egypt than across the channel, why why did they grant the armistice why, it was a puzzle to me and I asked everybody those who might answer and whose answer did not satisfy me and those who could not answer me and with whom I wondered together and those who said there should not have been an armistice but they I was sure were wrong and finally I asked an officer in the army whom I met accidentally and he made it all clear to me.

And this was his answer. The German army always works according to plan and they had planned an arduous and fairly long campaign in France and then an attack on England. In the last war they had been surprised by the strength of France this time they had been surprised by its weakness, but surprise is the important thing to disconcert the Germans any surprise will do if it is a real surprise, and this was a very real surprise. They came along so quickly that they lost their breath and it was going so quickly that they changed their plans, England this year instead of next year as it was intended and so they could not lose any more time so when Petain suggested the armistice they were delighted because now their hands were free to turn back to England, they knew Petain was a man of his word so they were not worried about what was behind them so off they rushed back to the channel. When they got there they found that their material was all in a very bad shape, they had gone so fast that all the plans for keeping everything repaired had broken down everything was used up, it was not made of very good material, as one returned prisoner remarked if the French had only had time to look at the German material they would have seen it could not stand long war, well anyway when they got back to the channel they saw that their armament was not equal to the task and so they had to wait. America came to the help of England in supplying material and by the time the Germans were ready it was too late too late. And then came the battle of London and it was too late. This is what Petain meant when once he was asked who was winning the war the Germans or the English he pointed to his own breast and answered I.

Between the armistice and the Russians fighting the Germans we all talked and talked and hunted for food, after the Russians began we continued to talk and talk and look for food but there was a difference, all the farmers got drunk with joy the day the Germans attacked the Russians and after that there were more points of view than ever in each one in every one.

We all talked so much and we all explained so much and we all talked to anybody, just to-day the end of October I talked to a man who is in the biggest railway station in Lyon, and he told me that all the workingmen who get leave out of Germany do not go back and they all tell the train-men, all about Germany. They say that three months ago the older workmen, a little sadly said of course the Fuehrer is always right, but perhaps, may be events will be too powerful for him, perhaps, and the younger workmen, were still chock full of certainty and pig headedness, and now after three months of bombardment they all say now we under-stand, now we want peace, peace at any price, we want peace the eleventh of November, '43, that is a date, so let us fix a date and that way we will have peace, and they count every day as just being one day less before peace. That is what he told me to-day, and you have to get to know which reasons are founded and which are not, during the time of the battle of London and the attempted invasion of England we found that when you heard persistent rumors coming from quite different sources there was something to it, and we all told each other everything and there was a retired customs officer who worked in his garden and every day we used to talk and we always talked about never who would win, that we always knew, it is extraordinary how many people always knew that Germany could never win, and could tell it over and over again, but the thing we all talked about over and over again was whether France should have gone on fighting when she couldnt

and only the other day Bernard Fay gave me a new explanation.
He said the mistake was in going into the war at all. But said I you
would have been attacked any way. No said he, Germany intended
to take Poland and then attack Russia, and if Daladier had told
the English honestly, that they had no material and that the army
did not want to fight which everybody knew and that is true we all
knew it before the war began that the army did not want to fight
and then if the English had answered that this was true then said
Bernard, the English would not have declared war, the Germans
would have beaten Poland attacked Russia, France and England
would have gotten stronger and then when they wanted they
would have come into the war. Perhaps said I this is so. That is
the point of view of those who said France should not have gone
into the war, and so from the armistice on we talked and talked
anybody everybody, and there were the collaborators as they were
called, but in France there always has been a party that although
they know they could not stand the Germans felt that they should
collaborate with them. Although everybody was sure that such a
collaboration would be sens unique as they said, a one way street.
Then there was the point of view of Georges Rosset. He said he
preferred that the Germans should win rather than the English,
but Georges I said you want your liberty, you know you would
never want to be under German control, Oh he said you dont
understand, we Frenchmen can always will always get the best of
the Germans that is the reason that although they win and occupy
us they can really not do anything to us, we can always get the best
of them, we always can, but the English, well it is not so sure, not
so certain, and I for one would rather not try.

I listened to so many in those days, and everybody's point of
view was so reasonable as they explained it, that is what the
French mean by saying they are logical, any point of view they
have which concerns themselves is so reasonable when they explain
it, they have no prejudices, they have traditions and a way of life
and they have a point of view, and they have a reason for it, of
course there are some among them not a great many but some

among them who simply want to be on the winning side, anywhere there are lots of people like that, and when they are like that it is simple but not logical, not as the French understand logic and as I understand logic with them.

This present war is so logical as I understand logic so much more logical than the 1914-'18 war, that was relatively simple and you had simple opinions and simple points of view but this war, well there are so many sides to be on all logical and the events in spite of their confusion are so logical, not nineteenth century at all not at all. The nineteenth century was completely lacking in logic, it had cosmic terms and hopes, and aspirations, and discoveries, and ideals but it had no logic, and I like logic I really do, I suppose that is the reason that I so naturally had my part in killing the nineteenth century and killing it dead, quite like a gangster with a mitraillette, if that is the same as a tommy gun.

But to come back to what we all thought about Petain. Bernard Fay and the chocolate cake.

Our neighbor's cousin has just been shot in the Haute Savoie, by a man with a rifle who shot him as he came out between his father and mother from church, and the man then put his rifle on his shoulder and walked away. The man shot was a son of a count, one of the old families of the country poorish but a considerable land owner and was he on one side or the other. There seems to be some doubt. He was an escaped prisoner and some say that he was in the German pay but his cousin says not at all he was strongly anti-German and did not want to have his younger brother join the special police whose business it is more or less to watch their neighbors, well yes or no, take it as so or take it as not so, it is all so mixed, his brother-in-law was killed fighting for the Allies in Tunis, it is all so mixed and her brother and her husband's brother had intended to betake themselves to the mountains instead of going to Germany but they did not because they were afraid of the long winter. And the man who was killed seems to have been a gentle and defeated soul, among his papers they found one saying that he hoped that if one of the four brothers, there were four should have to be killed in any way he hoped that it would be he because he had no future. He was just a simple man, and his brothers all were clever and they could have a future. His cousin who was telling us is married to a man whose family all say that Petain is a cretin, and she said she had to suffer that and now she is content that her brother is working in Germany rather than to be mixed up with all of them and even if he is killed by the enemy and she was all mixed up what between those who have betaken themselves to the mountain and those who are communists and Anglo-Saxons who are bombing and friends of Russia and they are suffering from the communists, and what will happen and I always say you can have any government you like but those who take to the sword will perish by the sword and if you persecute you will be persecuted, and yes she says I know, but you dont understand and a friend who was there said that the cousin who was killed had been denouncing his neighbors, not at all she said, the neighbors denounced each other, they were three of them who had been good friends with one another and they denounced each other and then to get friends again they came and denounced his brother who had turned special policeman and this had made her cousin who has just been killed reconciled to his brother being in this special police.

And all the time there is Petain, an old man a very old man and mostly nowadays everybody has forgotten all about him.

Marechal Petain then did save France and saving France defeated Germany and defeating Germany he just had to go on living until the Russians whom he feared defeated Germany and the Americans whom he liked defeated Germany and the English whom he mistrusted defeated Germany, he was an old man and he just had to wait and he spent every day and all day waiting but very actively waiting, he liked to wait and he liked to be active and he did them both at once. And while he was waiting anybody was bound to forget him and while they were forgetting he did not mind it because he knew he was actively waiting and so

actively waiting was a complete action and he did this not because
he had it to do but because to do it would do what he had to do.

And all the time everybody around him had so many points of
view so many points so many points of view so many things going
on inside them in each one of them. I remember some one coming
it was in the end of '40, and they said they had just come from
America and they had just seen Marechal Petain and Petain had
wanted to know how they felt about him over there and the man
answered and said they did not like his persecuting, and he said,
as for free-masons I hate them, as for communists I am afraid of
them, as for the Jews it is not my fault.

French people do like good fighting, they like it better than
anything and though they all are just as afraid as the Marechal
was of them it was very funny but even the speaker of Vichy when
he gives the news summary cannot help being proud of the
Russian fighting, they the French always feel that really good
soldiering belongs to them, they are as I am always telling them
hopelessly European about all this, they cannot get into the point
of America, that fighting consists in putting the other man out of
business, there is no use just in going forward or back and using
yourself up, it is just the difference between old fashioned dancing
and American dancing, in old fashioned dancing you were always
sashaying forward and back waltz or polka or anything but in
dancing as Americans invented it you stay put you do it all on one
spot. Well that is the American idea dont have your armies
running all over the place but stay on one spot, bombard and
bombard until all the enemy's material is destroyed and then the
war is over, but no European likes that, it is contrary to all their
past and it holds for them no future, because after all as I said in
Everybody's Autobiography, Europe is really too small for a
modern war, and there are not industrialists they are shop keepers,
they could get an enormous supply in advance put away in their
warehouses but when it comes to renewing that supply well there
is nothing to do it, France does better than most because she at
least can produce food, it is a thing which never ceases to surprise

me. How an average agricultural family in France counting a father a mother fortyish and not overly strong with one old mother or father sometimes both but nearer seventy than not with one usually sometimes two children and none of any of them very strong the amount of food they produce during the year is tremendous, potatoes and food for the cows and oxen, and wine, and wheat enough to feed France if the Germans had left it, and oats and barley, and garden truck, and fowls and rabbits, and quantities of it and they go on not very strong and not working very hard, and making hay, and selling quantities and they go on being neither rich nor poor and if their only son does not get killed in a war well then he goes on and they do produce a tremendous amount of food just like that.

I always do think that what the French really have most cause to be proud of but that they have no feeling about they take it as it comes and that is that Savoy and Alsace and Lorraine, and Nice and the Riviera, all which has only been French hardly a hundred years yet, they all wanted to stay with a defeated France they did not want to go to the victorious enemy Germany and Italy from which they had only been detached hardly a hundred years. Yes France has that.

And so this war goes on just like that, and it well not suddenly but certainly is coming nearer and nearer to not being a war at all. This war is like that.

Just now and here the war is mostly the struggle the mayor has in finding men to guard the railway lines, they do not want to go out on cold nights and be chilled and the mayor has to find them and they are so few of them left and they want to be in bed at night to be as warm as they can be and so every day the mayor tries to find them, he has a Swiss wife and they are very nice and he tries to find enough men to guard the railway by day and by night, and anyway as when they are there they shelter away from the weather and they are not around and it is cold at night even in November.

In Bilignin I know other people but mostly farmers here I

knew other people mostly railroad workers, they are not at all like farmers not at all. On the whole I think farmers more interesting, they are more interesting. They are not as generous not as kindly not as lively but they are more interesting, French farmers are more interesting.

It is natural to remember places.

In these days of October and November '43 it is natural to remember Modane. For so many years it was not natural to remember Modane and now it is natural to remember Modane. Here at Culoz is the place where the trains switch off to go to Italy, and that is where we are living now, in the days when we used to go to Italy every summer we went by Modane, I did not remember Culoz, Modane, the early morning at Modane, and then we went to Italy by the Saint Gothard that is by way of Switzerland and then we did not go to Italy at all but always there had been Modane and now and here the trains go to Modane all the time that Italy was in the war the coal trains went to Modane, coal and coal and coal went to Modane and then soldiers went to Modane and now Modane is bombed and trains do not go to Modane, and then the trains began again to go to Modane and now Modane is bombed again and the trains once more are not going to Modane and so any day and every day just now it is natural to remember Modane.

And we do still go to Chambery in the train and there was no window glass in the windows and they all said there were in the third class compartments but there were none in the second class compartments and they said however since they had paid for second class they would stay in the second class even if there were no panes in the windows. Basket our white poodle had his ear bitten and it was bleeding when we went to Chambery to-day, but everybody said he was very beautiful just the same. That is what can happen any day. And there are other things.

There is the son of our dentist. There is some more of that story. There naturally is as the days go on and a little fear goes on any day and a fair amount of excitement goes on any day, and a great deal of anticipation goes on any day, and a fair amount of food these days, in some places, quite a fair amount, and there is always a reason why, always.

No these days of ending the war have nothing to do with the nineteenth century nothing at all, not anything at all, every few days I read a play of Shakespeare and it is more like that tragedy, unless if you will that is everybody knows that there will be no progress anybody knows that there will be no progress everybody knows everybody knows that there will be no progress but there will be insecurity and there will be courage and fear, and hope and death and sickness and health, and strength and terror, and they will go on and nobody will want to give anybody what is not theirs to give nor theirs to take no nobody at all, and the nineteenth century is dead stone dead on this month of November in 1943.

Do not let it alone because everybody is patriotic, do not let alone because nobody is confused, it is progress that confuses, not patriotism and fear and struggle and life and death, not not at all and this is what happened to the dentist's boy.

It is the soothing thing about history that it does repeat itself, sometimes it has worse attacks of it than at other times, sometimes it is that history has a perfect outbreak of repetitions it always does of course repeat itself but sometimes it is that the repetitions are quite far apart but just now that is November 1943 it is just full of them full of repetitions of nothing but repetitions. It repeats all the Balkan wars all the difficulties between France and England all the German defeats, and it repeats all Italian history and it repeats well not exactly repeats it was in 1915 that it was said that Russia was a steam roller but then it did not roll, now it is not said but it is a steam roller and it rolls. The United States and Russia belonging to a new century do not repeat themselves, not yet, of course sometime they will but they have not done so yet, not yet, Japan yes, it was bombarded by the Americans to be opened and now it will be bombarded to be closed, that might be well called a repetition but to come back to the dentist's son.

We were very upset, some months ago to know that he had been taken away to prison, he had as a young fellow of seventeen joined the crowd in Savoy who were getting ready and getting ready meant preparing and preparing meant hiding things to use and hiding things to use meant hiding them in his room. And it came out and he was taken away and it was an awful day. The father was a Serb and the mother a courageous French woman daughter of generations of scientists and soldiers and she did everything to take care of him. But he was taken away and everything happened except that he was not dead. And this was done by the Italians and they took him far away into Italy. The next thing she knew was that he had been condemned to five years hard labor and she had seen him but once again and then she had given him his civil papers, then when everything had been done. She managed to do this. Then the Italians went out of the war and the prison was left open by them, go away the guards said as they were leaving and of course they all went away, some went one way and some went another way but the young ones naturally wanted to go where they would meet Americans, naturally enough. Then they got on the way but they found out it would be a very long way so some of them and among them two of them went another way. They got into the mountains and everybody they met was carrying large bundles, they were bundles of shoes and clothing, and so they went in the same direction and they found quantities of shoes and clothing belonging to the Italian army that had abandoned them and so they helped themselves splendidly. And then they had to go away, they found the quantities of shoes very useful, they traded them for food and guides and everybody was kind to them and one man who knew all the little roads took them high up in the Alps, and they got across the frontier and were back again where they came from and as his mother had given him his civil papers, that was the kind of a mother she was she thought of everything and had courage enough to do anything they went on. But their shoes the Italian army shoes made the peasants suspicious and they told the national policeman, who took them, now said he looking at them tell me

the true story and they did, and when they did he said all right
dont tell anybody about me, and then they went on, they got into
a German truck with German soldiers and the German soldiers
were eating bread and butter and the two of them were very
hungry and the German soldiers gave them bread but not butter
but all the same it was very welcome. And so they came home, and
the mother was so happy to have him and he stayed with her for
three days, bathing from morning to evening and eating and having
his photograph taken so she would have something to remember
him and then he said now we must go and she said where and he
said to join my comrades, do not worry he said to his mother it is
like being a soldier do not worry, and then he went away and now
he is gone again. She said you see the young feel differently about
it, if they are shot well it does not mean the same thing to them
that it does to us, not the same thing.

And so every day makes some people more cheerful and some
people not so cheerful and there is the same reason why. As for
instance.

Every day can be any day just now.

It was a dark day and a Tuesday and I went to see a friend who
was not well and she had four sons and one was still a prisoner of
war and the other on a boat in Indo-China and one who had been
a prisoner had escaped after trying twice and succeeding at last and
the other was not very well, well anyway when I left it was late in
the afternoon and there was a glow in the sky and I went up the
mountain there is a very big steep one right in back a real mountain and they bring wood down from the top of it by a cable. I went
higher and higher and the water was falling down the mountain
side louder and louder and it was very nice and cold quite
cold and getting darker. I like it getting darker and as I was
going up higher and higher and it was Sunday and nobody was
working as it was getting darker I began to meet groups of men
coming down from the mountain and I said how do you do and
they said how do you do. And then as it was really getting darker
I turned around to come down again, and it was very dark and

darker and it began to rain and snow and sleet, and I could not see but I could feel the crunch of the gravel under my feet and so I could stay on the path and all around me I heard others coming down too and there were in little groups about twenty-five men who passed me and they went quickly and I went slower and I was getting wetter and wetter and I wondered why there were so many men of a Sunday coming down the mountain and then as I came back very wet and they all passed me I supposed they were the men who are taking heather doing the maquis as it is called from Corsica where it has been done like in Scotland for so many centuries and they probably come down every night particularly in winter when policemen stay at home and they come down and have a good dinner with their family and get warm and spend the night and go back again before the policemen can think that anything is the matter, not that any of the policemen really are very interested in finding anybody that is hidden, not they.

And so every day is any day.

I was taking a sixteen kilometer walk, I do do this very often and sometimes when I have bread to carry, I sometimes do have white bread and cake to carry I sometimes take an autobus, and that day I had a good deal to carry and the dog to manage and some-body helped me and I knew her and just then I met the dwarf of Culoz and I shook hands with him, I always say how do you do to a dwarf, I say how do you do to anybody and I always say how do you do to a dwarf, and he shook hands with me and then he shook hands with her. She was surprised but any way that did not matter and when we both got out of the autobus and walked a bit together I said you are married now and have a child, yes she said and my husband is a soldier that is an officer, and I said where is he now while you stay with your mother and she said he is in a military prison in the rue Cherche Midi in Paris, in solitary confinement. And what ever for I said, Ah she said, I do not know nor probably does he, it is so easy these days to go to prison any indiscretion any little indiscretion and he was always interested in ameliorating the social condition of the soldier, but you hear from him, not at all, but I send him packages my sister, she does not see him, but he gives her his dirty linen and she brings him clean linen so we know well that is all I do know, she said and we said good-bye and she said it is useless to have illusions that they will let him out before the end and we said good-bye, and I had known her as a quite young girl, because they had a nice house where the exiled king and his sister were once supposed to visit her great grandmother. And the children used to play that they came on a white horse and were the exiled king and his sister and were paying a visit to their great grandmother.

And so going on.

We had a friend whose name was Gilbert and he was gone away and his wife followed him and the little girl Christine was left behind with some neighbors, we did not know them and one day a red-headed and active young fellow asked for me and I saw him and I said what and he said I have a message to you from Gilbert, ah I said is the little girl not well, oh yes he said she is all right she is staying with us, ah yes I said, do you need anything for her, I said and he said no she was all right and he was fiddling with a match-box and I said well and he said the message is in here and I said you had better go, and he said are you afraid of me and I said no and you had better go and dont you want the message he said and I said no you had better go and he said I will go and he had tears in his eyes and he went out and told the servant that we had not received his message and a friend said were you not curious and I said no not.

There are so many ends to stories these days so many ends that it is not like it was there is nothing to be curious about except small things, food and the weather. The funny part of it all is that relatively few people seem to go crazy, relatively few even a little crazy or even a little weird, relatively few, and those few because they have nothing to do that is to say they have nothing to do or they do not do anything that has anything to do with the war only with food and cold and little things like that. Anybody can talk and everybody does do that, even if they come in again or go out again which they do. And then there is Victor. We are very fond of Victor although there is no reason why and yet there is he is Victor and loved by his family.

The only ones who are really grateful for the war are the wild ducks, such a lot of them in the marshes of the Rhone and so peaceful, usually at this season they are very troubled, no sooner settled down then pop pop the country full of hunters hunting them and they have to fly away, now quantities of them sit there on the pleasant bits of water surrounded by high marsh ferns and they are so peaceful, nobody can touch them nobody, because all the shot-guns have been taken away completely taken away and nobody can shoot with them nobody at all and the wild ducks are very content. They act as if they had never been shot at, never, it is so easy to form old habits again, so very easy.

When I first came to France it was before there were automobiles in Paris, and almost everybody who was not otherwise engaged was pulling or pushing a push-cart and quite rapidly, the French move very quickly with them and then gradually the automobiles filled the streets and the roads and pushing and pulling of push-carts became too dangerous an occupation and so gradually nobody had one and nobody pushed or pulled them. In those early days all artisans had them all house painters and all plumbers and all sellers of anything, there are still a few who push them even in the days of automobiles but that is only to get to a corner somewhere and sell something, even that does not seem to be too legal because they are always being carried off to the police station, and there is nothing more helpless than a pushcart filled with vegetables or anything and standing all alone and neglected in front of a police station. I always wondered if anybody would ever push them again, but I suppose really their owners were never sent to prison probably they just had to pay a fine or something, or their licence was not right or something and they come back to push or pull it before the vegetables and fruit were too faded to sell.

But now in this year of 1943 push-carts every kind of push-cart on every kind of road and all ages pushing and pulling and so many kilometers and filled with anything and everything, the roads are full of them, every size and shape from small baby-carriages to almost a full sized wagon. They push them twenty kilometers sometimes when they go off to get chestnuts and besides that there is the constant carrying of grass to feed rabbits and goats and anything that can be fed and then eaten. Bicycles and push-carts, rarely anybody not carrying or pushing something so rarely that it just does not exist.

But to come back to Victor, Victor and his father have hunting dogs two of them but of course they cannot hunt and they grow vegetables and these get pushed in the push-cart and the family are bakers and Victor is the only boy and he has three sisters and how they all love Victor. He is very sweet is Victor and fond of children and now he is twenty years old and has gone to the Camp de Jeunesse, and he was always very well fed and he caught a bad sore throat and he came back and he looked very thin when he came back for twenty days' convalescent leave. And he was a little better but not well enough and he decided he did not want to go back, and his family who loved him did not want him to go back because any day he might have to go further, so he must hide himself and that is very easy, from one village you go to another village and in that other village nobody says anything and nobody hunts him up because it takes the papers a very long time to go forward and back and when he is not where he was the papers have to go back again and sometimes they just stay where they were and where their family is but that is more difficult, the time might come but going forward and back between these villages that is fairly safe quite safe enough for any of them except the mother who does tremble, they all love him but the mother does tremble, every once in a while she trembles a little every once in a while.

Anything can happen in such a time and to-day it was very funny, there are now everywhere and particularly here where there are mountains and wood is very easy to get, the automobiles go with wood, the engines are the same as they were, but anyway it works very well, there are lots of trucks and lots of autobuses and every fair sized town has several taxis. French people naturally like luxuries and although they are not supposed to take you except in case of great need, actually everybody takes them to go anywhere which is too far to walk, and if you have no bicycle. So we wanted to go to Belley on Friday and I telephoned to our taxi man and he said he had stalled just in front of his house and would his car go again, well of course it would sometime but would it go again by Friday and besides just now they had telephoned to him that he must go immediately and get some German officers who had to get somewhere immediately, and he said he could not his car had stopped going, and the authorities said they had telephoned to five different taxis and all of them had broken down and was his really not working and he said no it was not and it was not, not just then. It is an extraordinary thing so extraordinary that only we here notice anything but an extraordinary thing none of them not any one of the German officers have a car that goes, if they cannot take a train, they have to get the wood heated French cars to take them anywhere. It is the most extraordinary thing, I cannot say it too often it is the most extraordinary thing, the most extraordinary thing, really the most extraordinary thing of all the extraordinary things that happen, the most extraordinary thing, the motorised German army being carried around by French taxis.

Now that the end is more or less in sight anybody can be just foolish, not very happy, but quite foolish. They are foolish everywhere, everybody is just foolish anywhere, not funny but just foolish.

Really and truly this time nobody in their hearts really believe that everybody that anybody will be peaceful and happy, not anybody, not the immense majority believe any such thing and that proves that the nineteenth century is dead completely and entirely dead. Even the propagandists on the radio find it very difficult to really say let alone believe that the world will be a happy place, of love and peace and plenty, and that the lion will lie down with the lamb and everybody will believe anybody. They all know that none of them believe anybody that not any of them believe anybody. There is neither unanimity nor faith in peace and progress, the nineteenth century is dead but there is no particular peace for its ashes, although there is no resurrection none at all for the nineteenth century, none.

Everybody knows it, nobody says it, because the twentieth century is too troublesome and too certain to be difficult and distracted, but everybody knows that the nineteenth century is dead dead as a door-nail.

Now everybody knows that there is no use in being too successful, look at the Germans they began with the Ruhr, I will never forget that it was a Sunday evening and I was out walking and on the Boulevard Saint Germain and there were lots of people out and the eyes of the men had that troubled look that men's eyes have when they may have to go to war, when the last one is near enough so that there is no illusion and no glamor, none at all, and the women with them were talking and talking not about war of course nobody mentioned that and the men for French men were silent and the women were very talkative and their eyes were not as troubled as the men's eyes. And the Germans were successful and then there was Austria and they were successful and then there was Munich and all the Frenchmen were easier in their minds, no war, certainly no war, not for their generation, and then came Czecho-Slovakia's annexation and the Germans were once more successful and the French paid no attention, and then every year there was mobilisation and everybody was irritated and resentful and then there was Poland and by this time the Frenchmen kind of relieved, to really have war, and they knew the Germans would be successful but all the same it was a relief that they really had to begin war, and once more the Germans were successful and there was not much fighting and then very soon it was all over and the Germans were still successful, and then the Germans began not to be successful and now they are not successful at all. Now the wisdom of the ages, that is everybody really knows that if one thing goes well nothing else must go wrong, you cannot have a house, wood to burn and food to eat and the servant to stay, not all at once and there must always be setbacks, and there must always be the need of superstition to stop anything from going too bad or too well just like that, and people like the Germans never understand that, they dream fairy tales where everything is as it was or was not, and they make music which makes them feel like that but the French know that you must not succeed you must rise from the ashes and how could you rise from the ashes if there were no ashes, but the Germans never think of ashes and so when there are ashes there is no rising, not at all and every day and in every way this is clearer and clearer. And now almost anybody can again remember Petain, not that they say it, no indeed, once the French have stopped saying it they do not begin again, and they had and they have stopped saying it. All the same they are relieved that he wants a republic, there may be royalists but really the French like a republic, I imagine all Europe will be republican pretty soon, it is like South America, the Brazilians had a very nice emperor indeed, they liked him and he liked them, but they said regretfully it is no use it is not the fashion to have an emperor on the American continent, and we are so sorry but you must go away. And I imagine that is going to be true in Europe. The fashion is the fashion, and republics simply republican republics are going to be the fashion. You can see that the nineteenth century is dead, quite dead.

And now it is the first of December 1943 and everybody is cross just as cross as they can be and there is a reason why. Everybody well they did not think it but it was possible and they did hope it that the war would be over. Oh dear they say another winter, well but it is always winter in December yes but we did not think that this December would be another winter, we did not think there could be another winter and now it is December and there is another winter of war. And certainly there is another winter, everybody is so tired of having wood and not coal, of eating quite well but always worried of having it all be such a bother and not being able to go out and buy something if you have the money and worst of all well of course it is the worst of all, that it is is the worst of all, the worst of all.

How lightly the troubadour plays his guitar. How easily the radio tells you what they all say. How often they say what they all say, and how much there is to tell when well when very well there is nothing to tell.

The case of Petain is typical, he has so little to tell now November 1943 and he had it to tell and they would not let him. That made everything difficult, everybody remembered him because they would not let him tell what he had to tell over the radio, and everybody wanted him and he was just as peaceful about it is as if he had told what they would not let him tell.

If they believe it but they do not, Petain does tell what he has to tell even when they do not let him tell what he has to tell, and this time again the end of November 1943 it happened again and everybody almost everybody remembered him again and he went on peacefully again as if everybody did remember. How long will it last. Well that is not the end, not the end, not that.

It is funny they all act as if they believe what they say, and they do, they do believe what they say and it is so funny that they all act as if they believed what they say.

There is no use, everybody might just as well be funny, and some of them are, they really are.

We were talking and they said, that a good many people had for a year consciously tried to live on their rations, but now everybody finds that there is no use in doing it, no use at all and so nobody does, nobody does except funnily enough some timid grocery store-keepers, who are afraid. I know one family of them and they are the only ones around here who continue to be thin and to get thinner. Nobody else is, nobody else is thin and nobody else continues to get thinner, nobody not unless they are awfully poor and because of their situation in life unable to work. Nobody.

This is all another proof that the nineteenth century is over. England still believes in the nineteenth century yes she does, she almost wishes that she did not but yes she does. France never did very much belong to the nineteenth century not very much.

Such pleasant stories.

On the road I met a woman an oldish woman and we were going the same way and we talked as we walked. She said a little further along she had a house but she did not live there. She had had a sister paralysed for thirty-five years who had lived there and she died two years ago. She now lived with her brother-in-law somewhere else, he was all she had but of course some one stayed in the paternal house to take care of the chickens. Oh yes I forgot I had Basket on a leash because on the road as there is a cement works there are many trucks, of course there are quite a number of automobiles, no German ones, French ones the French always keep going somehow, well anyway I said I had Basket on a leash because he having worms was a little nervous he almost was run down by an automobile, so I told her and I said a dog is so easily killed, yes she said we had one at the paternal house and he went blind and so we had to have him killed, and I said we had a little dog we loved very much and he had to be killed because he had diabetes, and is he dead she said and I said yes, and she said it is different with chickens, she said just the other day a camion came along and he ran over one of our chickens and he did not notice it he just went on but a little later another one came along and he noticed it and he stopped and got down and gathered in the chicken and went on, just then my nephew came out and saw him and as he went away he noticed the number so a little later when the camion came back again my nephew stopped him and said you have to pay me for that chicken that is to say not money I do not want money I want the chicken, and the man said not at all I will pay you but I will not give you the chicken and my nephew said he did not want payment he wanted the chicken and the man said he did not have it which was probably a lie but still perhaps he had already eaten it, but anyway my nephew said well I will take the money, no said the other I am not paying you anything, why not said my nephew, because I am not said the driver and my nephew said well suppose you give it to the Red Cross to make a package for a prisoner not at all said the driver and he drove away and said I what did your nephew do, I have no nephew she said I only have a niece that is to say I only have a father-in-law, that is not my house where I live it belongs to my brother-in-law and just then our roads parted and we said good-bye.

There are so many stories. To-day I met a man on the road he had a hunting dog a pretty one a little thin and she and Basket said how do you do the man was pushing a cart filled with cabbages and we stopped and said how do you do, is she very young I said not so young three years old but she is a good hunter, and how he said, but alas now nobody can hunt and I said look there are so many birds of passage and wild ducks, yes he said we used to think them rather tough eating but now it would be a pleasure, I used to be a custom house officer and now I am pensioned and I thought I would spend my last days hunting, but it is not to be, well you never can tell I said December '43, perhaps it will be like '18, perhaps it will come suddenly, perhaps he said, but I said surely you were not originally from this country I said, he did not look it, he looked like a man from Normandy, and he said no my father who was a custom's officer like I am, had a large family, nine children and if you have a large family you want a job in a small town where living is easy, so he had a job here and I was raised here and when I was pensioned I came back here, but you have not a large family no I have only one son and he like I did enlisted in the army and was in it for two years and then the army was demobilised and they sent my son away at the point of a pistol and then they said he should go to Germany and he said he did not like them and he came home and the police took away all his papers, and then he went away that is he is here and he is not dead I said, no he said oh dear no. You see he said I was my father's second son the older one was not strong so my father said I should join the army young, and the years that I spent in the army would count on my time when I went into the custom's service as I had a right to being a custom's officer's son, and it was all right only the war broke out, not this war I am not a young man the other war, and I was a sergeant and I killed a lot of Germans a whole lot of them and then one day I was sent with a convoy of wood to make trenches, and I came along and somebody said, there is an armistice, and I said oh go along, and I went on, and then somebody else said sure the armistice has been signed to-day and I said I would not go on with the wood and I dumped it all on the side of the road and I went back, and they all said let us hit it up to-night, and I said no I was tired, really it was because being a member of such a large family and my father thinking I should help the little ones, I did not have any money and one of the comrades said let's see your purse and he took it and opened it and it was empty, and he said it's all right, and I said I know we are all comrades, but I have my pride but all the same we did whoop it up and then we shook hands and we parted.

One of our neighbors a charming boy went to Germany with his class and although he had never driven a truck he volunteered for that work, and so they gave him a tryout in Paris and naturally he stayed as long as he could and then he went to Germany and they gave him a job with a man who had a business of moving furniture. And sometimes it was with a camion and sometimes with horses, and Christian de la Flechere wrote and said it was not too bad only he quarreled with the wife of his boss because she did not give him all of his bread, but just the same he had a room to himself and it was not too bad and would his family send him some make-up and perfumes, because he could trade these things off and be much more comfortable, and they did and he was. Then one day his boss got the bill for the days in Paris when Christian was learning to drive the camion, and it was sixty marks and he said he would not pay it Christian should pay it, and Christian said he would be damned if he would and the boss could go further and the boss said he was fired and Christian should get out and get a job and he did he got a job in a dairy where he would be better paid and fed and he came back and his old boss began to apologise and said he easily got mad, but he wanted him to stay, and Christian thought a bit and remembered even if he was better paid at the dairy he would have to get up earlier and it was winter and any way it was better to accept the troubles you knew than to try out new ones and so he stayed. We were all after all we heard and knew we were all surprised at this story, it was so not like war at all, except that of course Christian would never have been there if there had not been war not at that kind of work if there had been war and yet it is just like any boy who went out to earn a living at any work he could get.

It is funny and his sister who told us the story, said and I have just met a friend and she was radiant and I said and what is it, and she said my son who was a prisoner in Germany has just escaped into Sweden and he was received with open arms and said at the embassy find me a job but you must find one for my buddy and they were both put to dish-washing at a big hotel and they liked it because there was lots to eat and they were not interned.

Yes yes.

Unconditional surrender very strange that.

Everybody is getting somber, the winter weather and the war not over, everybody is getting somber and a little dreary, in the summer they think it will be over this year but now that the fifth winter has commenced nobody can believe that it will ever be over. Nobody. The only thing that cheered anybody was the speech of General Smuts, against France, it made everybody feel alive, he said France was dead and as France does naturally rise from the ashes it made everybody feel very much alive. Naturally nobody was grateful to General Smuts but I was because everybody cheered up and it is better to have everybody cheered up rather than not. Decidedly yes.

Unconditional surrender.

The Europeans are fascinated with the idea of unconditional surrender. Nobody in Europe had ever heard of that, there are always conditions there have to be conditions, life in Europe is conditional and the words unconditional surrender is like a new thing, jazz or automobiles when they were new or radio, it is something new, and the Europeans like something new, it is an old civilization and they like something new. I like to tell them about it, about General Grant having the initials from Ulysses Simpson Grant. U. S. Grant and being called United States Grant or Unconditional Surrender Grant. I like to tell them about this but they really do not listen to me, they are not interested not even in its being American, unconditional surrender, they are just fascinated and find it very original and the meaning of it does not really penetrate, it is a new form of jazz, unconditional surrender, and when the Germans say the Japs wont and they wont they say but they will but even then it does not mean anything to them, because it is not really war, war is something else it is defeat and armistice and conditions, unconditional surrender has nothing, to do with war not for them.

There are so many refugees, roughly speaking one might say everybody is a refugee, nearly everybody certainly every city, town village and hamlet has its refugees, and plenty of them, this Culoz, is a little town of two thousand inhabitants and there are lots of them, Alsatians and Lorrainers and Poles and Americans, several besides us, working people that somehow are Americans and any town is like that and French quite a few French and Belgians, and anything else and lots of Persians so the Swiss Consul told us and every refugee is certain that he likes neither the climate the landscape the earth in which they garden nor the mosquitoes and if he does not say so certainly his wife does she most certainly does. To some it is a mountainous climate very cold and very savage, to some it is a warm moist climate never cold and the mountain disgracefully covered with rocks instead of pine trees and so many mosquitoes, as a matter of fact last summer there were none, however it was our first summer here, perhaps there are more sometimes, with all the marshes of the Rhone, anyway everybody is a refugee and it is a puzzle a considerable puzzle how everybody goes on living and spending money and looking fairly well fed and well clothed it is a puzzle, and then of course there are lots of Jews French and every other kind refugeed anywhere in any small place and then young men who do not want to go to forced labor and they change their town oh dear everybody is a refugee and how do they go on spending money and being fairly well dressed and well fed how do they. You never can tell who is going to help you, that is a fact.

French people are awfully careful of their money, so careful and so hard and yet so many of them most unexpectedly are helpful, not those whom you expect to help you but just anybody. Take our case. After we came into the war it began to get very difficult extremely difficult, and nobody among my old friends nobody asked me if we were in any trouble and it was getting a bit of a trouble, of course if we had wanted it we could have gotten some from the consul but with the price of things going up and up and up that would not have helped us, and so there we are, and so much worse than that there we were, and one day a young man his name is Paul Genin and we had come to know him because they had bought a house in the neighborhood, he was a silk manufacturer from Lyon and he was interested in literature one day he said to me are you having trouble about money, I said not yet I still have a supply but it is beginning to run pretty low and he said can I help you and I said what can you do, well he said write out a check in dollars and I will see what I can do, and then a little while after he said I have been looking into the matter and I think it might possibly get you into trouble and I think I had rather not have you do it, I could have it done but I would rather not so here is your check tear it up and let me be your banker, but, I said, Oh he said, why not, how much do you spend a month, I told him, he said all right I will give you that a month and I said what do you want me to give you in the way of a paper, oh nothing he said, I think it is better not, but said I if I died or anything you have no evidence of anything, oh he said let us risk it, and he did, and every month for six months he gave me what I needed to live on for the month and at the end of six months I sold a picture I had with me quite quietly to some one who came to see me and so I thanked Paul Genin and paid him back and he said if you ever need me just tell me, and that was that.

Life is funny that way.

It always is funny that way, the ones that naturally should offer do not, and those who have no reason to offer it, do, you never know you never do know where your good-fortune is to come from. The most experienced person can never tell, never never never.

At the same time you can tell that Secret Service is an amusement of peace it is not an amusement for war. I have just been reading a secret service novel a quite good one, in which the secret service agents save Hong Kong, to the British. That is all right in peace times like finding out all about new weapons and secret treaties and all that sort of thing and the other secret agents but once war begins well it is not of any use, really it is not, when it is peace time it is drama when it is war time it is melodrama. No information gotten within in a country is of any use to anybody by the time it comes out, anyway information like that is not much use, one does see and hear a good deal of the secret service, bound to, you just cant help hearing more or less actually about it, but it does not seem much good in war time, really not much good, when a country is in revolt as everybody is now who is occupied that is different, but that is not secret service in an enemy's country that is the organisation of resistance within the country, and of course when the whole country is in sympathy with them messages do go in and out, surely not otherwise, why are they not more often stopped and they never are, the conferences of the important people continue, why are none of the important people killed, nobody really finds out anything and all that secret service agents do in war time is to feel melodramatic and occasionally get shot up, it is indeed a peace time occupation, it really is. We know one of them pretty well, and he is supposed to be a pretty good one and beside upsetting his own nerves and changing his name constantly and his papers and occasionally frightening us rather badly by mysterious messages, which might have to do with him and perhaps might have to do with us, but would he know and being very frequently condemned to death but being still alive, well it is the changing of their name that is the chief occupation, I remember when I was young I was fascinated on the stage that anybody came on disguised by changing their wig, that is the way you knew they were the same but some one else. Well secret service people seem to achieve the same thing by changing their names, once they are Hubert and then they are Henry and then they Charles and the last name changes the same way. Why should it deceive anybody since they remain the same but it seems to, everything is peculiar but that seems to me one of the things that are the most peculiar, what is in a name, for a secret service man everything is in a name if they can find a new one and they undoubtedly always can, and that new name seems to completely throw the authorities out, I used to read about it and I thought it was just in the books, but no they do it they do do it and it seems to work in spite of the horrid suspicion one has that perhaps nobody is really interested in finding them but apparently they are any way it is very funny, a bit frightening from time to time but really very funny. The times are so peculiar now, so mediaeval so unreasonable that for the first time in a hundred years truth is really stranger than fiction. Any truth.

There are such funny thing, how can a nation that feels itself as strong as the Germans do be afraid of a small handful of people like the Jews, why it does seem funny, most strange and very funny, they must be afraid because as Edgar Wallace loves to say over and over again, hate is fear, and why, what can they do to them, after all what can they do to them. Everything is funny. Yesterday was a funny day.

Strangers always have to have papers to move about, they are supposed to stay more or less in their commune, nobody that is the French are not very fussy about it but you are more or less supposed to stay in your commune. We are rather favored strangers, and we can move about fairly freely in our department, but when we go to others we are supposed to have a special pass. Yesterday was a funny day.

To-day was a funny day we expected the son and the mother came. She did say that for the women of France to-day they were a great many who could not remember that there had been peace between '18 and '39 it all seemed war and war and no peace in between. To be sure her son had been born in sixteen in Paris, and she had to remain in bed, on the day he was born and risk the bomb but he had been wrapped up in absorbent cotton and taken down into the cellar with all the others who could move about, and now his son was born in 1940, and living in Lyon, when he hears the right kind of a noise he says reflectively that is a bomb, and it is a bomb. As I say to-day was a funny day but yesterday was an even funnier day. As I say we are very careful about having our papers in order. So many people wander about with false papers, one of our friends who has an automobile buys one regularly when he wants to go anywhere, and anyway anybody seems to be able to have one for the asking but we are not like that, we go to the gendarmerie and we get our papers to go where we want to go to be sure they are very nice to us and always give us whatever we ask for which is very nice for us. So yesterday we were to go to Chambery to visit the dentist, and off we started and all as usual. I like trains now, I perfectly understand why the French people never did care for automobiles, why they so much prefer trains, trains are so very much more adventurous, particularly now, when nobody really knows when they will go or where they will go, and when you get off of them whether you can get out of the station to go home, and then the dark stations, and the crowded train, it is all very exciting. So yesterday we started to go to Chambery.

I had to buy a jar of jam.

You have to buy what you do not want to buy in order to buy what you do want to buy. That is if you have nothing to trade and a good many of us have nothing to trade. Of course if you are a farmer it is all right you have lots to trade but if you are not a farmer then you have nothing to trade. Once when we were in Bilignin during the winter we wanted to buy some eggs and nobody wanted to sell us any because all the eggs their chickens lay they wanted to eat themselves, which was natural enough, and Madame Roux said can we find nothing to trade that is not to trade but to induce them to sell eggs to us, at last we found something, and it was our dish water. Madame Roux had the habit of carrying off the dish water to give to a neighbor who was fattening a pig, and as there was very little milk with which to fatten pigs, dish water was considerable of a help, this was in the worst days, '41-42, in '43 life began to be easier, well anyway Alice Toklas said to Madame Roux, no we will not give away our dish water, if the neighbor wants it she has in return to be willing to sell us a certain quantity of eggs. So Madame Roux went to the neighbor and told her she could have the family dish water only under the condition of our having the privilege of buying from her a certain quantity of eggs, well she wanted the dish water and we bought the eggs, but alas she killed the pig at Christmas, and everybody killed their pig at Christmas and so there was no need any longer of dish water to fatten the pigs and so our right to buy eggs was over, we had not had the idea of making the bargain for longer. Now in 1943, in December, well I do not know quite why but apparently for a number of reasons victualing yourselves is easier. In the first place so many trains being stopped tends to make all the food produced stay where it is made and there is an awful lot of food produced in France and secondly the transport being so bad and the Germans not having any essence and so not having any trucks, and the trains being stopped all the time the Germans are not able to take food out of France so it stays here and then besides it is a point of honor on the part of every one to steal the reserve that is gathered together by the government to presumably give it to the Germans and all that eventually gets back into the black market, and so now everybody who lives in the country at least complains of having to eat too much meat, too much butter, too much white flour, of course in the big cities it is a different matter, there just because of the difficulties of transport they have difficulty in getting material but even in the big cities curiously enough they seem to have many more provisions than they had before, and also it may be because the war looking as if it might be over, and peace might be upon us any moment, nobody wants to hoard any more, and as there were tremendous stocks of provisions everywhere, and as there are very few Germans in France these days to feed, there is a quantity of food, much more than there has been since 1940. Things work out so differently than one thinks for.

But to get back to train traveling more and more I like to take a train I understand why the French prefer it to automobiling, it is so much more sociable and of course these days so much more of an adventure, and the irregularity of its regularity is fascinating. As I said we were going to Chambery and we got ready and got to the station well ahead of time as is our custom and with all our papers in order as is our custom.

When we arrived at the station of course the train was not there it never is and we had a long conversation with our friend the gendarme who helps us get around and helps us get a goat, and helped us every way they help anybody every day often to get away, they do do that. Well anyway we waited for the train and at last it came and it meant to go to Chambery but not the car we were in that did not mean to go to Chambery and so all of a sudden the landscape ceased to be familiar and naturally I was talking to a young woman about Paris and Lyon and about her being a coiffeuse and having a studio in Paris some day, now she was only in Lyon, and she had a girl friend and we were all talking and I said dear me this does not look like Chambery, why no they said it goes to Annecy, oh dear we said what can we do and we all talked and everybody gave advice and a German officer looked as if he wanted to join in but naturally nobody paid any attention to him nobody ever does which makes them quite timid in a train, and they wanted us to go to the biggest town and we said no we would get off at the first town which after all was not more than ten kilometers from Aix-les-Bains and if the worst came to the worst we could walk there. And we got off dog and all because of course Basket is always with us he likes train trips he did not at first but he does now because they admire him and they feed him, French people even in these days of no bread and no sugar cannot see a dog without offering him some bread and some sugar if they are eating and in these days anybody in the train is eating. It is like America was during prohibition you never know when it will happen again so you eat when you can which these days December almost Christmas '43 seems to be about all the time. Well anyway we stopped at the small station and we asked advice of the station master and he said we were in luck there was a train to Aix in two hours and then at eight o'clock at night there was one from Aix to Culoz and we just had to give up Chambery and just try again later and we did and we were all talking so much that he did not ask us for tickets and we were talking so much that we forgot to give him tickets or pay him, and then we went into the town and they all told us where we could eat in a little café and eat we did and very well for very little and there were a number of us and there were two German soldiers standing at the bar and one of them looked like Hemingway quite a bit when Hemingway was young, he probably was not a German but a Czech or something, they mostly are these days and like Hemingway he was drinking, he had a brandy and then he had an eau de vie and then he had a glass of sparkling white wine and then he had an Amer Picon, and then he had a glass of sparkling wine and he looked more and more like Hemingway when he was young and the other one with him a shorter and fatter and a married man and frankly German only drank a glass of wine and when it came to pay it came to considerable and there was an Alsatian with them interpreting and the one the good-looking one who looked like Hem when he was young when they were leaving put out his hand to shake hands with the proprietress and the proprietress could not refuse of course but she was red in the face and pushed her daughter back and nobody said anything when they left, but everybody understood what everybody felt, to sell and take money is one thing but to shake hands is another thing and the proprietress knew it was not her fault and still she knew it should not have happened she did know that and so did everybody.

So then we bought some pears and went back to the station and then we heard that the proprietress was Swiss and not French and so we understood that though she felt the same way she did not know as well as any Frenchwoman would know to have a thing like that not happen.

So then back we were in Aix-les-Bains and there were so many

Germans there and there was an alerte but nothing happened and
we went to all the shopkeepers we knew and we know a great many
in Aix to pass the time and get warm because it was cold and we
bought real silk scarfs and a pair of woolen stockings and we went
to a tea place where they gave us chocolate and where funnily
enough there was a German officer who looked just like Goering
though surely he would not be there drinking chocolate too and
having bread and jam but there it was and at last everything was
closing up and we had to go to the station to wait two hours there
for our train.

We waited and I went in and out and walked up and down and
Alice Toklas sat on the bench near where they sell tickets because
the waiting room was full of everybody sleeping because you might
wait all day for a train or you might wait all night to leave your
train because the curfew does not ring but it is there any night and
every night and very often you have to wait all night to go home
until the morning. It is all like other times, the curfew and in
French it is cover fire, and it is cover light and they cannot have
midnight mass although it is Christmas because of the curfew. You
do not think much about it unless you are traveling because there
is nothing to go out for in the winter and so everybody stays at
home. So we waited for our train, and I went in and out and there
were a good many Germans about and German nurses in and out,
and the dog and I went in and out and then suddenly there in the
night and in the newsstand outside I saw a copy of Alice Toklas'
Autobiography in French there for sale on a shelf, and I was very
excited and went in to tell Alice Toklas and the ticket seller heard
me he was a pleasant young fellow and he said yes in ten minutes
in English he thought I was asking about the time of the train I had
already asked him and so I went up to talk to him, and he said and
these gentlemen, that is the way the Germans are always mentioned
and these gentlemen do not bother you and I said no we are women
and past the age to be bothered and beside I said I am a writer and
so the French people take care of me, and what may I ask he said
do you write oh I said it just happens that one of my books is for

sale outside on the newsstand and that is what I was just telling my friend, and the young woman ticket seller said and might I ask what is the name of the book and I told her and without any hesitation she took up her handbag put a scarf over her and went out to the newsstand and came back with it triumphantly and she said will you sign it? and I said why yes I will and I asked her name and I wrote it in and we were all very pleased and Alice Toklas thought it was all very funny, with all the Germans coming in and out and all about. Anything can happen in France and that makes it what it is, just that makes it what it is.

And now we are going to Chambery again the train was late again and it was raining, but anyway there were all kinds of them traveling, we and they and every one. French people love to get on a train and now the difficulties are just as they used to be in America in the early days when there were wash outs and snow slides, and train bandits and strikes, and breakdowns and everything, I once crossed the continent during the Pullman strike and traveling now is just like that, anything can happen and nobody expects anything everybody just goes on traveling. The government begs everybody to stay at home unless the reason for traveling is very urgent but of course it is urgent, why not as long as trains go and there is somewhere to go and so we went to Chambery again and it was raining. The dentist's son after having escaped from jail and having been all through Italy and home again and gone away again to join his comrades and be a commando, little boys in the streets play at that, after all that, he went to Lyon on business for his friends, and was caught by the Germans and now is in prison again and his mother is desperate. But he has written to his grandmother and says she cannot sent him food but she can send him clean linen which she does and he says he is with comrades and they are all well, and the only comfort is that he writes back-handed and people who do that usually manage to take care of themselves so perhaps he will get away although it is now more dangerous for him than it was his father and mother seem to worry less than they did, I suppose there comes the saturation point of worry and then

normal life begins again and just goes on being. I met another boy
he was an Alsatian and he was visiting in the neighborhood with
his mother and all that had happened to him, he had escaped from
a train and he had been let out finally and now all he had to do
was to avoid big cities not that he really did, they never do and I
asked him how he managed to get out of his troubles and he answered by patience and address, and I suppose that is the way to
get away.

Everything is dangerous and everybody casually meeting anybody talks to anybody and everybody tells everybody the history of
their lives, they are always telling me and I am always telling them
and so is everybody, that is the way it is when everything is dangerous.

Life and death and death and life.

I like to listen to the Germans talking English on the radio.
There was a very funny one the other day.

He said he was very much in earnest, he said that the English
were a terrible people and he gave two examples of their passion
for unusual cruelty.

In the first place there was the horrible fact that they killed
unborn children, they believe and they preach that most horrible
of horrible doctrines, birth control, can, said he, such a nation
remain in the ranks of nations called human, no he thought not,
and then he went on there is something almost more frightful there
is Malthus one of their great men who says people should be killed
off by plagues, by famine, and by wars, can went on the radio
speaker can a country whose acknowledged great men preach such
a doctrine, can they be called human.

And so he goes on and so they go on, and all the radio stations
interfere so that nobody can hear any one and in the midst of all
the misery it is not childish but very small boyish. It is strange the
world to-day is not adult it has the mental development of a seven
year old boy just about that. Dear me.

And so the world is mediaeval just as mediaeval as it can be.

They look like men they look like men they look like men-of-war.

I had that over the radio in 1939 and now it is January 1944, and they still look like men, and they still look like men, but and they still look like men, of war.

They do and they do not.

I often think that the real beginning of this plunge back into mediaevalism was the abdication of Edward, it was it undoubtedly was just like a bit of mediaeval history, and since then it has become more and more mediaeval, The abdication of Edward, Jew baiting, and the plunging every individual into mediaeval misery, and perhaps it will all have to be done over again until a new nineteenth century and a new plunge into mediaevalism, who can know, history does repeat itself, I have often thought that that was the really soothing thing that history does. The one thing that is sure and certain is that history does not teach, that is to say, it always says let it be a lesson to you but is it. Not at all because circumstances always alter cases and so although history does repeat itself it is only because the repetition is soothing that any one believes it, nobody nobody wants to learn either by their own or anybody else's experience, nobody does, no they say they do but no nobody does, nobody does. Yes nobody does.

It is very strange, for the last two years everybody was wearing shoes with wooden soles there were no others to be had and now there are no others to be had nobody wears shoes with wooden soles they all wear leather shoes like anybody did and there are none to be had but everybody wears them. It is a pleasure that it is like that, quite a pleasure, almost a contentment.

I was asking some people to-day how it happened and they said quite naturally, near Christmas '43 everybody knows it is bound to be over some day, this war in spite of the fact that a number of people say that it is to be a hundred years' war so why pay any attention to it, but nearly everybody thinks that now sometime there will be an end to it, as the peasant says everything that has a beginning must have an end so may not the war, and so everybody instead of keeping their leather shoes for later are wearing them now and besides that all the shopkeepers who have stocks of prewar shoes and in France there are always stocks big stocks of everything, why not, they are a saving and a secretive population why not, so now they are bringing out all these stocks to sell at big prices before prices become normal, so what between those who buy and those who wear what there is no longer any need of keeping, wooden shoes, which were really not very practical, have been given up and now suddenly everybody wears leather as if it were a fashion, now when there is supposed not to be any.

There are so many things that happened, we are burning peat, one used to read about that being done in Ireland, and here there are a great many marshes and there is peat and although it smells a little and smokes a good deal it is not bad to burn not at all, and as the windows in Grenoble and Annecy are all broken by explosions they all have paper windows, and as I say it really is like pioneering, we are all on the roads all the time going here and going there to find things to eat, in the country of course you do find plenty and at last there is so much that you can even refuse to buy more of it, of which we are all inordinately proud, up to date we all have bought anything anybody has brought us.

So many funny things one of our neighbors a very charming oldish lady who lives in a castle has three daughters and two sons, which is another matter. I am just now writing a novel about them Castles in Which We Live and the daughter Claude was in Chambery having her first baby, and she telephoned that the baby had come, the mother said she must go to her at once, but the husband said there is no train to-day, and she said but there is an autobus from Ruffieux, Ruffieux is ten kilometers away and she started off walking and she saw she would not get there in time so she stopped a man on a bicycle who was passing her and told him about her daughter and he said but the car will be gone before you get there and she said yes I know and he said I will take you on my bicycle and she said but there is no place behind for me to sit and he said no but I will take you on my handle bars and he did and she caught the car and she got to Chambery and she saw her grand-daughter.

If they say they believe it do they and if they say they will do it will they. That is what happens any day. Pretty soon there will not be any war and what will that be like.

Pretty soon.

I wonder sometimes why the English royal family lets any one who might come to the throne lets him be called George how can they, to be sure Shakespeare said a rose will smell as sweet call it by any name but will it. No it will not. Consider the name of George. Every time there was a George on the throne there was trouble bad trouble. The first two Georges gradually reduced England from the glory that Anne and Marlborough following William and Mary had given them, and then came George III and all misfortune, did he not lose colonies and go mad and then George the fourth and the first world war, with Napoleon and then no more Georges for a bit, and then after Victoria and Edward and Edward would not have a world war come George V a nice man but with all the misfortunes of a world war and then an Edward, would the world war have come had Edward stayed on but he did not, not, and a George came and bang a world war once again and plenty of misfortune and so will they again will the royal family again have the temerity to call a son who might come to the throne George. Better not, really better not. There is something in a name all the same.

To-day I was walking my usual twelve kilometers to buy some bread which is not dark and some cake which is very good, very very good and on the way I met a woman who was dragging a push-cart sometimes pushing it and in between she stopped to pick up sticks and I said to her well you will have a bit of a fire. Yes she said in the one sack I have some coal, I have picked it up near the railroad and in the other I have pieces of paper to light the fire and now I am picking up twigs to make it go. I do not belong here, she said, she was a good looking upstanding woman, I do not belong here she said, I come from the north, when I think of my lovely country up north where roses grow, but I and my son were put out without an hour's notice, put out by the Germans, they have my house and they have my furniture and I have nothing, and here, it is a wretched country and miserable people they would not give you anything even if you paid them and all I hope is that some day soon bombs will fall on them, bombs, she said and I laughed and she said my good lady, yes that is what I say, and we each of us went on our way, each getting provisions which we needed that day.

And the young are strange. It is all strange. I was talking to the head of our local bank and his daughter is studying social science in Grenoble and they are naturally bankers are very quiet and conservative, and I said now that Grenoble is so full of explosions and killings and reprisals I suppose you are keeping your daughter at home. Oh no he said, the young are not like that, they say, this is their war, that we do not understand, their professors can be shot as hostages, their comrades mixed up in aggressions, their windows blown out and all the rest, but after all it is their war let us alone it is our war, and said the father there is nothing to do but to let them alone, I guess it is their war.

One day is the same as another day and yet every day is different. And the girls tend to be tall, taller than they used to be but not the boys not taller than they used to be, I suppose there is a physical reason for this, I do suppose so.

What worries a great many is that when the young come back out of Germany they will all be old, quite old, that does worry a great many.

And any evening one can go on listening to any one propagandizing over the radio and one thing is very certain nobody seems to be loving any one. Do you love one another, is not at all true now. Nobody can, it is extraordinary really extraordinary how difficult it is just now for anybody to love their neighbor any neighbor, here there and everywhere it is very certain that it is not at all a natural thing for any one to love one another. This Christmas and New Year of 1943-'44 has made it very natural

indeed, that they do not do not at all not any one hardly any one
that no one does love any one, that is their neighbor, hardly any
one. It is like that now, this last winter was just one winter too
long, anybody knows that, last winter it was all right they could
still make the joke that the war was going to be over and when
asked why what reason had he, he said I have a very certain one, it
is that my wife has had enough more than enough. But now it is
another winter and nobody can make it a joke any more, it is just
one winter too much.

I was out walking this afternoon the first week of January '44
on the banks of the Rhone and there was a cold wind and I had
two layers of wool one very good and one not so good and a layer
of heavy linen very good and the wind came right through to my
arms and it was not a degree below centigrade zero in fact it was
one above and what are the German soldiers feeling over there,
there are a few around here young ones guarding the railroad line
and over in Belley they are that is they have been training young
ones, they are all gone now presumably to Russia, and they were
cold there in Belley where it is not so very cold and they were very
young and a great many of them were not Germans and they were
being trained to run tanks made of wood and that they worked
with their feet as the German army has no automobiles any more
none at all except those that are on freight cars, and yet it goes on,
well I suppose as the peasants say anything that has a beginning
must have an ending, and as Madame Gallais says it is she who
here gives us the little luxuries we need, she finds them and she is
very gay about it which is pleasant of her, she lived most of her life
in Paris and she likes to be Parisian which she is and you have to
learn to do everything even to die, and the young feel like that
about it too, they feel that the old ones cannot learn how to die in
this war, but they know.

While I was walking along the banks of the Rhone and the
wind was cold I saw a tremendous quantity of crows and of wild
ducks, there are so many kinds these days, to be sure for three
years now there has been no hunting but then on the other hand

there is no food, people gather in their crops more carefully than they used to, they do their own gleaning and so what is there to eat for all these birds and there are so many thousands more than there used to be and they are much fatter than they used to be there must be a reason for it but is there.

One dreams funny dreams these days. I dreamed one about Nathalie Barney. I dreamed that she always left the plants of her Paris apartment at a florist's to have them watered over the summer and returned in the winter and now would she have them back again, would she, would the florist would there be a florist, would there be an apartment, would there be she. I do not know whether she did do this ordinarily with her plants or whether she had plants but all the same I did dream it.

She is in Florence and it is January 1944 and everybody here well not everybody but a great many think that since the war did not end in '43, it never will end, never end at all and perhaps they are right, anyway that is the way a great many here to-day feel about it.

Everybody almost anybody these days is either dragging shoving or carrying something everybody along the road and I carry, it comes easier to me to carry than pull or push, although sometimes I do put what I carry on what they push and we push together but mostly I carry, not a great deal three or four or five kilos, and that is quite enough to carry quite enough for twelve kilometers more or less.

The other day I was talking to the baker, he does bake us cakes, yes he does, we like cake, and he does bake me white bread and he does give us jam yes he does, a good many do these days and he does. And we were talking. He said he had just been reading about Hungarian cooking. He said he was comparatively a young man he is forty-five or there about, and he said a man like himself had begun life being apprenticed to a very good cake shop in Lyon, from there he had gone to Paris, he had worked at all the best houses, all the most important cake and tea places, and then he had worked on the Riviera and he had a great deal of experience and now he had bought this little bakery in this little hamlet and perhaps he would stay there even after the war, after all he said a man like myself having had so much experience should remember a great deal of what he has learned from others but he should also keep just a little of what is only himself and then he has a small place and yet people will come because it is that. Now he said I can only do a few things for about fifteen clients of which you are one, but wait he said wait until the war is over then you will see what you will see and it will be very good.

And then we went on to talk about climate and the things each nation drinks and the food it eats. Yes he said I do understand that here in France we make normally a wine that is rarely more than nine degrees of alcohol, and we can drink that with our meals and indeed we can even put water into our wine as many do, and we drink a nice wine while eating, but the Hungarians who drink a heavy wine, they drink water with the meal and they drink their heavy wine after. As do the Spaniard and the Portuguese too, I said, it is all a question of climate. Now I said the Americans and the Russians who had more or less the same climate, they drink a heavy alcohol before the meal vodka or a cocktail, and during the meal they drink hot drinks like tea, coffee or cocoa, yes he said I understand the stomach has to have a shock and then has to be kept warm, but said he the only thing I do not understand is the German food and the German drinks, that is beer, ah I said the English and the Germans both suffer from the sea fogs of the North Sea and perhaps beer and their diet is the only thing that meets that sea fog, perhaps he said, all the others he said I find sympathetic but not that, he said, and then he sighed, he said they talk about the United States of Europe but he said that can never come about the food and the drink of each country in Europe is too radically different, they could never have a United States, oh no, he said. I sometimes think though, there could be all the Slavs together and all the Latins together, and then if we were fairly decently governed it might be all right, but he said even then very likely not, no he said I see that as long as each country wants to eat

its own food and drink its own drink and they do there can never
be a United States of Europe. It is strange, he went on, very
strange that in such a small continent as is Europe, there should
be so many kinds of climate, so many kinds of food and drink. It
is strange, he said, and I took my two delicious cakes and my two
loaves of bread and slung it on my back and Basket and I went
home as we always do in the winter evening.

It is January 1944 all the same.

All one's friends are going up to Paris for a change. There are
no trains but anyway all the time they all keep taking them. We
live the life of trains, so much more now that there are none. In
the old days of automobiles I never thought I would clink the
little gate and go through or put through the passage over the
railroads, the way I used to see people do while we waited in the
automobile but now I do do it just like that all the time, with a
basket on my back and I like it, why not.

There are little things too, little like an inch on the end of
one's nose, and that is tobacco. I do not smoke but Alice Toklas
does and she has to she just has to if not well anyway she just has
to. So when cards came in cards for tobacco and they only were
giving them to men, women were not being encouraged to smoke
not by the government and so what to do, well the tobacconist and
I agreed that since they did not ask if you were a woman, you just
inscribed yourself we would do so with initials and who would
know, well that worked for a whole year and helped out by an
occasional friend Alice Toklas did not do so badly and then the
next year they had regular cards and they had to be regular no
initials did not do and what could we do what could she do, we
did several things but none of them quite enough. Alice Toklas
found it very hard to bear, boys of eighteen had a right to
chocolate and they had a right to cigarettes too, that did seem
unjust, either they were too young to smoke or too old to eat
chocolate that was not reasonable but as foreigners even if not yet
enemies we had no right to protest, so we tried everything, and
one way and another way we got a few cigarettes, here and there

and in one way and in another way and friends brought some from Switzerland you could go to Switzerland then and come out again and there were some but not enough far from enough, and then a friend found a sergeant in the French army who would sell some that the army gave them and some more too and soon Alice Toklas had enough quite enough, and then we invaded North Africa and the French army was disbanded and the sergeant went away and it was a trying moment and then the Italian army came and that was fine, why the Italian army had so many cigarettes I do not know mysteriously the German army has not, but anyway whatever the way it was done the Italian army had them by the ton very nice little cigarettes they were too and the Italians loved to sell them, and everybody bought them and all the smokers were happy again. And then the poor Italians had to go away, just suddenly and and although everybody had a supply it was not a big enough one and something had to be done, In this part of the country tobacco was always grown, it has a climate that seems to suit tobacco one would not think so because it is mountainous and has a cold winter and a not too hot summer but it does seem to suit tobacco, and now everybody began to grow tobacco in their garden anybody and there were some who grew a very good cigarette tobacco and they were ready to sell us several pounds of it and I learned to roll cigarettes with a little machine everybody bought and mysteriously there was no lack of cigarette paper, everything is mysterious in this kind of war and that there is no paper but there is no lack of cigarette paper and so everybody and Alice Toklas was happy again. That is here, in other parts of France where tobacco will not grow they were not so happy.

A woman was just telling me about her grandnephew.

A great nephew had been sent to Germany to work and he was young and he was growing and he was not well and he was sent home to get better and they said he should go again now that he was better, and his mother and his father and his grandmother and his great aunt they all knew better and he knew better, and he went away to his grandmother and there he stayed and as yet,

as yet, it is always as yet as yet nobody bothered, neither to find
him or to tell about him but although he was young he had begun
to smoke and there was no tobacco, he of course had no care
because he was hidden so his great aunt who was in this country
part of the country where tobacco can grow tried to send it to him
but she never could it never started and it never got there if it did
start and so he has no tobacco to smoke. It says his grandaunt it is
a deprivation, after all, she said it does not seem much in view of
everything else but it is a deprivation.

To-day I was talking to the wife of the mayor, she is a Swiss by
birth and had a grandfather who was very Swiss. In a war everybody always knows all about Switzerland, in peace times it is just
Switzerland but in war time it is the only country that everybody
has confidence in, everybody. They are good for war time, all
right for themselves in peace time but good for everybody in war
time, and that is because they take everything seriously and
calmly, and everything is equally important and everything is
accomplished. That makes them very important when everybody
needs them and everybody does need them in war time.

So the wife of the mayor who is a Swiss was telling me about
her grandfather and she showed me a photograph of him and he
was just as Swiss as William Tell. She was also talking about people
becoming naturalised, Swiss and that unfortunately they are often
guilty of treason. It is she said bound to happen, she said her
grandfather had always said that naturalisation was foolishness,
consider he said no matter how much you naturalise a Savoyard
he remains Savoyard. Savoyards in his day were what Germans are
in our day. Well anyhow, I do think he is right, naturalisation is
foolishness completely. Nobody not born in a country or if they
are born in another country by accident must be born of parents
born in that country, nobody not born in a country has really the
ultimate feeling of that country. Let them have all the privileges
of residence, of earning their living in that country or of enjoying
that country but not of becoming citizens of that country. Citizen-
ship is a right of birth and should remain so, I think the old Swiss

was right undoubtedly right. I have lived in France the best and longest part of my life and I love France and the French but after all I am an American, and it always does come back to that I was born there, and one's native land is one's native land you cannot get away from it and only the native sons and daughters should be citizens of the country and that is all there is to it. The old Swiss was right, he certainly was and is. It would make everything go better. It certainly would.

Just now January 1944 nobody seems to think that the war will ever end. We all were hopeful in '43, but in '44 it is going much better but we have so much less hope of it ever being over so very much less hope.

Such funny things happen.

If the President of the United States has to be born in America then it is only reasonable that anybody who votes to make him president should be born in America, only reasonable.

The owner of the local drugstore is what they call a collabo, that is one who wanted to collaborate with the Germans, there were quite a few of them and they are getting less and less but there still are some and he is one. A German said a nice thing about that. It was in Paris and it was over a year ago it was in the beginning of '42 and he was talking to a group of French people who had met about some question of protecting French works of art, and he said the French are a pleasant people and I like them but they none of them have three qualities they only have two. They are either honest and intelligent, they are either collabo and intelligent or they are collabo and honest but I have never met one who was collabo honest and intelligent, everybody laughed and it is true there is no such thing as being collabo honest and intelligent. Well the drug store man was collabo and honest but certainly not intelligent. He had already been sent a coffin and other attentions and the other day the Germans went to his house to make a search. Of course he was terribly upset. Apparently some one to tease him sent an anonymous accusation against him to the German authorities giving the detail of explosives that he had concealed in his premises. As they always investigate these accusations and as naturally they do not know the local political opinions they examine which is natural enough. The unfortunate man went to complain to the gendarmerie, and of course they told everybody and everybody roared with laughter finding it an exceedingly good joke, on all of them.

Around here it is getting to be just like Robin Hood. The young men in the mountains come down, they they took two tons of butter from a dairy and the other day to the delight of everybody they took a pig weighing one hundred and fifty kilos, he had two small ones and they told him to fatten them up and they would take one and leave the other, they took this from the local aristocrat who had been highly unpopular because of his political opinions and because having been a poor man and been put at the head of the local food distribution, he had only given supplies to those who had his political opinions, and they took his automobile from him, saying that he could go to mass on foot the way the rest of the world did and as he had no more food to distribute he did not need it, they also took eight hundred litres of eau de vie, which he had on hand, and as everybody says as they always pay the government prices for everything they take nobody has any cause for complaint. Everybody is excited and pleased, the young men are so young so gay so disciplined and they have so much money, presumably English and American gold and everybody is pleased, naturally enough, as nobody can stop them everybody takes it to mean that it is the beginning of the end of course all except the collabo who say they are gangsters and what will happen after the war. Everybody says the war will go on forever but in spite of that everybody does think that the war is closing in which it is the end of January forty-four.

Everybody wanders and it is interesting to know how much they wandered even before.

I was talking to two young workmen, they had gone twenty kilometers for provisions and I had gone twelve and they walked along quickly and I walked with them and they told me their own and their families' history, at least one did, the other only came along.

He was all alone he said, and he did his own cooking. He was a good cook he said, he had even cooked in a restaurant, he had been in the army in Algeria and he had had leave to come back to France to see his family and the day he was to go back the Americans arrived in Africa and so here he was all alone. To be sure his father had been born in Italy in Bergamo and so had he, his father had come to France to earn a living and then had brought his family with him, and he this boy was six years old then and so he too had been born in Italy. He had seen while he was doing his military service the lovely cathedral of Albi he knew it was beautiful although he had never been inside it and now he was all alone. And have you no brothers and sisters, I don't know where my brothers are and I have a sister married in Italy, to an Italian I asked, no he said to an American, South American I said, this I do not know he said and I have never heard from her since my mother died and I am all alone, and not married I said, no he said I am only twenty-eight and one should not marry before one is thirty, a cousin of my father he said, made a fortune in America, where I said, ah that I do not know, he said, and then we said good-bye and parted.

Workmen have always wandered, just as they did in the middle ages, they wander until they marry and then some of them begin to wander again. In the last war we had a Negro wounded man whose name was Hannibal and he said that he had been a great wanderer he had wandered all over Staten Island, well here in Europe they are just wanderers, they wander all over Europe, and very often they end up all alone very often. And now there is war, and they wander so much that they seem to be not moving at all, not anywhere at all.

I was talking to a woman the other day we were both walking carrying our baskets and intending to bring home something, and she told me of her two brothers and her husband who had all three escaped before the prisoners were taken to Germany, she said some

families suffered so much and some not at all, she said it was fate.
She herself had five children four of them girls. That too does
happen very frequently in this country we both agreed. And then
we got talking about the strange thing, that so many of the comparatively few Frenchmen killed in this war were only sons of
widows whose husbands had fallen in the last war. Why I said.
Well she said, it is probably because they went into the war more
worried than those whose fathers had not been killed in the last
war. It could be that. And she said might it not be that being
raised by a widow they would naturally be more spoilt and not so
active as those raised by father and mother. Naturally she said, a
mother can never really dominate a son, a mother is bound to spoil
children because she is with them all the time and she cannot
always be saying no so she ends up by not saying no at all. And
besides she said, if a mother had lost her husband in the war her
little boy had been impressed by her crying so much and that
would make him nervous, when he too had gone to war. It certainly is true that a very considerable percentage of the relatively
few Frenchmen killed in this war were the only sons of widowed
mothers who had had their husbands killed in the last war.

To-night Francis Malherbe who had been sent to Germany to
work came to see us just back and very interesting, January
nineteenth forty-four. One of the things he said was that in Paris
he had come home that way they all said that there would be a
landing on the twentieth of January. Of course everybody supposed it was going to be in France, and at the same time we had
word that the man who always knows what the Germans expect to
happen said that there was to be a landing between the sixteenth
and the twentieth of January forty-four and he always knows what
they know and so we were quite excited and there was a landing
only it was in Italy instead of in France. Pretty good deception
that, because and that must never be forgotten people do know
what is going to happen and so far the Americans have been
pretty good at it, twice we have known it was going to happen and
the right date and everything but not the right place. We are very

pleased with our countrymen, it is a good poker game. Very good indeed and we like them to play poker well. It pleases us.

However that was not all that Francis Malherbe told us. He described Germany the way it is now and the way the French who are compulsorily working there are. He gave such a good description, he said of course there was no food no fat, and the cooking of vegetables always in water, the German workmen were given fats but not the Frenchmen, but I said is there no black market no way of getting any, oh yes he said plenty of that among all the foreign workmen but never with the Germans, but I said where do the foreign workmen get it, how do they get it, they steal it, he said, each one who can steals a certain quantity of something and sells it or trades it with others for something else, and that is all the black market there is but and he laughed it is considerable, and we said how do they the Germans feel, still convinced of victory especially the young, he said but why should they not the world is made for the young, the fifteen year old boys have older men get up in the street cars to give them seats, naturally they are convinced that they will win, if you have such a position in the world as that at fifteen of course you are bound to win. And really we said really he said they certainly can hold out six months longer, certainly. My brother he said he is a military prisoner a lieutenant, and as I was what they call the man of trust, that is to say I had to judge and patch up the incessant quarrels between French and German workers they gave me leave to go and see my brother. He had been a prisoner for four years and of course I had not seen him and now I saw him. He came in with two soldiers with guns and fixed bayonets at his back and it upset me so I began to cry but he said to me sternly control yourself do not show emotion, and we sat down at a table together and we talked and we compared photographs those he had of the family and those I had with me, and the adjutant who was there to listen to us said suddenly he is giving you photographs, how dare you said my brother accuse me of such a thing, apologise I insist that you apologise, first examine these photographs and then apologise, and the man said but it is all right, no said my brother look, look at them count them and examine them and then apologise, which the adjutant had to do. I was proud of my brother. When he told us this we were of course much moved, it was so real so normal, like a piece out of Dumas and yet happening, happening to a boy we knew very well and are very fond of, and then he went on describing, and telling about the different nationalities with which he was working and making it all real and the Russians he said, they are the most interesting, we Frenchmen get along better with them than with any others except Frenchmen, and they do impress us with their courage and their tenacity and the simple way they say naturally we expect to occupy this country and when we do and we think we will, we will make them very unhappy. And so he talked on and then he had to leave and he has to go back and he has to go back because he has two officer brothers as prisoners and something might happen to them if he did not and so he will go back. We hope to have him back again we are very very fond of him. He is a nice neighbor.

These days everybody hears from their sons or their nephews who are working there, one who really was too small and too weak to go but go he did, his father had been in the navy and then had been in a garage as electrician and we had liked him and when the French were defeated the shock killed him he could not believe it and this only son writes to his mother dear mother I am hungry, I was never hungry before but I am hungry now always hungry so hungry. And then there is a nephew of some one here we know he is an intelligent fellow a designer of machines, and he writes that he is in the capital and that the sky is sad, it is a cold sad sky, and he he plays the violin and draws a little and hopes not very much but a little as most of his compatriots have been killed in a bombardment, and so every day is another day which passes in that way.

Yesterday I went my usual twelve kilometers to get some bread and cake and I met three or four who were on a farm wagon being drawn by a mule and they said come and sit, and I said can the mule stand one more, why not they said and I sat it was very comfortable. Basket the white poodle was completely upset but finally he decided to follow along and we jogged along and it was a pleasant day although it was January and I said you know you French people you can make a pleasant thing out of anything, but we are not rich like the Americans no I said but you can go on working the kind of working you do until you are ninety or a hundred and you complain but any day is a pleasant enough day which it is not in every other country, and they said perhaps but they would like to be rich like the Americans and then we were on the top of the hill and I went to get my bread and cake and they went on to get their flour and it was a pleasant day.

The young ones who come back from Germany on leave are puzzled by one thing, any Frenchman would be why are the Germans so sentimental, when they are what they are why are they so sentimental. No Frenchman can understand that.

Yesterday I was out walking and I met a man I used to know, a casual country acquaintance, that is to say he and his family were cousins of some very old friends of ours, and they own a place around here, they used to be here for only a few weeks in the summer but now, things being as they are, they live here altogether. The father is a big gay man about town, who has lots of property is a good business man and used to spend all his life between here and other places and the Cote d'Azur. His wife was born in Washington U. S. A. her father having been in the French embassy and he is an amusing man, of course he says we live here now, the country is lovely in winter, I never saw it before but it is, it is like English pastels such a delicate color, and besides we all get all we want to eat, dont you, and I agreed that we did, as much of everything that we want, butter eggs meat cake and cheese, and I had to agree that we all did because we all do. Just why we do now when the years before we did not nobody seems to be able to explain but we do, is it because the army of occupation is getting smaller and smaller or is it, that everybody knows how now better and better, anyway it is undoubtedly true everywhere in France now, everywhere and nobody seems to know quite why. Well any-

way, the other day I met him M. Labadie, he saw Basket and he
waited for us he was on his bicycle and I was on foot, and we
stopped to talk together. I thought he had very funny clothes on
and when I came nearer I said to him these are funny clothes that
you are wearing what are they. Ah he said you would never guess
look at the buttons and I did, they were large American army
buttons with the eagle and the shield, nice brass buttons on a
khaki coat and I said when in the name of wonder did you get
that. Ah he said I bought it after the other war from the American
stocks and I kept it here in the country and now it is very handy,
and it was, some German soldiers on patrol had just passed but M.
Labadie did not mind that, you know he said everybody wants to
buy one off me, look he said counting them there are twelve of
them, quite a little fortune, just to-day again they offered me forty
francs for one, but not I, I keep them and wear them. Well we
went on talking and I said your boy who is twenty-one, has he gone,
oh dear no, he said, you see I keep him traveling, that is the way
you do you either go off to some little bit of a place and stay there
quietly and nobody bothers you or you keep moving, now I keep
my boy moving, I have lots of business to attend to, and I send him
around to attend to it, and if you keep on traveling for business
your papers all always have to be in order which of course they are
so no one bothers, that is the way he said, and of course he is right
that is the way. And then we went on talking. We talked about the
war, why not since there is this war. He said of course the Germans
cannot win, which is natural enough because their country is so
poor they know nothing about cooking and eating, people who
know nothing about cooking and eating naturally cannot win. He
went on reflectively, France always seems to be beaten but really a
country that can see and shut one eye and then shut the other eye
opening the first eye, is bound to come out of any mess not too
badly, you see he went on meditatively, one must take care of
oneself and be brave and be excited and at the same time must
take care of one's business must not be poor. War said he is
inevitably connected with money and naturally when two people

want the same money or more money they must fight, and he said reflectively nowadays when one wants to spend so much money when everybody wants automobiles and electrical installations and everything else well naturally the more money everybody wants to spend the more men have to be killed when it comes to a war. People who spend little money when they make war kill few people, but the more money you want to spend, the more men you have to kill when you begin to go to war. And there is another thing if you can really spend the most money then you have less of your own men killed than the other side who wants to spend more money but has not got it to spend. And so America has less men killed and Germany more and that he said is natural enough. And just then another man whom we both knew was coming along, now said M. Labadie he is a poor thing an unfortunate man, he has a wife but one never sees her she is always away and a forsaken man and he shrugged his shoulders and we each of us went on our way.

To-day was another day, as usual in France feeling gets more and more complicated, and now when those who have taken to the hills come down and take food off the railways, well will it get them in the habit of stealing and should it, and they all worry, and there was one woman who was visiting and she quarreled with every one in Culoz, and when she left she said they needed the Germans to come to whip them into subjugation, and some one said and she an idler who has money what does she think will happen to her. Well anyway one thing is certain every day brings the war nearer and nearer to an ending but does any one around here believe that, certainly not, so little do they believe it that although we know it we do not really believe it ourselves. As one woman said well now as we have all made all our arrangements to live in a state of war I suppose the war will go on. We all suppose it will and it does this the first day of February in nineteen forty-four.

I have just been listening to a description of how the mountain boys captured two Germans and took them to the mountains as hostages and now the Germans even when they want to buy a piece of bread in a store they are all armed and always at least six of them and one standing outside as a guard for them. It makes everybody laugh. Every tenth birthday makes a man afraid and a woman too and even children every tenth birthday does that. Be careful everybody.

Everybody is feeling a little more cheerful about everything to-day even though it is a dark and gloomy day.

Breathes there a man with soul so dead who never to himself has said, this is my own my native land.

Well yes, yesterday when the Swiss radio announced that the Americans had landed on the Marshall Islands and that these islands had belonged to Japan before the war I was so pleased. It was midnight and I was so pleased. As an American and as a Californian I was so pleased. I went up stairs and woke up Alice Toklas who was asleep, and I said we have landed the Americans have landed on the Marshall Islands, which before the war belonged to Japan and Alice Toklas opened one eye slightly and said, well then they are invaded, and slept gently again. Of course that is what every one wants them to be that they are invaded, when that does come to pass it will be a comfort to every one, yes every one but them and they do not want at least their feelings arc of no account no account. So that made this day a nice day. Otherwise not such a nice day because they are trying to take younger and younger men away to work but mostly they do not go this is undoubtedly so.

And then to-day when they said, that is to say the announcers said that the Marshall Islands were on the way to the Philippines, it did make all one's youth come back the days when we saw the American soldiers preparing in San Francisco to go that way. They were more unformed than they are now, their character is more affirmed it was more so in the world war than in the Spanish-American war and now we have not seen them but we hear them they are as simply direct as they were then but not so unbaked, the national security is undoubtedly stronger, we are hoping to see

them soon, yes we are. To-day we were in Belley my birthday the
third of February and of course everybody was upset most horribly
because there is preparing an effort to round up the mountain boys
and as everybody's boys are there it is rather horrible. One of the
Bilignin women cried to me what can I do, my boy was always so
fond of you what can I do, and what can she do with a nineteen
year old boy, go or not go, stay or not stay, go away or not go
away, who can say. Who can. I said the only thing I can advise is
to do nothing, just now it is the only thing to do and mostly it does
succeed, do nothing but he wont eat, and he got up at four in the
morning to work because he says if I have to leave I will have as
much work done for you as possible dear me. Our Swiss grocer he
is a nice man, he has three sons but as he says they just did not give
him his naturalisation papers before this war and now they are all
Swiss and so comparatively safe and all the same he said to me, they
must come the Americans must come and they must come soon to
save the boys to save the boys, oh yes to save the boys. Everybody is
unhappy and ashamed, ashamed because French are arresting
Frenchmen, the taxi-man said the other day, three of the guard
mobile who are going up to the mountains missed their train and
they asked him to drive them. For you personally he said or by
order, no they said there is no order, well he said if I take you,
you who are going to shoot up our boys, if I take you you will
have to pay for it, and they asked me how much, and I said double
the ordinary fare, and pay they did, the pigs who are going to
shoot up our boys. Everybody is ashamed, everybody is crying,
everybody is listening to everything and the trains go on, with
Germans who are not Germans and French who are not French,
oh dear me, there is no nineteenth century about this, hardly the
twentieth century, it is terribly the middle ages, and in the meantime Alice Toklas came along with six lemons, that seems nothing
but for years there have been no lemons, and there were a few
while the Italians were here, and since these have gone none.
Where said I did you get them. From the grocer she said, and

where did he get them, he said he had them because there had
been a wedding in Tunis.

What that meant nobody can know, of course there has been
no communication of any kind with Tunis since the Americans
landed there, so what did he mean. Of course one never asks anybody what he means.

We get more and more excited about the Marshall Islands and
being on the way to the Philippines, we cannot help wondering
how the American commentator can speak so quietly about all
that, shows he is no Californian, for us all of it is passionately
interesting, Alice Toklas remembers the man who was second in
command with Leahy who took possession of Guam coming back
from Manila. They liked that island so they thought they would
take possession, and as they had never taken possession of anything
before they did not know how, and two of the native girls fell in
love with Leahy and as he was reading the preamble to the constitution which he thought was the right way to take possession the
two girls right in front began biting each other and as Leahy
finished the constitution his second in command Spear hit him on
the shoulder and pointing to the girls said you're it. Well anyway
it is all real to us here in a little town in France and everybody
fighting. And then there was the young boy Ned Hanford that
Alice Toklas knew then and he had volunteered and had become
an orderly to General King who afterward wrote novels about it
and in one he said and I threw my bridle to my orderly Ned
Hanford, well everybody was a hero then and everybody is a hero
now only none of it was sad then and it all is pretty sad now and
just here, just here now. It is sad when at nineteen and twenty
you have to decide for yourself, shall you betake yourself to the
mountains, shall you stay at home and risk it, shall you go to
Germany and hate it and perhaps be bombed working for your
country's enemies and shall you what shall you what can you do,
what will you do, it is hard at eighteen or nineteen to have to
decide all these things for yourself, each one for himself, in a war
it is comparatively easy, you are drafted you go you are with a

crowd and you are all more or less of an age and you are all together and even if it hurts it is not so bad, but now these French boys have to decide each one all alone by himself which has he strength for, has he people to whom he can go, will he get there, can he be fed, and all the rest, and the winter and the mountains and will he find any one, and if he has not gone what will happen, it is hard at nineteen and twenty for each one to decide things like that for himself. Very hard.

We are in the very thick of it now, rumors and rumors but some of them are true, they have suppressed the use of the telephone all through the region, nobody can go anywhere without very special leave and just to-night we have heard that the captain of the gendarmerie and our very good friend and the father of the most charming little girl, who has a charming curl in the middle of her forehead and a very sweet and attractive wife has just been carried off, whether by the mountain boys whether by the Germans nobody seems to know and we are most awfully upset, everybody is trembling lest anybody is taken as hostage and if they are dear me if they are. Whether it is to put down the mountain boys whether it is because a German colonel has been killed whether it is because they are afraid of a landing whether it is because they expect to retreat into this country out of Italy whether it is because they do not know what to do, whether it is because it is coming to an end and an end has to be like the end at the theatre when the piece comes to an end a state of confusion, whatever it is our good and gentle friend has been taken and we are very sad.

In the nineteenth century we all became accustomed to permanence. Permanence was natural and necessary and continuous. Permanence and progress were synonymous, that seems strange but of course it is natural enough. If things are permanent you can believe in progress if things are not permanent progress is not possible and so the nineteenth century believed in progress and permanence, permanence and progress. And now. Well now there is neither the one or the other. England and Germany who strangely enough are more nineteenth century even yet than any other part of the globe do still hope to believe in permanence and progress, progress and permanency, but nobody else does and nobody else is interested in their believing in progress and in permanency, nobody else.

In these days January forty-four, here where we are, we are once more as we were in nineteen forty—we have the terror of the Germans all about us, we have no telephone, we hear stories and do not know whether they are true, we do not know what is happening to our friends in Belley, except for the life of this village of Culoz we seem separated from everything, we have our dog, we have the radio, we have electricity, we have plenty to eat, and we are comfortable but we are completely isolated and rumor follows rumor, and on the road for the first time now in two years we meet automobiles with German officers, motor bicycles with Germans on them going by quickly quickly, and at the station are long trains of railroad trucks marked Italy, and Munich and Breslau, and we none of us know why, why this little corner of France which is so very peaceable should be harassed. In the newspapers they say it is Savoy but actually it is not, in Savoy they can telephone they are peacefully left alone and here one little town and another little town is surrounded and the principal inhabitants are taken away and nobody knows why, nobody can think of any reason for it, what is the reason for it, nobody knows, and those who do it, naturally do not say so that makes it that nobody knows. Why. Nobody knows. The young men are getting restless, they stand around and laugh and their fathers and their mothers are very nervous, but the young men just stand around and watch them go by, and they laugh, they laugh at them, and it does seem as if it were not they that are being sought, but others and older and why. Nobody does know why. Nobody can go in and out of Belley, such an innocent town, and for so long there has been a German garrison there, learning its military lessons, and nobody interfered with them and they did not interfere with any one and now they came and surrounded the town and took fifty men away and nobody knows why, nobody knows.

As I say everybody feels as if it was like the beginning of the invasion in forty, but then it was a beginning a long beginning and a very long middle and now everybody feels that it is an ending and the French have always felt that a wounded beast is always worst when it is cornered, and the winter has been pleasant and long and now it is snowing and dreary and everybody feels it so except the young boys who are up and down on their bicycles on their feet all day long and they stand and laugh as the others go past. Everybody else feels like crying but not they, and so it is to-day.

And so it is to-day. Yesterday I went to see the mayor and the mayoress of our little town and we talked about everything. Naturally she is very nervous. These days, nobody knows why the Germans surround a town take the mayor prisoner and sometimes they let him go and sometimes they do not. So naturally the mayor's wife is nervous, the mayor too a little but he does not say so. The mayor's wife does. And they have been doing all this to the towns around here and about and will they do so here.

Here they are. Our neighbor a nice old maid who lives alone in a little house and has plenty of land and has plenty of everything and is sometimes double faced and can be called a viper by our cook but mostly is very kind and nice. She came in to say that they had come. They knocked at her door, she was not dressed yet and she called out what is it and they said it was the German army so in fear and trembling she opened the door and they said are there any men here and she said no, and they said honestly and she said yes honestly there are no men here, and they said pointing to our house are there any men there, and she said no two ladies and two servants all women, and they said honestly and she said yes honestly there are only four women there and then they went away. Later in the day naturally we did not go out but later in the day I saw her going out to look every time any soldier went up or down the steep mountain road, and I said what's the news, and she said I am so scared, well why said Alice Toklas if you are so scared do you go out to look. I go out to look she said because I am so scared.

Then later the boy that carries our wood up-stairs three times a week came in. He was very sad, his father who is an Italian has been taken and is being sent to Germany, but said I he is more than forty-five, yes I know said he sadly but although he has always lived in France he is an Italian and they have taken him. They are still here the Germans and Basket our dog has gone out for the evening it worries us but we expect he will come back again. Although you never can tell with soldiers, they like dogs and he is a very pretty one. And nobody knows why they are here nor how long they will stay, and no one can come in to the town and no one can go out not even the priest, and nobody knows why, all this country is so peaceful. Of course there are a great many young men who have not gone to Germany who have been called but that is all yes dear me that is all. To be sure those who go up into the mountain and do behave a good deal like Robin Hood, they carry off a doctor and his wife and all their possessions, so that the doctor can take care of them and his wife take care of him, and his possessions so that nobody takes them away to punish him. They are careful to choose a doctor who has no children. Everybody says and that too does sound so like the middle ages, we are between two armed forces, the mountain boys shoot if you do not do what they say, and the Germans shoot if you do not do what they say, and what can you do, each side blames us if we do what the other side tells us to do but what can we do. And indeed what can they do. Anyway it goes on and it goes on just like that. And how many have been caught, here and in Belley, oh dear we do not know, everybody says something but nobody knows.

It is funny why do the Germans wear camouflaged rain-coats but not camouflaged uniforms now why do they. The first I saw was the other day, they went by on bicycles, and they reminded me of the chorus of the Tivoli Opera House in San Francisco, it used to cost twenty-five cents and the men in mediaeval costume looked so like these camouflaged coats, with sort of keys and crosses on them in contrasted colors. Oh dear. It would all be so funny if it were not so terrifying and so sad, this in January forty-four.

Ma foi it's long is what they say. Everybody in the country in France says ma foi, a nice mediaeval expression, you say anything to them and they say ma foi, that can mean yes or oh hell, or no, or just nothing. At present any of them can say, it's long, and the answer is ma foi, which also means to be sure. In this particular part of the world they have another thing, they say taisez-vous, or shut up, or shut it, and they say it as they are talking, they are talking along about something and they say, oh shut it, and it is not to themselves, nor to you, it is of the facts of which they are speaking, sometimes they say taisez-vous, taisez-vous, and the sentence goes on, it is rather delightful, I do not quite know why, they may say and the war is long and the Germans might be coming this way again oh shut up oh shut up and do you think it is possible that they will. This is a kind of a sentence it makes, and it is enjoyable. Ma foi.

And now once more the telephone is working and we can see people and the roads are open and the Germans are gone from the village and everybody is breathing a little more freely not entirely so but a little so, although some few unpleasant things did happen, oh dear me. Everybody looks at their neighbors and says oh dear me or ma foi, and anyway everybody is relieved. Nobody knows what it is all about excepting that it is to find out who is supplying the mountain boys with food. So many strange things the curfew at seven o'clock instead of ten o'clock, two young fellows who had sling shots and had themselves taken away, one young fellow who tried to run away was shot, and one old man who was drunk and out at ten o'clock was killed, and as it was very bad weather, snow and sleet and wind the rest of them stayed at home, it is so difficult to make a French population realise that it is dangerous not to do as they are told, they like to do what they like, and they do. As one Frenchman said to me in France a civilian is always more important than a policeman unless he happens to be a criminal, but just any civilian is always more

important than just any policeman. This is ingrained in every
Frenchman and so it is almost impossible to make them do what
they are told. Such strange things happen, a funny little man who
was known as being a collaborator and had even gotten a coffin,
the kind they send to them, had all his things taken by the Germans, it seems that his father in days long gone was a receiver of
stolen goods, naturally enough as this town has always been an
important railroad junction a small town but an important railroad junction, and his son, well perhaps he did not receive stolen
goods, but he had stores of forbidden provisions here there and
anywhere, and among them some very ancient fire-arms from the
revolution, or Napoleon collected by his father and somebody
mentioned them and the Germans went to look for them and they
found them and so naturally they took away all the soap and iron
and wine and spirits that were there too naturally enough, and he
the little man was away and they have given him three days to
give himself up, but where is he and does he know, and how can
he or anybody else know why they went to him. There are also an
elderly man and his sister, here, and it has just been told us that
their father who had been a railroad worker, once stole precious
jewels and tried to sell them in Geneva and was given five years
prison and the son and daughter now quite old were never
married and they live together, and the son for all that was
employed by the railroad, he still is as a night guard, and she after
a long life of domestic service has stomach ulcers, and anyway
these stories did distract our minds from anxiety and the distresses
of one of our neighbors whose son was finally killed in trying to
run away. To-day now that it is all over everybody went to the
funerals of every one who had been killed, and now to-day it was
Sunday and the sun shone and the snow was on the ground and
the whole population were out skiing and sledding and the mayor
was tired and so was his wife, and with reason, it is no fun being a
mayor these days. The mayor finally persuaded the Germans that
there were no mountain boys in the mountain back of us because
as he explained there is no water there. In the days when he used

to go hunting we always had to carry a flask of water to refresh the dogs with because the dog could not find any water there so how could men stay there. No it is not possible, and finally the Germans were convinced and they left. They left. And the telephone goes again, and the people can move around the streets again, and I can let the dog out again the dog Basket and we can go walking again and the snow is beginning to melt, and to-day is Monday in February nineteen forty-four.

Tired of winter tired of war but anyway they do hope and pray that it will end some day.

I was talking to Madame Gallais, she keeps a little shop, she was born in this country, but spent most of her life in Paris, and she is Parisian and it is a pleasure. Landscape is all very well but you do long to see a street any street. Once in Belley I went in to see Madame Chaboux and she was not home and I was tired and I lay down on her couch, and she lives in a street, and opposite was a wall just a wall with windows, it was a relief from trees and fields, I remember Janet Sayne, she was a friend before the 1914 war, and she always used to say that she could never understand why trees which look so pretty in a city look so ugly in the country, and in a way she was right, in a way she certainly was. Well Madame Gallais, manages to get anything you want in a small way, they all come and they all go the people of the country and they bring one thing and they are given another thing and we are given something and we give something and everybody has a fair amount of something and life goes on. We do suffer from a lack of dental floss, seems a funny thing to suffer from but we do and we decided whenever the Americans coming up from Italy pass in front of the door we will go out and stop the first dental ambulance and ask them for some dental floss, and Alice Toklas says that they will not have any and besides will they come and I say yes they will have some and they might come. All of which is pleasant enough this cold February day.

Well as I was saying I was talking to Monsieur Gallais, he had fought the last war the 1914 war, of course everybody of that age

in France did, and we were telling each other stories as veterans do
about how sweet everybody had been then, ah yes he said the
French in those days were a united people, and he told about how
every one shared everything with their comrades, and one poor
man, who had very few packages and was always joking said when
he went on leave that they would be surprised by what he would
bring them back, and the others paid no attention but sure enough
when he came back he brought with him an enormous turkey that
his wife had been fattening up for them and they all ate it and
said Monsieur Gallais everybody was like that then, the French
were a united people. And his wife said but after all the young
ones are just as much comrades, look at the mountain boys look
at the forced labor ones in Germany, they help each other, yes
said Monsieur Gallais but think of those at home who denounce
them. Well after all, of course there is disunion, there are the
scared middle classes afraid of communism, there are the military
people angry that the army has been taken away from them there
are the religious old maids and widows who are afraid that in the
future there will be no religion but as Madame Gallais says the
young generation are just as united as the poilus in '14-'18 and she
is right they are. Just to-day I met a woman who was on the train
to Lyon the other day and there were two hospital coaches on the
train with wounded men from the police who were supposed to
have been in upper Savoy fighting the mountain boys. They said,
and that we had already known because only about half came back
through here that had gone there, they said that a good half of the
special police had joined the mountain boys and the rest of them
the mountain boys had very carefully wounded in the legs, they
wanted to put them out of business given an excuse to go on
drawing their pay and yet not have a wound that might later stop
them from earning a living, only one was wounded in the arm and
that was a mistake, they were very careful to wound them in the
leg. Of course they were harder on the militia, they hate them, and
they kill any of them, well no not exactly and not any of them were
hurt, no not exactly, it's all right, they said and laughed. So after

all the French are a united people, of course there are the Germans, and of course that is completely another matter.

I said the Germans were here and all along here, and here in Culoz, two young ones were killed who tried to run away and one man an elderly man who drank and who was shot by the Germans because he was out on the road after the curfew hour, and what hurt everybody was that he had been left there by the Germans all night, and everybody went to his funeral, but what excited everybody the most was that a woman was found not far from here on an island in the Rhone, and when she was taken out they found that she had a bullet in her head. They then found out that she was a schoolteacher from the town of Seysell where there was the most shooting by the Germans because there the mountain boys were always being fed, and this woman was a schoolteacher there, and it seems that when the Germans came she was badly frightened and wanted to go away and the head teacher said no, he said a teacher was like a soldier a doctor a nurse or a mayor, his or her business was to remain at her post whatever happened but she said she must go to her people and she tried to take the train and they would not give her a ticket at the station and she got more frightened and she put on the trousers of her skiing costume and she walked away to go to another town to take the train and the next thing that happened was that she was dead on an island in the Rhone where drowned people are always found with a bullet in her head.

Just at present we are all quiet in very wintery weather here toward the end of February, and if or where or when or if the Americans will be coming soon, well will they.

Of course these days when there is no way of getting new books I have to read the old ones and fortunately I have great quantities of detective stories and adventure stories and each one of them now has a different meaning, it is one of the real most important things about war, the making geography come alive, and lots of places in the story books are real now which is a pleasure. Of course getting frightened again and again is not always a pleasure, is not at all a

pleasure, when I heard last evening that the primate of Poland
had been taken away from the abbey of Hautcombe it was frightening, one is always a little frightened just a little and this evening
the maid said that there were some people in the kitchen would
Alice Toklas come down to see them, who are they, we asked, and
she answered passing strangers, well actually they were American
citizens a brother and a sister who had been here for some time, in
the village, American born of French parents who had come back
to Marseilles and the boy had already been rescued by the Swiss
consul and now once again they were taking him, so we told the
sister, to take the train to-morrow to Lyon and to see the Swiss
consul, which she will do, and as I say everything is a little frightening, and then there are stories well they are a little frightening,
enough said, they are a little frightening, especially if the dog stays
with them, well it is a little frightening. The Swiss are very comforting, they really are, they have just given us a passport of pro-
tection, and the mayor's wife is very comforting, she is Swiss, and
she and I sit and talk together, and she tells me, that she does not
care for the higher clergy she thinks they think more of palaces
than of humanity and that the lower clergy think more of eating
and drinking than anything, to be sure she said the poor dears are
very poor as they have to give so much to the bishops, well anyway
that is the way she feels about it and she is a little frightened too
but she is very comforting. Last night the local baker was bringing
us some beans and some flour, and he came late and banged at the
door of the kitchen which was closed and the cook came up frightened and said it is Germans, no I said I guess it is Bonaz which is
the name of the baker and to be sure I was brave because I knew he
had intended coming, so the two servants went down and opened
the door, and Jeanne the maid said that they were neither very
brave their legs shook inside their skirts, and the baker laughed,
he likes a joke and he knew that he had scared them. To-day the
end of February things look as if things might be going faster, and
the birds have come, they all say here they have never seen so many
spring birds, including quail, and they suppose that the fighting

has scared the birds out of Italy and out of Germany and that is the reason there are so many of them.

Rabbits have no habits that is the reason that we prefer hens. Besides hens lay eggs, which is a pleasant habit.

To-day a man said to me the hunting dogs are all going crazy because they cannot hunt, because we cannot hunt, the time will come I said and he said yes this autumn.

Spring is here, it is the first of March nineteen forty-four and spring is here, well not quite here but pretty well here, and everybody feels a little more hopeful, they are all wishing that it would be over without France being invaded, and I guess we all feel like that, it is all right to be liberated but it would be so nice if it could be done without bombs and fighting on the soil of France. Madame Gallais says we are all selfish we cannot help feeling that way about it, but anyway it is not for us to decide so why worry, all you want to do is to buy as much as you can so when it does come every one will have enough to eat in their cupboard, so that even the poor dog can have a bone. Everybody is coming back from Paris, that is to say everybody has been there and everybody has come back and they all say life has gotten pretty normal there and they all also say that you can have all the vegetables you want, there are lots to buy and not dear. Well in the country you can have meat and fish and eggs and butter but no vegetables, vegetables do not come until June, so in every way the French people defend themselves that is they lead their normal life. I remember once Virgil Thomson saying that the only thing the French respect is longevity, the power to go on, indeed it is the only criticism French people ever make, if they think you have talent they say continue like the nice story of the nigger, in all the schools that is all any master ever says is continue, keep on, and once in a military school, the master came along and one of the students was a Negro and the teacher said in surprise, why you are a Negro, yes said the Negro, well then said the teacher, continue, in other words go on being it. And so the French continue their normal life. The Topses the other day told us that the German authorities were complaining of the aspect of Paris, nobody would know that there was a war, and it discouraged the German soldiers who were there on leave. The prefect of the Seine said but what can I do, French people will lead their normal lives whatever happens, and they do lead them, what can I do, whatever you do they will lead their normal lives it is their way, and that is why the French can always rise from the ashes, they rather like it to be like that, it makes the leading their normal lives just that much more exciting.

It is very funny the way everybody and anybody can feel about anything. Take the mountain boys, did I meet two of them when I came back from my walk up a part of the mountain this afternoon, they both looked rather tired and then we said how do you do in passing, everybody carries heavy sacks on their backs these days, nothing means anything, and some say, that they are back in the region and some say no, and some say the Germans are back in the region and some say no, and anyway it is evening and nearly midnight and I will be listening to the last news just before going to bed, again. It is funny the different nations begin their broadcasting I wish I knew more languages so that I could know how each one of them does it. The English always begin with here is London, or the B. B. C. home service, or the over seas service, always part of a pleasant home life, of supreme importance to any Englishman or any Englishwoman. The Americans say with poetry and fire, this is the voice of America, and then with modesty and good neighborliness, one of the United Nations, it is the voice of America speaking to you across the Atlantic. Then the Frenchman, say Frenchmen speaking to Frenchmen, they always begin like that, and the Belgians are simple and direct, they just announce, radio Belge, and the national anthem, and the Frenchman also say, Honor and Country, and the Swiss so politely say, the studio of Geneva, at the instant of the broadcasting station of Berne will give you the latest news, and Italy says live Mussolini live Italy, and they make a bird noise and then they start, and Germany starts like this, Germany calling, Germany calling, in the last war, I said that the camouflage was the distinctive characteristic of each country, each nation stamped itself upon its camouflage, but in this war it is the heading of the broadcast that makes national life so complete and determined. It is that a nation is even stronger than the personality of any one, it certainly is so nations must go on, they certainly must.

Spring seems to find it impossible to come, we are all getting sad, this is the middle of March, neither spring nor the end of the war can come, but boulders cropping up in meadows is always romantic and makes it look like a park, even if it is on the side of a mountain, and the fact that it is romantic is consoling, I do not know quite why it is consoling but it is consoling, boulders great big ones with ivy on them or tiny trees are always consoling when they are scattered about in a meadow, they are. The wind blows and the wind is icy cold and the spring does not come, they say that the seasons cannot come as they should, because cannon changes the clouds about, first they change the birds about and then the clouds, there is no doubt that they the bombardments do change things about. The days follow one after the other and the time passes so very quickly, it is hardly possible to get accustomed to one day before it is over and then it is the next day and then it is Friday and we listen to the resumé of the week by the Swiss commentator and then the week is over, just like that. Then Chinamen did invent gun powder, there seems to be no doubt about that, and the French and the Americans automobiles and flying, and the Italians wireless and there does not seem to be any doubt about that, why not, there does not seem to be any doubt about that. Just now nobody thinks about what century it is, they just wonder when it will be over, they just wonder. There is no doubt about that.

I was just listening to an account by one of the American generals of the simple things for which Americans are fighting and the first thing they mention is that you can be in your home and nobody can force their way in and authoritatively frighten you and do whatever they will, I think it is very extraordinary that an American general can so simply understand that that is the horrible thing about an occupied country, the uneasiness in the eyes of all young men and in the eyes of their fathers mothers sisters and brothers, and wives, that uneasiness because at any moment they can be taken away at any moment, their papers can be all in order and yet, and then papers can not be in order and also, and just now our neighbors were telling us of a young man we had known him very well in Belley and later here, and he would go out to the nearest town to buy bread, and his mother said no do not, and he said but mother my papers are in order and he went and he did not come back, he was sent, his mother does not know where and his papers were in order and yet, and it is extraordinary that the American general should understand that that is what any American could fight for, that nowhere in the world should those who have not committed any crime should not live peacefully in their home, go peacefully about their business and not be afraid, not have uneasiness in their eyes, not. I do think it very extraordinary that the American general should have so simply understood that. It is now the middle of March and spring has come and with it a little courage, they do think now that it is not going on the war is not going to go on for years and years yet, they do begin to think that, they are not hopeful yet, it is hard to be hopeful, after five years very hard, they are not hopeful yet, but they do lead their lives, and they do think that now perhaps it will be over some time. It is Sunday to-day and our maid Jeanne who is not a hopeful person came in just now and said they say in Culoz that the Germans are retreating, where we said, why in Russia, she said, so they say, they say it in Culoz, but of course we said, ah yes she said, they do say it to-day in Culoz. Well that does mean they do not any longer expect it to go on forever, and as I went walking to-day, they all began to talk crops and potatoes, and planting, to be sure when the French people can begin to dig up the soil and plant vegetables they always feel more cheerful, and to-day is the day to do that, so even if Culoz had not decided that the Germans were retreating in Russia, still they would begin to feel more cheerful they just naturally would now that they can dig and plant, they must do that.

The middle of March and it is as if it were almost most likely to end some time, the winter and the war, the war and the winter.

We like to take the train to Chambery, we always see something or somebody, everybody travels, the French people do like to go up and down on trains, and to stand and wait in stations, and there is so much of that. Day before yesterday we were waiting at the station at Culoz and among them all was well he certainly was an American, only an American could wear his hat like that, only an American could balance his body like that, and he had a pinched nose like a certain kind of an American boy has and he was about twenty-five and he had a pack on his back and he did not notice anybody and he stood on the edge of the platform very near where the train was to come along, and I said to Alice Toklas do not notice him, we naturally of course did not want that anybody should notice that we noticed him, but if any of the French people did notice that he was not a Frenchman, well nobody noticed him and we supposed he was going somewhere probably into the Haute Savoy, perhaps yes, and we carefully did not notice where he went but he undoubtedly he certainly was an American and it was the tenth of March nineteen forty-four here in the station at Culoz.

It made us feel funny, and yet it was so natural it certainly was. It reminded us of nineteen eighteen when we used to see the American soldiers in the south of France a. w. o. ling absent without leave and they would say to us are there any military police around here, and we used to tell them well not just here but they had better look out in the next town, but that was a joke compared with this, we do hope he got safely to where he was going.

You meet so many people from so far away any day and you meet no one, but then railroad stations and trains are made to do this thing and they do it.

Spring snow is prettier than winter snow. This the first real day of spring and I can say so. Spring snow is prettier than winter snow. Yes and no. This spring it certainly is, there was no winter snow and there is spring snow and everybody well not everybody but quite a few are beginning to be hopeful again, that spring snow is prettier than winter snow.

Some one in the village just told me that the German station master, they have two at the station here, which is for a small town an important one because you change there for Italy and Switzerland and Savoy and the south, and so it is important and as many very many German troop trains go through they have a German station master. To-day the middle of March nineteen forty-four he said to the French trainmen, in three months Germany is going to go smash caput, and then instead of going back to Germany I am going to stay here to celebrate with the French, back there in Germany they have nothing to celebrate and they do not know how to celebrate but you French do, so I am going to stay here and celebrate with you, naturally nobody said anything but it was comforting not that he was going to stay to celebrate but that in three months time he thought the French would be celebrating. When I tell the story everybody says a little sighfully let us hope so. Hope deferred, we have felt sure so often but at last the Russian steam roller that was to roll in the last war and did not looks like being one really being one. I have to explain over and over again that the Americans even if they have not taken Rome have the airplane bases where they can go a bombing and without that bombing the Russians would not be able to roll, I get impatient and I say you French you have such old fashioned ideas of war, you just think about land fighting and taking places but we Americans we believe in destroying the production of the enemy. Yes they say, yes that is true, but, well they do wish that we would take some and go faster, but I tell what I always told them that Americans like a long preparation and then when they are really ready then something does happen, look at Tunis I say you complained just like that then, yes they say convinced but not believing and I understand I do understand because five years is a long time for their prisoners and themselves, and said one of them and if the allies win will our prisoners remain in Germany as hostages, hostages to whom I asked indignantly, I do not know she answered, I just wondered would they stay on as hostages, no America will insist that they be immediately released, oh she said if America will do that. It is always hard to understand anything but at the end of five long years understanding gets more and more difficult there is no doubt about that, yes and no, spring snow is prettier than winter snow, certainly this year we all do say so.

And in between there is our goat. We have lots of food now, really more than we can eat, lots of everything butter cheese eggs meat sugar everything but milk, and so we had and still have a goat, but a goat has to have kids so as to go on giving milk, so ours went to the male and now in a week she is to have kids, and so of course we ask everybody what to do, they say, she should have an infusion, the kind the French take whenever they feel badly, of linden tree, or mint or verveine, or something, and somebody says either she or the kids should have warm wine, and she should have bread with oil and a certain herb on it, I think both mother and child and it was all a confusion, and some said she could manage to have the kid all by herself, and somebody else said we should be there but how can we if we do not know when it is going to happen and the stable is far away from the house, and some say we can have milk as soon as the kid comes and some say not, anyway, I took her out for a walk this afternoon and she seemed a little heavy but cheerful so we are hoping for the best. In the meanwhile day before yesterday I saw the first yellow butterfly and to-day I saw the first white butterfly and to-morrow so they tell me is the day the birds begin to find their mate the day of Saint Joseph, and they have two days to decide about husbands and wives and then no nonsense they go on to building their nests, to be sure it was a nice sunny day so perhaps they all did get it done but if not, well if not nobody tells me anything about if not, there is no if not, in country life in France, there just is not any if not.

And so everybody is beginning to feel a little cheerful again except that young men and young girls are newly being rounded up to go to work in munition factories and where, well nobody is certain about that, they say in France but is it to be in France, and everybody has to decide something and they say, oh they say so many things, they can be worried about so many things, there is no logic to this war in nothing that is a war, well if and when the war is won will the prisoners be kept where they are as hostages, hostages to what I ask impatiently, so they say, they answer me, so they say. That is what makes it so extraordinary, everybody listens to the radio, they listen all day long because almost everybody has one and if not there is their neighbor's and they listen to the voice from any country and yet what they really believe is not what they hear but the rumors in the town, by word of mouth is always the most convincing, they do not believe the newspapers nor the radio but they do believe what they tell each other and that is natural enough, all official news is so deceiving, so why not believe rumors, that is reasonable enough, and so they do, they believe all the rumors, and even when they know they are not true they believe them, at any rate they have a chance of being true rumors have but official news has no chance of being true none at all, of course not.

We spend our Friday afternoons with friends reading Shakespeare, we have read Julius Caesar, and Macbeth and now Richard the Third and what is so terrifying is that it is all just like what is happening now, Macbeth seeing ghosts well dont they, is not Mussolini seeing the ghost of his son-in-law, of course he is you can see him seeing the ghost of his son-in-law, his last speech showed that he did, and any of them, take the kings in Shakespeare there is no reason why they all kill each other all the time, it is not like orderly wars when you meet and fight, but it is all just violence and there is no object to be attained, no glory to be won, just like Henry the Sixth and Richard the Third and Macbeth just like that, very terrible very very terrible and just like that.

A long war like this makes you realise the society you really prefer, the home, goats chickens and dogs and casual acquaintances. I find myself not caring at all for gardens flowers or vegetables cats cows and rabbits, one gets tired of trees vines and hills, but houses, goats chickens dogs and casual acquaintances never pall.

The children of course play funny games, yesterday I saw a little girl of seven putting two little ones of two and three under a piece of tin and saying now that you are safe I will say good-bye.

What are you playing I asked, we are playing abris, shelters she said and that was that.

I was talking to Claude Malherbe she had just come from a widow whose husband had died suddenly, yes she said they do now, they were very young men in the last war, they were in this war, but what is so terrible for them is that France was beaten, it eats them she said, I sometimes say to my husband but after all France was beaten, and he says do not say that, it is not true I cannot hear it, but said Claude it is true but of course women cannot suffer from it the way the men do, men after all are soldiers, and women are not, and love France as much as we do and we love France as much as the men do, but after all we are not soldiers and so we cannot feel a defeat the way they do, and besides in a defeat after a defeat women have more to do than men have they have more to occupy them that is natural enough in a defeat, and so they have less time to suffer, yes said Claude I do understand that.

Sometimes it none of it is very real, but what is real, what you used to do or what you do now, well I used not to sit in a field and watch the goat eat, but I do now, which is real what you do now or what you used to do.

It is funny that men who are supposed to be scientific cannot get themselves to realise the basic principle of physics, that action and reaction are equal and opposite, that when you persecute people you always rouse them to be strong and stronger, as the French say, sugar attracts bees more quickly than vinegar, or the fable of the wind and the sun to make a man take off his overcoat, it is funny it has been going on so long, persecution to make men weak and it makes them strong, and if you do not persecute them then they do get soft, well naturally if action and reaction are equal and opposite what else can they do, when people have too much peace they want war and when they have too much war they want peace, what else can they do, just now nobody seems to really know what they do want, peace seems to them almost as dangerous as war, it was the last time, and war is not dangerous any more it is endless and miserable, miserable and endless, and peace will peace be endless and miserable too or just miserable and not endless, and still yes still they do want peace, at least they want it different from what it is now. Some one was telling me, we were talking about eating, one does naturally frequently talk about eating or not eating, and we were saying how difficult it was to know whether people in any given place were eating or not eating, some who come from there, say there is plenty and some say there is nothing and anyway how can you tell. Yes they said eagerly, there is a woman of ours a neighbor who kept saying there is no trouble in getting anything one wants, why she said I can even get candied fruits, oh dear, they said and then gradually they found out that the woman had very little to eat, and it was not to make others believe that she talked that way but just to make herself believe it, and she did believe it. Generally speaking here in France more people eat than not, but then the French are pretty good at eating and eat they will, if one way of getting food fails they try another, and one way and another they do achieve food that is their way, they must eat and in order to eat, they must find food, so they find it, if at first they do not succeed try try again but incidentally they do succeed somewhat even the first time, but certainly they do succeed ultimately to get a good deal of it, they certainly do, it is their way, as they called it in the last war, the system D, debrouillez-vous, that is look around and find the way.

Our goat died in not giving birth to her little one. Domestic animals so often die in childbirth, which is very discouraging, it does happen again and again, and now it did happen to our goat, our neighbor sat up all night with it and he and another neighbor worked three hours over it trying to get the dead little thing out of it but they did not succeed, this is what can happen even now, when each one of them is working in a factory and do special duty in guarding the railway, the French are like that, you must always do what you can to save the life of a domestic animal whether it does or does not belong to you, they are like that.

It gets more and more perplexing about what they are feeling more and more perplexing. Was there could there be anything more dangerous than a war that is finishing, nothing, that is to say a war like this last one, not a war like '14-'18 which was still a nineteenth century war but this thirty-nine to something war which is undoubtedly a twentieth century war undoubtedly.

I like what they say here in this country, in the spring the trees weep, they shed tears, they do not say that the sap runs they say the trees weep and actually they do, they exude drops and the newly cut vines they weep too, they let fall a drop and another drop, that is what they do, I keep telling the French people that they do not understand twentieth century war-fare, I get angry I say after all if the Anglo-Americans had not blown up as they did everything in Germany and in the countries working for Germany the Russians would be still where they were in the elbow of the Dnieper but all you French people can think about is taking a little more or a little less territory, no destroy the provisions of the enemy and they must die of attrition, cant you understand, they say yes but really not, what they want is nice eighteenth century fighting that is what they really liked, not even nineteenth century fighting the French liked it best in the eighteenth century. Sometimes I wonder was Kansas before the civil war like it is in France to-day and like during the revolutionary like it was described by Fenimore Cooper in The Spy, everybody denouncing friends and enemies, everybody being hidden in the mountains, patriots false patriots, bandits making believe being real or false patriots, the trains being blown up and now the French say it is being done by the Germans to make the French angry with each other and to-day at the station there was a whole train full of gendarmes, the national police and they had brand new automobiles and all sorts of armament and what were they going to do, and trains going one way or the other nobody ever knows what they are doing where they are going and do they know, very likely nobody can say so. All the French people are on the trains all the time, French people do like trains they are always going even for no greatly important reason, just to keep going, they like to move around, they like the social life of the trains and the stations, they like the regularity the irregularity and the coming and going, it is more sociable and more regular than an automobile, very few regret automobiles, very few indeed, they really do not worry about that.

No thank you, and then so sadly because the little girl was tuberculous and they loved her so and the doctor said he could do nothing further for her and they bought a place in the cemetery for her and she began to get better and began to move around and they were so happy that they bought her a radio apparatus to amuse her, she had had a little one and now they bought her a bigger one. These things can happen when everybody is busy with perhaps the end of this war. They can happen because they do.

To-day when I was out walking there were five German soldiers repairing an automobile, but nobody paid any attention everybody came and went and nothing happened, this can happen when this war is beginning to look like ending, it can happen because it does. Spring has come, April is here, the birds are singing and a hawk came down in the grass in front of the house to find not a chicken but a bone that a dog had brought there. The hawk seemed a little disappointed but perhaps he was not, April nineteen hundred and forty-four, that is Easter week.

Publicity, that is what we hear them say publicity, and is not that the real meaning of persecution, publicity, it is not nearly as complicated as it seems. There always has been a great passion for publicity in the world the very greatest passion for publicity, and those who succeed best, who have the best instincts for publicity, do have a great tendency to be persecuted that is natural enough, and here I think is the real basis of the persecution of the chosen people and just now more than ever because as publicity is more and more a conscious process those who have the greatest instinct for publicity are naturally those of whom the others who would want to be masters of publicity are jealous, at least I do think so, and perhaps yes.

It is very interesting but the end of the nineteenth century and the twentieth century realised the beauty of publicity for its own sake as an end in itself, this is very interesting.

It is now the eleventh of April the Tuesday after Easter-Monday and everybody had hopes that something would happen and in a way it has, bombardments have been bombing and the Russians have been moving and everybody is expecting everything to be happening and we all talk while we are out walking to find eggs and spinach and cake and everything, one does find everything and I met one of my neighbors and he had a little boy on his bicycle and I said what are you doing with him, I am taking him up into the mountains to be a shepherd, how old is he I said he is nine, and he has two brothers and they are refugees and up there he will be well fed, and said I does he not mind leaving his family even where they are, and he said he is reconciled to it, he was a round faced blonde little Alsatian with a little suit case with him and he was going nine miles up the mountain. To-day it was Easter-Monday that is it was yesterday and we had lots of visitors and they asked about Americans, since Eisenhower is to govern France for a while naturally they want to know all about them, and I was telling about the doughboys in the last war, and one of our visitors said yes I remember in the last war, I was nine years old and my father was a doctor and we lived opposite his hospital in Vichy and there were Americans there and one of them used to take me out fishing, he used to call for me every other day and we used to go fishing, he could not speak a word of French and I could not speak a word of American, so we never said a word to each other but every other day for two months he used to call for me to take me fishing, he had a funny way of fishing, he always had a little bottle of cream in his pocket and when we got to the fishing place he would take out a piece of absorbent cotton and he would twist it around the hook and then he would pour a little cream from his bottle on to it and then he would drop it in the water and our visitor added it would catch fish and after two months he went away and we had never said a word to each other because I did not know any American and he did not know a word of French. This same visitor had a little daughter with him a little seven year old red-headed girl and when she was given cake the plate had painted on it some fruits, oh said the little girl, that is a banana, I remember bananas, but my younger brothers and sister do not, they have never seen them but I remember having had a banana, I remember it very well.

And so now Easter week being over pretty soon something is going to happen, pretty nearly everybody here has now forgotten about the Germans everybody forgets very quickly but nobody forgets quite so quickly as the French, and although the Germans are still here they have pretty nearly forgotten them and they only think about Americans, yes says our cook, I will cook for them for the Americans, is not that so Madame says she to me and I say yes and I do hope so I certainly do hope so, yes says she we will strew flags everywhere to meet them even on the ground and I will cook a dinner for them, and we all do hope so most certainly most sincerely hope so.

Every day it comes a little nearer, and we do all most certainly and very sincerely hope so, we do all of us most definitely do hope so.

I remember being always so interested in the emigrés after the French revolution going to England, and in spite of everything immensely enjoying the complete change in their lives, anything is better than nothing more than more of the same only nobody knows it, and that is what makes pioneering but then those are the adventurous people who would be doing something anyway, but a war that puts an end to a century that makes one century change to another century that kind of a war always makes a considerable part of the population get moving and in a way they enjoy it, the Russians did after the Russian revolution, but now this is on a much larger scale, everybody is moving around, they are on the roads they are everywhere and nothing is as it was, in America and England and the few neutral nations but everybody else is moving around moving around. And now Hungary and Roumania are joining in and it goes on more and more, that is what makes the end of a century, nothing is as it used to be, nothing at all, and that does make an end of a century. I was walking this afternoon up to Ceyzerieu, it is quite a walk fourteen kilometers up and back and

I get a little tired particularly as I have a little rheumatism in one knee, one is bound to have rheumatism somewhere in a world cataclysm, but anyway, we got some very good cake there and cake is a comfort, cake certainly is a comfort. I usually talk to somebody on the way, they even sometimes get off their bicycles to walk along a way with me and she did, she was an oldish woman and we compared family histories she was married and had no children, but she had a great-nephew staying with her and she wanted to know all about me and she told me all about herself and then she said her niece from Bourg had just been to see her, she was the mother of the great-nephew whom she had kept with her and she had a young baby and she brought the baby with her and she told her that a woman in the Maternity at Bourg had just been brought to bed that is she just been delivered of six little puppy dogs, not possibly I said, but yes she said, not often but quite often, you see she said, in times like these women do console themselves with dogs and this does happen, of course the dogs dont survive they are kept in museums, but it does happen, not really I said, oh yes, she said, in Bourg they once had it happen to a nun, and when the doctor went to see her the dog would not let him come near her. Did it really happen oh yes, she said it does happen and it did happen.

Well so life goes on, we had just been reading Shakespeare Richard the Third, and the things they say there do sound just like that, so why not, anything is so if the country makes it so, and a century makes it so when it is so, just like that.

They have just been telling us over and over again that they are going to bombard all the railway stations and we are quite near a fairly important one, are we to be frightened or not we have not quite made up our minds, this afternoon there was an alert but nobody paid any particular attention but that was easy enough because nothing happened but anyway conversations went on.

Our cook was just telling us that the way to cure dysentery is by taking the white of an egg and beating it up in a cup of water and it stops diarrhea immediately, her sister and it is true that her sister did have a bad colic and she got over it at once and Clothilde

said it was done like that. She had it from an old book of medi-
cine written by Raspail, after whom the boulevard in Paris is
named and I said but I would like to see that book, ah that she said
is not possible, because it was packed away in a case and there are
cases and they are old in a little lodging that I have always kept in
my native town and all this putting away happened in 1918 and
that is the story of my life, she seemed to want to tell some more
but her sister Olympe would certainly have been angry just why we
do not know but we know she would so we did not encourage
Clothilde to go on with the story. To-day the baker who has just
had his shop closed for three months because his eldest daughter
has been selling bread tickets instead of giving them to the miller,
well to divert his mind he went off to find morilles the best of the
spring mushrooms and he only came back with six and we said
what happened to the rest did your wife cook them with a cream
sauce, and he said no he was in the woods looking for them and his
dog was with him, and suddenly his dog began to growl and bark
and act strangely so said Bonaz certainly there is a dead boy from
the mountains there, there were those that died in the snow and
there were those that were killed there, and so he slowly ap-
proached not liking to look but his dog made such a fuss that he
went on and there he found a wild boar that had been strangled
in a trap, and was not dead very long so of course he gave up
looking for mushrooms and got the butcher and together they took
it back to the butchers, that is to say they butchered it there where
they found it and did we want some of the meat. Well we like wild
boar but I dont know, I guess we had better not and we did not,
but we did want some of the mushrooms and would he go off again
and get them and he said he would but as yet he has not.

Everybody is so excited about everything but nobody is very
certain that there is anything to be excited about. We were in
Belley to-day the nineteenth of April nineteen forty-four and there
were a great many German soldiers there and everybody suddenly
seemed to hate them rather more than they ever had hated them
before, everybody suddenly began to hate them a good deal more

than they had ever hated them before. It is so. It is happening quite suddenly just like that.

When you are weak and brutal you are very much more hated than when you are strong and brutal, that is natural enough and that is what is happening now, nobody says of them now all the same they are still strong, and so although I am not sure that they are any more brutal than they were their not being strong any more and just as brutal makes them more hated than they ever were before.

Every day well every day we do not listen much to the accounts of the bombardments, naturally enough when you are among the objects to be bombarded it is not as interesting as when you are not, there was always that amusing story of the earthquake in San Francisco, and a young fellow who was one of the group appointed to dynamite to meet the fire and in that way stop it and who was very ardent and very lively about it and well in the front of the group suddenly realised that it was his own home that they were about to dynamite and it was a shock. Well that is the way we are feeling now toward the end of April when they are beginning to send thousands of bombers down our way. It was all cheerful when they were doing Germany but now not, I must say we were not really enthusiastic about their doing Italy either, but then after all but then.

There are so many stories so many stories and so much confusion. I have just been rereading Cooper's The Spy, and there like later in Kansas anybody could be an enemy and anybody not. Are there really many boys in the mountains, nobody really seems to know, this is what happened to our friend the captain of gendarmes who has always been so nice to us and he says in spite of what happened he does not know if there are a lot of boys in the mountains or not. It was still winter and lots of snow and some mountain boys in a truck were going somewhere and they met some German soldiers in cars and they began to shoot at each other and some on each side were killed and wounded and the people in the village were so frightened they would not come out of the cellars where

they had taken refuge, so hearing about it the captain came in his
car to be a comfort to them and when he had gotten the mayor and
the priest out of the cellars and they had commenced to do their
duty by the living and the dead he went into the post-office to telephone all about it to his superior at Bourg and just then at the
door were four mountain boys with tommy guns, they all have
them and they took the captain away with them right up into the
snow up the mountain, and the first night it was all right but the
second night it was colder and colder and they climbed higher and
higher and then at last they the mountain boys began to stop noticing their prisoner, so he ran away in the snow stumbling along
until finally after a good many hours he finally got to a village
which he knew and so he got home to Belley, and there he had
pneumonia and was in bed and the Germans came to take him
away to Germany but he was too sick and he went to a hospital and
now the Germans seem to have forgotten, anyway he has had a
promotion and for the present he is not very well but not too
worried. He says that the mountain boys do not know what to do
and if they could only keep away but how to live, it is cold in
winter in the mountains very cold. And now it is the end of April
and to-day I heard the first nightingale twittering they first twitter
in the day-time before they sing in the night time. And of course
there are the bombardments, a young fellow whom we just met
said that the factory of his father at Lille was just destroyed and
he said I have just heard that my mother and father are safe, I did
just escape becoming an orphan he said. Everybody is so uncertain
as to what they hope for and what they despair of, so confused that
it is not necessary to know what they think, they think so many
things, so very many things and all of them at once, one thing is
certain sure, and that is that the French have not a single track
mind, that is absolutely certain. How they can have such a variety
of emotions and convictions at the same time and so many of them
completely opposed is perfectly wonderful, but one opposition
they all have, they want the Americans to come and drive out the
Germans and they do not want the Americans to come because

in destroying the Germans they will destroy France. That is all reasonable enough. Some one has just come in and said he saw in one town where the Germans had been executing people and they put up a placard signed by the German commanding officer saying that he regretted all these horrors but they were necessary because the civilian population had gotten in the habit of making mock of the Germans and of course that would not do the French would perfectly understand that so what could the occupying forces do than do what they did do.

The trains are going less and less but still everybody goes on traveling, to be sure they all say it is safer to walk and a good many are walking, the French are good walkers, they have to be because when wars come, they have to walk, yes they said when the Germans did not take Moscow with all their motorized army, yes but the French under Napoleon did get there and on foot, and they always repeated and on foot. It is more certain they say and they are right if you keep walking you are bound to get there but with other things so the French think it is not so sure. They really have more confidence in their legs than in any other form of locomotion, they really have.

Oh dear we do have from time to time to take a train somewhere just to change the scene, that is to say also to go to the dentist and to buy some English books so we do from time to time go to Chambery for the day or Aix-les-Bains for the day and we did yesterday, only when you do you come back having seen something and it is a change but in a way just saddening. When we got to the station there were about thirty young fellows standing each with their suit case and an overcoat and one does not see that so often, they are Italians who have been taken to go to work or French who have been taken to work in Germany, but they usually go in ordinary passenger trains but these were going into freight cars and that usually is only done with soldiers, any soldiers the German soldiers as well as in the old days French soldiers and American soldiers in the last war, and so it did look rather sad, and they told us they were young men and girls that had been rounded up in

Annecy and were being taken well somewhere, did they have any reason for being taken, well probably and where were they being taken nobody ever does know and every day is another day and Pope did say hope springs eternal in the human breast, and it better had certainly just now and it does certainly just now. And then at Aix well there were at least ten thousand German soldiers in the hospital there and everybody was so depressed, they are not real said one woman to us they are phantoms and she was right they were they were just phantoms depressing phantoms who when they marched around singing like automatic phantoms, it is very strange and if it were not true that they are phantoms it would be so depressing that hope would have a hard time to come springing but they are phantoms and real life can go on just the same and it does.

To-night that is this evening I was taking a long walk up the mountain and of course it was bright daylight and as I was coming down far beyond any houses, Basket began to bark at a man and I called him and when I came near I saw he was not a man from around here, he had on a grey suit of cloth and a cane and a stiff brimmed hat and a rain coat over his arm, and he had bright blue eyes and a large nose and was very sun burned and had the button of the legion of honor and another decoration that I could not make out and he wore a wedding ring, and Basket continued to bark he does not at the country people because he knows what they are and I said in French he is not dangerous he is only barking, and he said is he a caniche and I said yes and he said in English he is a good doggie and I said in French no he is not dangerous, and it did seem to me that he emphasized the last e in doggie and what naturally did that make him and one always is a little nervous you never know and we went on down Basket and I did and he went on up and after a while I looked up and he was looking down and I came home and I asked Alice Toklas what she thought about it but naturally there was nothing to think about it, there never is, no there never is.

How the wind blows but it always does blow in the valley of the

Rhone and we are in the valley of the Rhone, and we are still in
the period of the red month where although it has been very hot
it can freeze and nip everything and there are in this lunar month
three days of the three saints or are they only two saints of snow
and ice and until these days are past nobody can be sure but for all
that there are nightingales and there are swallows and there are
cowslips and even a few bats and they ought to know but do they,
well and they all also say that this is a month when a landing should
take place, there seems to be some reason for it connected with the
sea, but will they neither you nor I nor nobody knows and that is
certainly true enough.

To-day it is almost at the end of April and the bombs fell on
Paris and Petain went up and flew the French flag upon the top
of the city hall of Paris and had a triumphal entry into his capital,
and, and you see the woman at Aix is right, they the occupants are
phantoms otherwise how could it have happened. The Germans
are right in calling Petain a foxy grandpa, he most certainly is, the
country had forgotten him, so many other things seemed to be so
much more important and he seemed since the young men had
been taken away so frightfully helpless and not interested in doing
anything and now little by little the interest has been coming back
again and when he so simply went in to Paris following his flag met
everybody in the streets and said I am coming back of course he
was real and the others were the phantoms. It was Virgil Thomson
who said that the French can accept everything that has the vital
principle of longevity in it, in other words they dont like anything
to die on them, death should be durable like everything else, their
great men, like Jules Ferry, Clemenceau and now Petain they all
have this quality of longevity, they are in a way like Chinamen,
they are not in a hurry, it's other people whom time kills not they,
they are the only ones to persist that are like Chinamen about that,
they do just go on, they do rise from the ashes, they do just go on,
Petain's going to Paris was really wonderful so simple so natural
so complete and extraordinary, it was all that. Sometimes we complain of the French as is natural enough many strange things

happen in these days but when they do what they have just done, it is like Verdun again it is complete and incomparable.

To-day we had the first lilies-of-the-valley and that is a pleasure, the room smells sweetly even if the wind is blowing a hurricane, and we are all waiting for everything.

And then the next day we were all disappointed because Petain had to go on talking about the partisans and all the rest of it but I suppose he had to to quiet the Germans after what he did do, whatever the intention to every one it is a sign that the Germans are weakening. Here in Culoz the Germans have gathered themselves together from the surrounding country and have shut themselves in with barbed wire defences at the station and put in mines to blow up and they flatter the population or try to and say that they have never done anything wicked here in Culoz they have always been very nice and the population say perhaps but look what others of you have done and they say that was only Hitler hang him but not us, but this time really this time it is not the same, as the farmer did once say to me, the Germans are like that it is not their leaders who are to blame, they are a people who always choose some one who will lead them in a direction which they do not want to go, it is their instinct for suicide, the twilight of the gods, they are always going to pieces and when that happens they have neither pride nor courage, and that is the reason as a farmer once explained to me that he preferred that the Germans should win rather than the English, you see he said, the Germans after all even if they win we can always get the better of them, but if the English win well we are not so sure, and they really prefer that the Americans and the Russians win because these two have other things to do and they will not very long bother them, that is the way they feel about it and from their point of view there is a good deal of sense to it.

It is darkest before the dawn at least we all hope so, we are all terribly worried these days, alerts and airplanes and everybody wondering if everybody in Paris and Lyon are starving and indeed it is not impossible because with all the transport cut what can happen to them. Of course we in the country here are better off for food than we ever have been, we have as much food and as much variety of it as we can eat, because now that there is no transport all the food that the country produces remains right here, and the quantity of food that the fields of France can produce cultivated by a few oldish men and women and young children is perfectly extraordinary. It is a miracle that never ceases to amaze me, a father and mother not very strong with a very aged parent and one or two young children, and the amount of food, of wheat, of wine, of brandy, of potatoes of vegetables of cows and goats of butter and milk of pigs and chickens and ducks and geese and oxen and food for all these animals and for themselves, the amount of food that these five or six people can produce in a year and not working very hard, all the time but not awfully hard, the quantity of food that they produce is an eternal miracle, and we even after this fourth year of occupation by an enemy which takes the biggest part the amount that there is still here to eat is extraordinary, it is extraordinary, it remains extraordinary. Of course every work-man has a garden and that garden does produce a lot of food, for himself and family, of course and I forgot rabbits, everybody keeps rabbits and eats them, it is extraordinary. We are wondering and we are waiting and we all say to each other but of course it cannot be to-day or to-morrow, and one old man said to me when I said that well you mean that it is going to last two years yet not that I said and he laughed, any way it is the first of May nineteen forty-four and certainly it will not last two years yet certainly not, cer-tainly not. I am wondering well better not wonder, better wait than wonder, and we are all waiting.

We have had two hens and it is very nice because every day one or the other of them have laid an egg and sometimes both of them and for these months now between them they have given us ten eggs a week and now one of them is setting and I have not had anything to do with a setting hen since I was very young, and at first I had to get a neighbor to take it off its eggs so that it could have its food, but now I am courageous enough to do it myself to.

take it off and to put it back again, it would appear that they should always sit on thirteen eggs, that is the most lucky but we only had eleven but anyway it must be an odd number and now there are only ten because she broke one getting back on them again but nobody suggests that we should take one away to make it nine nobody proposes that so we hope that she will think there are eleven even if there are only ten and they will all come out and about and later on we will eat them, in the meantime we have found plenty of eggs round about, as I say now that the transport has stopped, all the food remains in the country where it is made and while we eat omelets we worry about our friends in Paris who have none. It is funny about chickens, they so naturally are themselves to themselves and to us and to the other chickens, more so even than dogs are. Dogs have much more social than individual sense, and the most definite thing is the difference in their feeling toward a dog whose acquaintance they have made while visiting in a house from their feelings to the most intimate acquaintance picked up on the road, the difference is complete and when they meet the one they have met in the home on the street, the greeting is completely different from that they have for the even very continuous acquaintance of the road. Everything about a dog is social more than individual, but a chicken not at all, god bless chickens eggs are so nice, I had a fresh egg to-day, to be sure meat besides and potatoes and carrots and apples, so we are not suffering for food, but the poor people even the rich ones in the big cities, it is very bad. Everybody is cheerful because it is spring, and to-day is the first of May and they were all walking about little very little ones as the parents said the new France with sticks and on the end of them banners and that is to say a rag and the front one of course a piece of red rag, it is funny and everybody so pleased, to be sure the birds are singing, and every night and every day the airplanes come over our heads but you get used to everything. If only too many of the young men would not be taken away that one does not get used to, and every time you hear of another one it is awful, a woman was just telling me to-day that her brother was taken, they said he was in a truck with the mountain boys but he had not been but it is necessary that somebody says that he has been and they take him away, and put him in prison and I used to say when the women in Bilignin complained but after all you still have your sons and your husbands but now they have not got them any more no indeed they have not and it is very sad, nothing makes a country so sad as all the men taken away, when they go away to be soldiers it is not so bad, they come to and fro they have leave or they are wounded or something but when they are taken away like this, to be sure the large majority of them will come home again but oh dear it is awful.

It is still the first of May to-day and little by little we are expecting something every day.

It is certain that in this mountain country winter does most completely suddenly turn into summer, everybody is enjoying that, it is such a pleasure that summer is summer even in the month of May but, and then they all sigh if we could only enjoy it but it is difficult to know that summer is summer with all the boches that are around and about us. I must say that on the whole they are awfully decent about the bombardments even the one in Rouen which by some mistake destroyed the cathedral and the prefecture in the center of the town where there were no factories or railroad stations and incidentally almost killed the favorite niece of our ex-mayoress and even she when she was telling about it was very decent about it, there are a few that are very bitter but most of them do keep saying well you cannot make an omelette without smashing eggs and they admit that if the omelette is well made it is desirable, and indeed an omelette is good, including the surprise omelette that our cook makes with whole eggs inside the omelette, well anyway to-day when I walked my fourteen kilometers to get the cakes a nice country baker makes us and they are mighty good layer cakes, he made a nice one for each of our birthdays, with congratulations written on it in sugar, well anyway he gave me a warm handshake and said it is going to be over soon, what, I said, the war he said, ah I said, yes he said the landing in France is to

take place on the fifteenth of May the thing is to be all over the
fourteenth of July, it is to be a national celebration and an international celebration, and he said, how many stars are there on your
flag, well I said I do not know exactly how many now but certainly
a lot, why, I said, well he said I am going to make you a wonderful
kind of a wedding cake for the happy day and I am going to
decorate the cakes with American and French flags, and I felt it
was very pleasant that he was so certain that he could begin to
worry about the number of stars on our flag, and I came home and
told Alice Toklas about it and she was very pleased too. On the
way home I met a man who was a refugee from Lorraine, he had a
shop there and had been very prosperous and now he was working
as a day laborer but his brothers helped him and he was sending
two daughters to good schools because after all after all, and he has
one brother who is a designer in a railroad works at Noisy-le-Sec
and he has just been bombarded and the whole place completely
destroyed, and he has another brother at Nancy and he was fore-
man at a factory and that has been completely destroyed, and there
is another brother in Algeria but he does not hear from him, and
anyway well we said good-bye and each one of us went on our way.
In the meantime there are Germans here in the railroad station as
station masters and one of them the one that is always hoping that
everybody will be nice to him after the German defeat because he
has always been very nice, now comes in to the park here of the
property to rest himself, it is a nuisance we do not know how to
get rid of him, he wants to be friendly but of course we do not, of
course we do not, certainly of course we do not. And so we do not
forget to remember that they are here, very little just here but still
always ever here.

We have very pleasant neighbors and one of them has just had
a baby girl and they had to name her Madeleine because the only
safety pin gold of course that they had had the name Madeleine on
it, you cannot these days buy a pin to suit the baby's name you
name the baby to go with the gold safety pin. We were all pleased
with that.

Passing by the railroad tracks there are of course a great many freight cars because the trains go through here all day long and the freight cars seem to come that is they have the name of the town where they belong printed on them, the other day I saw a whole train with Breslau and Koenigsberg and Luxembourg and all the Polish and East Prussian towns that are in these days in the news, it did seem strange to see these freight cars here in this country so far away so awfully far away, and how do they get here and why, well this I do not know nor does anybody else here, but here they are, war is funny because here they are. War is funny.

These days you keep hearing rather worse stories about German atrocities against the civil population particularly in the farming regions of the higher mountains, are they worse than they used to be because they are like rats caught in a trap or are they not any worse and people believe worse things of them because they are hoping to get rid of them, you never can tell or is it that when they were more afraid of them they did not tell of the things that happened, the mental workings of people in a time like this are so simple and natural that they are completely surprising, you cannot tell who are the ones that are feeling one way or another way, you simply have no way of knowing or learning except unexpectedly what some one is believing, it is all very calm and very mixed up just now, every day has something to say, such little things but they do make a day. Every one who is helpful is very helpful. This is so.

It is now nearly the fifteenth of May and we all having been feeling rather low in our mind, the Russians have not been making those cheerful announcements which call for a celebration from Moscow guns and we have all kind of gotten discouraged about the landing, it is so long now that it has been promised, just to-day again the sister of our cook who is here on a vacation from her job is worried about traveling because of the coming landing and suddenly we remembered that just a year ago the same thing happened, she was afraid to go on the train for a long trip because of the imminence of a landing, it kind of made us gloomy that a year ago we thought it was just as imminent as we think it now, it does make you kind of gloomy but to-night the Russians have once again announced cheerfully that they have broken the German lines at Sevastopol, so perhaps after all, the wolf did finally come after he had been announced so often so perhaps well yes perhaps.

We are getting a new lot of occupants that is Germans in our village, the mayor was telling me all about it this afternoon, he says it makes him tired and it undoubtedly does make him tired, quite weary and worn, and of course complications happen all the time, refugees come and he has to find a place to put them and sometimes it turns out to be quite comic and then again it does not, he told me a long story about one this afternoon, a family for whom they had found an apartment, and who then offered the landlady twice as much as the apartment would have rented for to a native and paid in advance besides which is never done, and the landlady was disturbed, she was pleased, she took the money but she was confused, but of course she said you must never interfere with people's habits, and a good time was enjoyed by all. Oh dear well yes it is oh dear.

So we have been talking a lot about after war, and the future organisation of the world. We have a friend who has lots of convictions, he is a big manufacturer in Lyon, and he suggested electric force to replace gold and this and that and suddenly last night I realised suddenly and completely, that really gold has almost a religious quality it really has and that is the reason it is always the standard of money, it has to be. The reason why is this, it is the only metal in the world that is of no use, it is purely a luxury, you cannot use it in industry, dentistry which did make use of it, gave it up because it was not really useful, and think of it, even the Germans, who can turn anything into something useful with which to make war, can find no use for gold in war industries. It is really marvelous that the only metal in all this world of ours that is absolutely entirely and completely useless is gold, and therefore it must have the mystic quality of aloofness which makes which always will make it the standard of money. And beside it

has the extraordinary coincidence of just when there is too little
of it of enough new being found to make the quantity necessary
for its value to continue to go on. So how can there ever never be
a gold standard. There has to be. The only metal that has no
possibility of being made useful, must be the measure of all things,
in short it is not utility that is mystic it is the thing that has no
possibility of being useful that is mystic. It really is very extraordinary and very comforting, completely comforting and completely
extraordinary.

One of our chickens is just hatching out its little ones, one of
the egg-shells was a double one, nobody had ever before seen a
double egg-shell and yet in some way, the outer shell had broken
away leaving the inner shell intact but we could hear the little
chicken moving, it is nice to have a chicken have little chickens,
very nice in war-time when we are all waiting for the landing.
There are a number of Germans here now and they say we cannot
go walking up the mountain because if there is an alerte, then
maybe there will be parachutists and so everybody that is away
from home will be shot on sight, the Germans seem to be very
nervous about parachutists and everybody is very polite to us just
now, well they always are polite and say how do you do but now
they all take off their hats as well as say how do you do, and so
many stories and so many rumors and so many dates for a landing
and so many dates for the end of the war, and to the disgust and
amusement of the population the German soldiers here have two
cows and goats and some pigs and they take them out grazing
sitting there with a gun on their back, the French can never get
over the fact that the Germans seem to be so afraid, so completely
afraid of the population although the population is unarmed and
peaceful, but that is the way it is, and it always is that way. Down
in a field there was a woman with a goat and she was not just
feeding it along the road the way everybody does but she took it
into a meadow and she was heard to say feed little goat feed well
little goat feed without tickets just feed little goat, after all the

people that own this field are rich people so feed well little goat. She was a very religious woman and does a great deal of good.

And so many people are afraid and some cry all the time but most of the French people just go on taking trains and traveling about and really do not stop to bother about anything except how to get something extra to eat. We all do, we all keep on doing it, and everybody does it and now nobody really pays any attention to it. But really what they all need now is a little rain, quite a good deal of rain, the ground is dry and the wind blows dryly, and that at the present moment that and the landing and the bombardments seem to be about all there is that is going on. It is funny about dates, the last time we all were told and the information I imagine comes generally through the Germans, that there was to be a landing and the Germans expected it in France so did we all and then not at all, it was the landing at Nettuno in Italy and the day that we were told to expect it, and now once again we were all told definitely that there would be a landing on the tenth or eleventh of May and instead there was the general offensive in Italy, it is funny that we are always being given the right date but the wrong event. There is nothing stranger than the way everybody knows everything, everybody does, but there is always a catch to it, that is the way it has been from the beginning and I suppose will go on being.

To-day when I was crossing the railway track I saw a long train filled with soldiers and each freight car had a flag that at a distance looked like the tricolor of France, and I had a funny feeling, naturally, but when I came near I saw that instead of red white and blue, it was black white and red, and I did not understand because the German troops never have flags, it is funny, I just realised it now, but all the German soldiers that we have seen and gracious goodness we have seen an awful lot of them on foot in cars and in these last years on the railroad, but never never at any time did any of them have a flag, it is rather strange that and strange that I never was conscious of it before until to-day the fifteenth of May nineteen forty-four, when I did see a flag hanging out of each freight car filled with soldiers, the train had paused and I asked the woman at the crossing what that flag was, oh she said those were Italians and that flag is the one they use for the soldiers that fight for Hitler, so that was the flag of the new fascist republic. At least they have a flag, even if German soldiers have none.

I suppose these Italian soldiers are being brought into France to fight, but well they never not any Italian soldiers that we have seen and we have seen a lot of them were ever very enthusiastic about fighting even when they looked like winning and now, well it certainly is and now. We all are impatient but hopeful, and the three saints of ice and snow have brought the cold weather back into this mountain country, and everybody says what is the use of a war when the war is over, why does not everybody know that it is over when it is over and it is over.

Just now everybody here forgets the war because of the red moon. The April moon that is the after Easter moon is the one that always is dangerous for agriculture because it has in it the days of the three saints of ice and snow, and Assumption which is always dangerous for harvest because it is in the middle of the saints of the three saints of ice and snow and besides it had the further difficulty that if it rains on Assumption then it will rain when the hay and the wheat are cut. We first heard of this dreadful lune rouge or red moon from Mildred Aldrich who during the last war lived in the country and thought agriculturally and in this war we are living in the country and thinking agriculturally and alas to-day the second day of the ice and snow saints everything has frozen and as Easter was late and that made the red moon come late it is now the middle of May alas all the grapes were forward and the potatoes well up and they are all as the French say, scorched they use the word cooked for the action of freezing, and indeed the frozen vines and the frozen potato plants down in the plain do look as if a fire had passed over them. And of course as they all say ordinarily it would make a difference but not such a difference as now when all that they have to eat is what they grow, on the hillside the freeze cannot freeze so badly but in the fertile plain oh dear me. It is extraordinary though how philosophically they all take it, they are sad and they did work so hard, but as all French people are terrien as they call themselves people who think and act and work in the ground, it is because of that that they can so well resist the disasters of war, they are so used to think in terms of farming, and a harvest is in constant danger until it is gathered, and so war is like that it is in constant danger and you are all in constant danger until it is ended and so it is like a harvest and it is all natural enough, and so French people take it as it comes and recover from it so quickly and go on to the next harvest so naturally.

To-day on the road I met a woman from Modane a refugee, and she said although her home was still standing though it had no roofs and no windows it was useless going back because as it was just at the railroad tunnel leading into Italy it was bound to be bombarded again and again. She had two goats and three black faced sheep and she said her father was a government employee, and she said as all refugees say, ah there again there is something not like this barren country where nothing grows. All refugees have a firm conviction that their home was in that favored part of France where agriculture develops admirably and here where they are refugeed the soil is bad the people ignorant and the animals starving. Undoubtedly this was true in the last war and it is true now, and also undoubtedly this conviction that where you live is the real right place makes the will to live, without that conviction anybody could give up the struggle but as long as everybody is convinced that where they live is God's country there will be the will to live. A little later two little baby goats followed my dog Basket and there was great trouble in sending them back because their mother having died they had been mothered by a sheep, and they took Basket for a sheep and their mother. Basket was not flattered, he was very annoyed.

It is funny, all this time the French population managed to ignore the Germans round and about them, the younger generation even made a cult of not knowing that there were any Germans existing, either in France or at home, but now that the Germans are being defeated and defeated by French troops everybody is willing to be conscious of them. Said one woman to me, they all say the German soldiers say that they are not Germans that they are Poles or Serbs or Czechs or something but that is too easy, naturally they are getting ready to be spared but after all there have to be some Germans in the German army said the woman. It is true they look longingly, when people are talking together. Basket the dog and I were standing before a window talking to a little boy and his aunt, and we were laughing together and three Germans came past and they wanted to look friendly and nobody noticed, of course nobody noticed but we knew they were there and wanted to be friendly and for all this long time we would not have known they were there and they would not have wanted to be friendly. Any thing changes even a German and nothing changes not even a German. We are all a little nervous these days a little discouraged because will it ever end and a little happy because the news from Italy is so very good and a little troubled because our friends in Paris are having a good deal of difficulty in keeping alive, we send them a large cheese from time to time but it is only from time to time and they have no gas and no electricity and no wood and no coal. Here in the country we have all we want to eat, more than we need to eat, such funny things happen some one sold us the other day a pound of rice. You have no idea what a pleasure it is to have a little rice in the soup, I used to be very indifferent to rice, but rice has become so rare that it is really angel food now, food for the gods, wonderful rice. When the Italian soldiers were here they always used to have rice in their soup and we used to envy them but just at this minute we are having rice in our soup. And not because we have lots to eat, butter and cheese, and bread, white bread and fish and meat and vegetables and cake and honey and plenty of it but as I keep saying on account of the lack of transport, everything that is produced in the country stays there and that is the way it is here. You certainly do not want to live in cities when there is a war, the country is the place, but the two things that we think of the most besides is rice and orange marmalade. Well life is like that and appetites are like that.

Can you think that two makes three after a war, that is as to nations and eating, I wonder.

Certainly nobody no not anybody thinks that this war is a war to end war. No not anybody, no well no certainly nobody does think about it, they only think about this war ending, they cannot take on the future, no really not, certainly not as warless certainly not as a future. Better get through with this war first.

To-night I was listening to the wireless from America, and they began to give us directions in English how we should know all about roads and places for landing and woods for hiding and depths of rivers and it was just like being in a theatre with a romantic drama, the things we heard when we were young, Secret Service and Alabama and The Girl I Left Behind Me and Curfew Shall Not Ring To-night and Shenandoah, they were real American voices talking American and from headquarters and here we are in the heart of the French country with near a hundred German soldiers right in this village and wire entanglements and little block houses all around the railway station and it is exactly like a novel or a theatre more theatre than novel, and very exciting, and will they ever come well anyway I have always been quite certain that there will be no landing until Rome is taken, I have been certain of this more than a year more and more certain, certain because it is reasonable and then there always is Saint Odile, and a saint having a vision has to be reasonable and it would be reasonable to wait for the landing in northern Europe until Rome is taken, and Saint Odile did say that when Rome was taken it would not be the end of this war but it would be the beginning of the end and that too is reasonable. It is very reasonable to be a prophet if you see a thing completely and reasonably and even if it is five hundred years away that makes no difference being reasonable and complete and have a complete vision is all right and natural, and anybody is more or less a prophet more or less more or less, but Saint Odile is quite completely a prophet and Rome will be taken and then a week or two after there will be a landing and we are listening in American English as to what everybody is expected to do.

Everybody is so tired of darning everything, that is of course Alice Toklas who does all the darning, and darning darns and then darning the darned darns everybody is getting tired of darning everything, everybody is.

Just now near the first of June and there is a moon, only the bombardments the worst of them are done in the daytime. It was rather awful, when there are other places that are bombarded places one only knows a little there is not so much feeling about it but Chambery, we do know Chambery so well we go there so often everybody there is so kind and nice and obliging and just as it happened René Reulos was lunching with us and there was an alerte, and we paid no attention to it as one does not, and then we left to go in a taxi to Belley and he left to get back to Chambery and when we got to Belley we heard that Chambery had not only been bombarded but all the shops we always go to and nice elephant statue and the arcades were all wrecked bombed to bits and burned and then we thought of René on his way and his mother there alone with her invalid husband it was all so awful, to be sure it is necessary because well because it is necessary but oh dear me, it is so near and dear, I mean the places one sees every few days so pleasantly. They are courageous about it, they complain but who would not and a railroad employee whom I just saw this afternoon and who had been in Amberieu when the station was bombed and I said it is dangerous and he said no bombs always go down into the earth and we are not in the bowels of the earth we are on top so why be afraid. We have a shelter here in the garden and the children and the women are supposed to go into it but of course they do not, they pick daisies in the field instead and the women stand around and the siren takes so long to blow the second time and the littlest boy said but why do they not press the button. Naturally he knew that. And then yesterday a German soldier came to ask if the German soldiers could come into the cellar or into the shelter and Alice Toklas said no that was for women and children he should go and ask the mayor, and then they decided to make trenches for themselves but when they started to dig they found that the subsoil in this country is granite so they came back to-day to say that they would just come and sit in the park when there was an alerte and Alice Toklas told them if they did they should not make a noise and they said they would not.

Day before yesterday when I was out walking, I heard behind me some one whistling the Madelon the marching song of the young recruits of the other war, and I said to him, I recognised him as an employee of the railroad of Lyon whom I used to talk to last year, when he came to work in his vegetable garden, and I said you are singing the Madelon and he said we will all be singing it in a month, in a month it will be all over and I said do you think so and he said I do not think it I am certain of it. Well anyway he told me how in the last war he had been taken at seventeen just after Verdun and when he and his baby comrades went to the front the Arab soldiers all chanted, look at the seventeen year olders they are not men they are infants and when the cannon commences to roar they will begin to cry for papa and mama. It was no fun he said and then I was made a stretcher bearer and I was taken prisoner and then thanks to the Spanish ambassador I was sent home and then I went back to the army and I was with the Americans at Saint-Mihiel, and they were great guys, they advanced to the charge smoking their pipes and with their guns on the shoulder at carry arms not at the charge and the Germans shot but not they not until they were on top, they were great guys he said and how we got drunk for armistice and at other times and how we talked French German English but we always understood each other. I can just see them in Italy now, and I asked how about the Germans at the station, he used to tell me funny stories about them last fall, how are they, how are they he said, well he said now if we step on their toes they say I beg your pardon.

Just to-day they told us again about the date of the end of the war. There was a woman in a hospital, and she said one day to the doctor, it is useless to work over that woman in the bed next to me, she is going to die to-night, and the doctor said nonsense she is doing very well, I am telling you said the woman, and the other woman did die that night, she did other things like that and finally the doctor said to her well since you are an extra-lucide, which means you have second sight, tell us when the war is to end. Ah that, said she I cannot tell you until the day before my death, and one day she called the doctor and she said I am going to die to-morrow, so to-day I can tell you the day the war is going to be over, on Friday the thirteenth, which is in July, and the thirteenth of July the war will be over, and the next day she did die. Well we will see. Anyway Saint Odile did say that when Rome was taken it would not be the end but be the beginning of the end, and she certainly was right certainly was and is.

One of our friends who is a manufacturer in Lyon used to be of silk and now does rayon and glass to make textiles said that one thing was certain and sure and that is that after the war cotton will be king, everybody he said now has a passionate desire for the real thing, no more substitutes, everybody wants real cotton real coffee real chocolate. They want real mustard real oil real butter real sugar they want things made by nature and not substitutes created by man and they will have them they certainly will.

One of the things that is most striking about the young generation is that they never talk about their own futures, there are no futures for this generation, not any of them and so naturally they never think of them. It is very striking, they do not live in the present they just live, as well as they can, and they do not plan. It is extraordinary that whole populations have no projects for a future, none at all. It certainly is extraordinary but it is certainly true.

From war to war. I learned how to drive in the last war and I did drive and drive into this war and now for two years I have not driven and now I have sold my car just to-day and looking at it in preparation of giving it up I seem to have forgotten what a number of the gadgets and buttons were for and so it goes from war to war, you begin a thing in one war and you lose it in the next war. From war to war.

Yes just like that you can almost say thank you for not troubling me before and during and after a war.

The siren that warns for the bombardments is not working any more, I suppose it was worn out as they say here they have succeeded in putting it out of order, but who the they are nobody knows and now the Germans are to warn us by trumpeting but after all that does not really wake one up if one is really asleep so everybody prefers it, that is all everybody talks about is bombardments and naturally nobody is pleased, and whether the aim is good or not is hotly discussed, they say they should not fly so high, though they do admit that the precision of hitting is very great, nevertheless they say if they flew lower there would be less destruction round and about and as the defence is practically non-existent why not fly lower, others say they should not bombard at all and, everybody will hate them and they did love the Americans but I said you know how they are here the French forget the past and enjoy the present yes they answer but our towns and all the dead, oh dear they say to me can you not stop them, alas I say I hate to have lovely places all smashed up and French people killed but what can I do, well they say, anyhow it is going on so long so long, and sometimes we that were most optimistic are getting kind of pessimistic it is going on so long. One woman told me to-day her brother-in-law who is a retired government employee wont even now spend his money all his money on food, he says that he has always been keeping his money in case of necessity to see him through a bad time, well said his sister-in-law indignantly what do you expect, can you expect anything worse than this, and he did not answer.

Anyway in this little town a hundred and sixty children were confirmed to-day but the bishop did not stay long, after all there are the bombardments and it is just as well not to stay too long anywhere. We have lots to eat except bread, but that is because there is no transport, oh dear say all the French people oh dear if they would only land and fight on land, we would prefer it. Well I say I am sure that a week after Rome is taken they will land. Oh dear says everybody, anyway Saint Odile did say that when Rome was taken it would not be the end but it would be the beginning of the end and this evening the allies are in sight of Rome. I have just sold my automobile to a friend whose own was smashed to bits in Lyon last week in a bombardment, and as he is in the Red Cross he has to have another, and I was sad to see it go but nevertheless there will sometime be lots of others, it is hot weather and we are all waiting yes waiting.

To-night Rome is taken, and now that Saint Odile's prophecy is being fulfilled it is a pleasure and such a pleasure that it is not the end but the beginning of the end and it has taken everybody's mind a little off their feelings about the bombardments in France about the civilians killed, it really is funny that feeling about civilians, well not funny exactly because it comes from the time when the army was not only made of professional soldiers but very often of mercenaries, and so the difference between soldiers and the inhabitants of a country, civilians were important, but it was really in the American civil war that they first began not to make that difference, the army was a civilian army and when Sherman made his march through Georgia and said war was hell, he said you had to destroy the granary upon which the enemy depended, and that was the quickest way to finish a war, but here in Europe, the armies are civilian armies that is to say made up of the whole population the whole male population, and so what is there really different between civilians and the army. Our little servant in Bilignin when some one began to speak about the bombardments in Germany killing women and children said but every German woman means ultimately seven German soldiers, in other words, scotch the snake in the egg, but actually almost every one does not feel that way about it, not here, they still think of the civilian population as a population entirely apart from the military one, and as they are very unhappy about it naturally I do not explain to them that we have the same thing now that we had in the civil war, we are the granary which now is the munition producing material of the enemy and their railroad communications and they are destroying them just as they did in Sherman's march to the sea, by pulling up the railroad tracks everywhere, only now it is by means of bombardments, at the same time of course everybody does make fun of the Germans who always are the first to betake themselves to the fields and the mountain for safety, they are not courageous no they are not they all say of them, those birds as they call them, our visitors as they call them, no they say they are pantless Sadies, they are not courageous. It is funny and yet it is true, they are not courageous as other men are courageous they are not, it is true. But to-night Rome is taken and everybody has about forgotten the bombardments, and for the French to forgive and forget and forget and forgive is very easy just as easy as that. Rome is taken and Saint Odile says it is not the end but the beginning of the end.

To-day when I was out walking with one of the women and we found some German soldiers they said most pitifully how do you do, we naturally said nothing, later on I was sitting with the wife of the mayor in front of her house a German soldier passed along the road and he politely bowed to us and said how do you do, what is it I said they have never done this before, do you think that they have received orders to do it now, no said she no, it is only Rome.

She told me a story. Her husband has of course to always supply the Germans with whatever they ask for and they are always asking for something, very often they do not want it after it has been gotten for them. One day they wanted something and they asked the mayor to go with them to find it, he said yes of course politely as he always does, and they called for him in a closed car, and she was standing at the gate to see him go, the officer who was going with him said to her, Madame weep because we are taking your husband away. No said she her eyes sparkling courageously no I do not weep, no, but said he you should weep because we are taking your husband away. No said she no. I do not weep. And then the car went away, she said to me if I was going to cry I would not cry in front of them, But said I, did you cry, no she said because I did not believe it but my husband stayed away about three hours and the last hour was hard to bear but at last as I was standing at the gate I saw my husband coming around the corner. It was a relief. He said nothing to me about what had been said so I supposed he had not heard it so of course I said nothing. But said I why did the officer do it, to see if he could make me cry. Sadism I said, yes to make themselves feel masters.

Well that was yesterday and to-day is the landing and we heard Eisenhower tell us he was here they were here and just yesterday a man sold us ten packages of Camel cigarettes, glory be, and we are singing glory hallelujah, and feeling very nicely, and everybody has been telephoning to us congratulatory messages upon my birthday which it isn't but we know what they mean. And I said in return I hoped their hair was curling nicely, and we all hope it is, and to-day is the day.

While I was out walking to-day I talked to a little girl who looked nine but was really fourteen, her people came from the neighborhood of Rome but they had been French for some time and the children all born in France, she said they were all small, she certainly was and we talked about eating, and she said she would like an orange, and I said how about a banana do you know what a banana is oh yes she said I used to eat them, but my younger brothers and sisters they never saw a banana, and some of them cannot remember an orange, well she said sighing the time will come yes it will of course one does need bread but one does need oranges and lemons and bananas too.

To-day is only the third day of the landing and what a change, everybody openly making fun of the Germans, the girls leaning out of the window and singing the Marseillaise, and all the people in the village, so pleased because it has been said that this department the department of the Ain will be the first to be free and then the Savoy and the Haute Savoy, and indeed the mountain

boys are at it, Bourg the biggest city in the department has been
completely cut off by them from contact with any one, they have
cut the railroads, they guard the railroads and they have interrupted the telephone, and they have occupied quite a few important towns round about, and the few Germans that are left are
getting mighty uncomfortable, the fifty who are here were called
to go and fight the mountain boys and they said they did not want
to and their officer harangued them and then they had to go, but
there were no trains and so they requisitioned the French trucks
and some autocars and away they went, I was sitting with the wife
of the mayor and we saw them going off to fight and it was a very
great contrast to the German army of 1940, my gracious yes. They
have just told us that when the Germans started to attack the
mountain boys the mountain boys just climbed a little higher, and
sometimes they do not trouble to fight, they just throw stones
down and call out cuckoo, cuckoo, of course to the French a
cuckoo is some one who has stolen somebody else's nest. The
Germans did not like being called cuckoo but what else can they
do. The young people are all feeling very gay, the older ones
naturally are worried but the young ones are feeling very gay.

The mayors now have to have the whole responsibility of their
towns, there are no communications, so they cannot get into touch
with a higher authority, and so they are the ultimate authority,
and they are very capable the French mayors, even in the smallest
places. Ours is taking care of us very well, he has managed to get
flour for bread and that is important because French people do
not like to live by bread alone but without bread they cannot live
at all, potatoes they say are filling but an hour after you are as
hungry as before while bread is really sustaining so they must have
bread and so far our mayor has managed it for us. It would be nice
if ours would be the first department to be completely freed of
Germans, perhaps, the mountain boys around here are very active,
and it would be nice.

A buzzard has carried off one after the other three of our baby
chickens, that is natural the hunters usually shoot enough buzzards

every year so that they do not steal baby chickens, but after three years of not hunting, the air is full of buzzards full of buzzards.

And full of everything just now but mostly rumors. There are however some funny true stories, the mountain boys the other day came into Amberieu and one of them got into the post office and sounded the alerte, the whole population and the Germans ran away supposing it was a bombardment and the mountain boys went into the round house and blew up a quantity of locomotives and left before the Germans got back. The latest rumor is that Belley is held by the mountain boys but one thing is certain at the station here no trains pass, I was around the station this afternoon and I never saw a railroad station so dead not since in my youth I crossed the continent during the Pullman strike and what else can we do, it is the third time that we have been deprived of the telephones and this time fortunately they have left us electricity and the radio, which is a pleasure. But for how long this we do not know, anyway the landing goes on and when we hear the official French announcement that the Germans are perfectly calm, we know better, they are not, what we are afraid of now is that German deserters will try to get into the house, one did to-day, he said he was looking for a German lady, but as we are well up the mountain and not in the town it sounded fishy. Basket barks and barks as if he were a savage dog instead of a lamb which is just as well. Everything is going on that is to say nothing is going on no trains no mail no telephone, nothing coming and going except a few unfortunates, I saw one to-day who seemed a little queer, and there is a noonday hush all over the place all day long, the Germans are requisitioning more and more enormous logs to get themselves barricaded, away from the mountain boys and everybody chuckles they say much good that will do them, there are according to all calculations about three thousand of them in the whole department and as the mountain boys are killing them a few at a time it may take some time but on the other hand, they are stuck they can go up and down the road a distance of about fifty kilometers and then they have to come back again, all the youth are joining up with their friends, the police too, our friend came to see us from Belley yesterday Sunday and everything is peaceful except that everywhere the mountain boys guard the roads but they are very polite and help shove the cars when they get stuck, everybody for the moment is very polite, the mayor on his bicycle goes around gathering in food from the surrounding country to feed his population and so far has succeeded very well, the only thing that is a great trouble, is when there is a need for surgical operations and it is very difficult to get a conveyance, the men with the taxis are always getting their cars out of order to avoid going around with the Germans and they are frightened of putting them in order in order to take the French, but by the end of the week it is now the first Sunday since the landing everybody expects that the Germans will be gone. And they will, yes they will. My gracious they are all happy not the Germans but the population, even those who were collabo as they call them are happy why not they were collabo because they were afraid afraid of communism and afraid of Germans and then too the Germans to some French people did seem to be so strong but now well they are weak nobody uses the phrase that used to annoy us so they are still strong, and so there are no collabos because now that the Anglo-Americans have proved themselves so strong they are less afraid of communism and they are not at all afraid of Germans not at all so the rejoicing is practically universal, a little frightened still but complete. Some one has just told me about how the mountain boys in Bellegarde have taken German prisoners and have put them to work picking potato bugs off the potato plants, the only agricultural activity that every French man woman and child hates, they are looking forward to the clearance of the pests completely by the German prisoners. Everybody is delighted they say potatoes came from America and the potato pest seems to have come over these recent years from America and now because of America they have been able to take German prisoners here very far away from the Americans to be sure and these prisoners can spend their days destroying the potato bugs off the potato plants.

Are we excited yes we certainly are all around us there is fighting, the conversation in the village sounds exactly like the communiqués of the Yugo-Slavs in their early days of guerrilla fighting only we have we hope one great advantage, the Germans cannot get reinforcements because all the railways are cut and all the roads guarded by the mountain boys and anyway these days the Germans have other uses for their men even if they could send them here which they cannot. All day long the Germans rush forward and back through the town they requisition all the trucks and alas with their French drivers and then they go first in one direction and then in a very short time back they come with guns sticking out in every direction, the other day they stationed such cannon as they had everywhere in the village and we all a little fearfully went down to look at them and then later in the day they took them all away, there had been no fighting, they had been told when they were elsewhere that the mountain boys were here but they were not of course they were not, that is what wears the Germans out to be continually going where there is nobody and then when not expecting having a truck with its German contents blown off the road suddenly, we are in the high hills and of course that kind of thing happens easily with everybody against them and helping the others, it must be pretty awful to be surrounded but completely surrounded by hate, it must be pretty awful really pretty awful. One German told the baker who had been a prisoner in the last war and so had learned a little German that the population had better be a little careful, he himself did not mind very much when the children called him a pig but there were others of them that might and there might be trouble. Sometimes there are a lot of them in the village and sometimes very few but few or many they certainly do look worn out, and the mountain boys do kill and wound a lot of them there were five ambulances came over from Aix, German ones of course and big ones, to take off the wounded in yesterday's fighting, and the German captain who was here has just been caught at Amberieu. The mountain boys do not stay in the towns, they keep to the hills descending into the town to barricade all the roads and then they go back to the hills, they are always up and down, they have cut all the telephone and telegraph wires, and so the Germans cannot communicate with each other and they have to go on the road, the other day just a little further along an Italian in the ditch at the side of the road killed two motor cyclists as they were going along, and then he quietly got out of the ditch and went on, how can the Germans tell which is which, they cannot, it is most exciting, nobody works except in their gardens because the railroad and the few factories that are here have stopped working there being no material and no way of sending things in or out, it is a mighty effective blockade and the Germans who are gradually getting killed can really do very little except move forward and back they should have gotten out as soon as communication with Italy was cut, because after that there was no reason for their staying here, but they are slow, they always manage to do everything just too late, just too late, thank heaven they do. I suppose they are human but they do look pretty awful, and even in their most uppish days they were awfully dead and alive more dead than alive. This is not a prejudice it is a fact.

We are excited.

Perhaps the department of the Ain will be the first department to be completely cleared of the Boches. That would be nice.

They are fighting all around us this afternoon I was raking the hay with a neighbor and we heard the sound of cannon fairly near, nobody seems to know very much of what is happening, the mayor who is usually very well informed has no time to think about things like that, he has to find calves to butcher to give us all something to eat, we ourselves are very well off because they have been bringing us fish and nice lake fish they are, the bread question not so serious for us because we do not eat much bread but terribly serious for the French population, potatoes no matter how many they eat after an hour or two leave them hungry, but since either the mountain boys or the Germans cut down trees to bar the roads that lead to the mills that grind the corn even if the mayor can get some wheat together how can it turn into bread, but there is always the Savoy, mysteriously the Savoy always has everything, some one has just given us a kilo of delicious fresh butter from the Savoy and the mayor is hoping he really is hoping to get flour from the Savoy, the Savoy is always rich in food no matter what happens you can always get meat and fish and fowl and butter and cheese and honey from the Savoy and meat, I do not know why this is so but it is so and as we are just across the river Rhone from the Savoy we do not fare too badly, even if we are completely cut off from the rest of the world which we certainly are. To-day for the first time since the landing we had some letters from Lyon they came from the Swiss consul who has charge of American interests and they solemnly ask us to make out a paper stating if we wish or do not wish to be repatriated. It is a charming thought, ten days after the landing in France the American authorities seem to be quite certain that as soon as they like they can repatriate all Americans still in France. We giggled we said that is optimism. Naturally American authorities not really realising what it is to live in an occupied country ask you to put down your religion your property and its value, as if anybody would as long as the Germans are in the country and in a position to take letters and read them if they want to. The American authorities say they are in a hurry for these facts but I imagine that all Americans will feel the same better keep quiet until the Germans are gone just naturally play possum just as long as one can. Just that.

It is a queer state living as we are all doing, you have no news except for the radio because there are no newspapers any more and no trains no mail no telephone and even going to Belley is impossible there are twenty-three barricades between here and there a distance of seventeen kilometers. As I say we live within the village completely within it, the Germans rush forward and back there are distant sounds of cannonading, some villages have been burned and that is all anybody knows. The Germans threatened to make a curfew at six o'clock and keep all vehicles including bicycles off the road, but the mayor told the Germans it was impossible as it is too hot to take the animals to pasture before half past five it is too hot and nobody can work in the fields until four because it is too hot, and as in France fields are a considerable distance from the house and now it is haying time carts have to move around so the Germans agreed and now the curfew is at nine o'clock.

Is life real is life earnest, no I do not think so, it certainly is not real.

This kind of war is funny it is awful but it does make it all unreal, really unreal.

They must have been lonesome in the middle ages and that was natural enough because busy as they were with getting enough to eat they were pretty well cut-off from communication with everything and it is kind of lonesome in this present war which is so much like that, with trees cut down to block the roads and everything but still our friends did get over in a pony cart from Belley to see us and it was a pleasure, and besides they brought us some money which was also a pleasure because the traveling banker who used to come once a week to this town has not come and money is certainly a very great necessity these days.

To-night the Americans have just had a victory and are going to take Cherbourg and that is a pleasure. To be sure in the middle ages they did not have a wireless and although it was threatened that they would take them away from us they did not and now it would be rather late for it to happen and I do like to hear their American voices. Everything is quiet around here now, nobody seems to know just what happened but it is all quiet around here now and we even had letters from Lyon to-day.

Bread and cake cake and bread which is better, I myself think that bread when there is good butter is better than cake, bread and butter but when there is no bread and butter then there is cake Marie Antoinette was quite right about that.

Some refugees have just come here from Normandy, they are friends of the wife of the mayor, they left Normandy just seven days ago and they progressed partly by bicycle partly on foot and partly by train, it took them seven days to get here, they were a party of seven with three children and the mother just about having another baby, they stopped at night and dug themselves a trench in which to sleep on account of the bombardments they describe the railways all through the north completely blocked and the German material scattered all about, and the Germans take the little roads because the big roads are bombed all the time, it is like well like nothing, although Wells did describe it in a kind of a way, and nobody says anything except it's long c'est longue, which is I suppose the inevitable human cry, in the meantime the eagles are carrying off all the baby chickens and ducks because not having guns nobody can shoot them, we had seven baby chickens and now we have only two, and the poor hen screams and goes pale but what is the use, there is no use in screaming or going pale when nobody is allowed to shoot the eagles in the air. On the other hand the wheat the vines the potatoes all are growing well, and so if there is anybody there to eat when it is all over there will be eating for them, the refugees from Normandy said you could buy a kilo of butter for ten francs in that part of Normandy but there was nobody there to buy, there seemed to be people to sell but nobody there to buy, and it made us all sigh naturally enough although we did not want ourselves to be there to buy.

Now they have made the curfew at six o'clock of the afternoon it was just to-day and all windows that face toward the street have to close from then until seven in the morning, and everybody is pretty unhappy because domestic animals will not feed in the heat of the day and farm work in the summer is from sunrise to sunset and everybody is worried, naturally enough and nobody knows why but really I imagine it is because the Germans are afraid of the mountain boys or the parachutists, but really since it is day-light until ten o'clock why should they make it at six. Of course the French population take it very simply that it is done to annoy. They take this for granted with all the German regulations, they only do it to annoy because they think it teases. Oh dear as the French say of the allies all the time if they only would hurry up.

It is their only cry hurry up. The Germans are convinced of the efficiency of the new bomb, but not any Frenchmen, one German was telling about it to some Frenchmen and one of the French said to him but you are silly if you believe that, any soldier ought to know better they all say, but the German did not take offense, he just went on believing or did he. After all any hope is a hope to a dying man. All the French population can say is of the allies is if they only would hurry up, although they do admit that two weeks after the landing a great deal has been accomplished. One village to another is full of rumors. In Belley they think we have guns all around us, here we were told that all sorts of things have happened in Belley, but so far it is all rumor, the latest rumor is that the maquis the mountain boys have caught a colonel a captain and two ladies with whom they were out walking, and that is the reason they have made the curfew at six o'clock. The hide of a German comes high, said our cook why don't they send them back, they are no use to anybody and then we could go and take the potato bugs off our potato plants. Well life in an occupied country is like that.

I am going on cleaning the weeds off the terrace so when the American army gets here it can sit comfortably on it, Alice Toklas thinks the weeds may get a chance to grow again but I hope not, anyway I am making it nice and neat, and as the terrace is not on the road side of the house, I can go on working at it after we have to stay indoors, that is to say that we cannot go out of doors on the roads.

In all these years I never had a wrist watch, watches to wear never particularly interested me, I like clocks and I am always buying them any kind of clock any kind of fountain pen, but watches seemed kind of dull, I like to know what time it is in the house but out of doors it is less interesting to know about the passage of time and in a city particularly in France you see so many clocks you hear so many clocks to be sure they do not tell the same time but no matter they do tell some time and when you are going to an appointment sometimes you go quickly because you are late by one clock and then you go slowly because you are early by another clock, but now that the curfew is at six o'clock, and I am sure to be out on the road somewhere and they do shoot you if you are out I thought it best to have a wrist watch and so out I went in our little village and asked the local jeweler lady whether she had a wrist watch, yes and a Swiss one and brand new and made for sport for women and men and I thought it perfectly lovely and I came home proudly and now I wear it with immense pride and joy and it seems to keep time and I get home in time and do not get shot by the Germans.

The maquis are beginning to fight again, there was a lull for a bit and now it has commenced again and the Germans are taking all the gazogene automobiles and they are threatening to take away some of the radios from some of the people not to prevent the people listening they do not seem to care very much about that but presumably to get ready to get their orders that may come by radio when all the telephone and telegraph lines are cut which they certainly will be soon. Everything does seem as if something is going to happen that is what everybody keeps on saying. In the meantime our mayor has most efficiently gotten meat and bread and wine and corn meal and butter and everybody is very cheerful because they stand in line for hours but they finally get something and that is a pleasure. How they love a piece of bread. They certainly do. And I am going on scraping the weeds off the terrace so as to be all ready for the American army when it comes, one boy who came to-day and brought us fish said that he had seen an English soldier with his own eyes we none of us believed him naturally but it was a pleasure to hear and he did believe it.

The Germans are very uncertain in their minds now, they decided to-day to give us the curfew at ten instead of six in the evening, it was posted up at the mairie and everybody was happy and then at half past five they sent the local policeman around to announce that they had changed their minds and it was back to six o'clock again, then a half hour afterwards they sent him around again to announce that it was changed back to ten and that is

where it is now, or so we hope. But that is the way they are about
everything, they come and go and they are afraid of their shadow,
it is very hard to believe but it is true, and now everybody knows
it, guerrilla warfare gets on their nerves it is so darn individual
and being individual is what they do not like that is to say what
they can not do.

It is exciting to me to hear over the radio about Lake Trasimena, when my brother and I were still at college we spent one
summer some weeks in Perugia at a pension and there were lots of
us there and one day some of us went off to see Lake Trasimena
because there was supposed to be a whole army at the bottom well
an army of ancient days naturally with gold chariots, and we
thought we would like a swim in the lake, and the young men
took the boatmen with them at one end of a little island in the
middle of the lake and we girls went to the other end to swim, and
we swam without clothes in the sunset in Lake Trasimena, and I
have swum in lots of lakes and oceans but there was something
special about that and now well it is being mentioned every day.
And Cherbourg, when my eldest brother was coming to Paris with
his family, my brother and I had been living there some years
already, my eldest brother was a little nervous about the trip and
he had not much confidence in the ability of my brother and
myself getting to the station in time to meet his train from Cherbourg, and so for several months my eldest brother wrote letters
and each one of them ended up with a postscript it is six and a
half hours from Cherbourg to Paris, six hours and a half. We used
to laugh about it, it was a family joke six hours and a half from
Cherbourg to Paris. Well perhaps, anyway it is Cherbourg, yes it is.

Everybody is excited so very excited and all around us there
are explosions, we do not know what they are whether they are
cannon or bridges blowing up or avions or just thunder but there
is a lot of it and everybody hears and tells of a different lot, the
Germans in French local trucks, not having any of their own, rush
forward and back, and nobody seems to know just why or where.
When I was out yesterday, I met five Germans with guns on

bicycles and they were followed by a truck from Grenoble with soldiers having mitraillettes pointing in every direction and then followed by a local taxi-cab containing two officers of a higher rank than we are accustomed to see around here, and where they were going nobody knows, do they, and then there was a private car that went to Aix, and in this was an officer who had been here and was not popular and he was in a car with two soldiers each carrying a gun and the officer was driving and the car swerved and one of the soldiers dropped his gun which went off and killed the officer. And then there was his funeral with all the officers present. Then I have been seeing a German soldier working lately in the local carpenter shop, and I asked the carpenter why, well he said he told me in his own country he was owner of a carpenter shop and had six men working under him and he said as he has nothing to do he would like to handle tools and as I am short handed I let him, he says the war has settled his hash all right, when and if he gets back to his home he certainly will find nothing there for him.

It's a funny life all right, so far we ourselves have not seen any maquis, I went on a long walk yesterday and went over a road that had been barricaded, just trees pulled to the side of the road, all the telegraph and telephone wires down, they had not fought there but it was certainly like a battle field, it is hard to tell who is maquis and who isnt, they have an arm-band but naturally when they come home to see their people and they all do they keep it in their pocket and then there are still some firm reactionaries who are convinced that all maquis are terrorists, we have some charming neighbors who are like that and it worries me because after all people get angry and things might happen to them and we are very fond of them, it kind of reminds me of the description of the marauding bands in Cooper's Spy, but that of course is the extraordinary thing about this war it is so historical not recent history but fairly ancient history, not I suppose where the armies are actually fighting but here where we are. The mayor keeps us pretty well fed, there are no more tickets because there is no contact with the authorities, there is only the mayor, there are no police but we are all peaceable and we are very well fed, we seem to have everything but sugar. We even had a lemon and an orange which should have gotten to Switzerland but did not, the bridges keep being blown up and nobody wants to go out to repair them it is too dangerous, the Germans tried to pass an armored train through the other day, but did it get there, nobody seems to know.

They just blew up the electric line between here and Chambery and now everybody is walking, they walk to Grenoble they walk to Lyon, even children of three and five walk along with their elders, and sometimes somebody lends them a bicycle and sometimes the children fall off but not often they stick on holding on to anything in front of them, and so they still move around, everybody has to go somewhere and French people always find a way, they are wonders at always finding a way. The death of Henriot killed by the militia or somebody in their uniform has been an immense excitement, it is hard to make any one who has not lived with them realise how really tormented the population has been in its opinions and Henriot did perhaps more than anybody to turn Frenchmen against Frenchmen, he was a very able propagandist, he used the method not of a politician but of a churchman, he had that education, and he knew how to appeal like a revivalist sermon, and he did do it awfully well, and he held the middle classes they could not get away from him, what said I to one friend whose mother always listened to him, what will your mother do now, oh she mourns but at least for a week she will be busy with all the funeral orations, but after that, good gracious after that what will she do. A great many of the middle classes feel like that, of course the immense majority of French people are delighted at his putting off, they breathe more freely, there was no one else in the government who had the power he had, no one else. I do not think outside of France this was realised, I do not think so.

And now he is dead and except a few of the die hards everybody is happy and relieved and everybody can now get ready for the end of the war that is to say for the evacuation of France by the Germans.

One of our friends wants to be taught to say to a parachutist who comes to her door, and upon whom she has closed the door, she wants to say to him in English through the keyhole please break down the door and come in by force and take everything you want by force in that way you will have what you need and the Germans and the government cannot blame me and now said she just how can I say that to the parachutist through the keyhole. The rest of the population just wants to be taught to say we are glad to see you, and some of them are learning to say it very nicely, every one is certain that a large party of Canadians have been parachuted somewhere in our neighborhood and that they are only waiting the arrival of an English general expected any day this is the first of July for the advance to begin. As a matter of fact the forty-odd Germans who are here and who no longer get their pay are getting more and more peaceful, they ask for work they wander around unarmed and they used never to stir without a gun on their back and never less than three together, now they wander all about the country alone and unarmed. It certainly is a change this conquering army this occupying army now wandering around hoping some one will speak to them and that some one will give them a job. It certainly does look like the beginning of the end. The breathlessness of the situation is a bit on everybody's nerves but the most selfish of all the women here did to-day in a great burst announced that it was all right there must be no bread, no money no anything and then the Germans would leave, that is the way it was going to be. There are no more trains here any more, and this Culoz where we are was a very important railroad junction for Italy, Switzerland the Savoys and Lyon, but not a train not one single or solitary train not one. No wonder the Germans are meek, here they are and here they must stay until the maquis come and take them away.

They are getting away from here, the last lot that were in Artemarre are leaving and they are trying to sell the wagons that they had attached to their horses and all that is left in the region are right here in Culoz, we still have forty odd and when will they leave very soon we are hoping, they do not do anything very disagreeable here but oh dear what a relief it will be when they are gone, as everybody says even when they are not doing anything they are an oppressive burden, they are.

The Germans still eat sausages, just like the old jokes, the Hitler regime has not changed that, they borrow a sausage machine from an old woman here who is called the old Maria, and they tell her all their troubles and how they are all going home very soon now, and the soldier who accidentally killed his adjutant and who has been crying ever since locked up in a room and he wanted to commit suicide but the officers decided instead of shooting him he would be sent to the Russian front and we all laughed and said by the time he gets there there wont be any Russian front.

And now the cook has just come up to say that the maquis are on their way and may get here at Culoz not any day but at any moment of to-day. I wonder. It is now the fourth of July and things certainly are moving.

It's the fourth of July and everybody is on the broad grin. The French black troops with regular French officers are now within eight kilometers of us, they have been parachuted in the region and the Germans scared to death are packing up their bags and moving away and everybody stands around and laughs and with reason. It is a happy day.

To-day I took a long walk and all along there were groups of people telling each other all sorts of things, some had seen Canadians and some had seen English and some had heard on the radio that this department of the Ain was going to be completely emptied of Germans by the fourteenth of July and others had seen the black troops and anyway there was a sound of cannon firing and somebody had heard one of the German soldiers say, the only thing to do to shorten this war is to kill our chiefs, and sometimes when you realise that there have been twenty-four German generals killed or imprisoned in three weeks are they doing it, are they.

There is one thing certain now it is very bad form to mention maquis or mountain boys, you speak respectfully of the French army, in two days the word maquis no longer exists it is with great pride the French army. There are such funny things the new prefect was talking of having he himself been condemned to death by the maquis and the wife of the mayor said yes he will write about it in his memoirs and then she added meditatively condemned to death we are all condemned to death.

It is very pleasant to have a new army with an old name or an old army with a new name, very pleasant.

We were in Belley yesterday and there everybody was excited the night before the maquis had come into the town and walked off with the sous-prefet with the chief of police with a thousand kilos of sugar that one of the cake shops had and lots of other material, and everybody of course was excited and upset, six of us had gone over in a taxi including our mayor, and it was very exciting and then we came home and then that evening the maquis came very near to Culoz and the Germans took out cannon to shoot at them and all to-day they were firing around the mountain and we all stood around talking and everybody said if the maquis come they bring food but if the maquis come and do not succeed then the Germans will take hostages and burn up the farms, oh dear do they want maquis or do they not want maquis, it all is very exciting we now have one hundred and sixty Germans in the town and they are not leaving, we all hoped that they would leave and that would be very comfortable for everybody and they would like to leave but Hitler likes everybody to stay where they are until they are all killed, he likes it like that, so I suppose even these few will stay until they are killed so that now that the railroad is not working any more there is no use in staying but their orders are to stay anyway. A lot get killed when there is a lot and a few get killed when there are a few but the idea is to always stay and get killed. That is the way to create the last battalion which will then be killed and we will all be happy, yes quite happy.

I had seen many things in this war a great many but I had never seen an armored train and to-day as I passed the railroad track I saw one, with the engine with a sort of tea cosy made of metal over it and behind cars with sand bags and Germans and we wondered

because there was no way to go the railroad being all broken up
except just to Chambery and I came home to tell about it and it
was almost nine o'clock of summer night just a little later and
Basket barked and I looked out and there was a German officer and
a soldier and they said in French they wanted to sleep and I said
have you a paper from the mayor because they are always supposed
to have and he said like an old time German officer I must see the
house, certainly I said, you go around to the back and they will
open, and I called the servants and told them to attend to them, I
thought with that kind of a German it was just as well to keep our
American accents out of it, and then they were at it, the German
said he wanted two rooms for officers and mattresses for six men
and he did not want any answering back and he did not care how
much he upset the ladies of the house, and the servants said very
well sir and he left and as soon as he left the soldiers were amiable
and they carried around mattresses and they had three dogs and we
locked up as much as we could and took Basket upstairs and went
to bed, finally there were fifteen men sleeping on the six mattresses
and the two dogs the third one would not come in and in the morning after they all left we could not find my umbrella it turned out
that it was used by a poor devil of an Italian whom they kept outside all night in the rain to sit with the horses, and they took away
a new pair of slippers of one of the servants and they broke the lock
and stole all our peaches and they took away with them why nobody knows except to be disagreeable the two keys of the front and
back doors, and then they left but the third dog would not go with
them and he is here now, there were six hundred of them in the
village and they are supposed to be on their way to fight the
maquis, but actually they themselves thought they were going
home, they were sixteen and seventeen years of age and when they
were alone any one of them with the servants they told about how
hard their life was and what an unhappy country it was where there
were maquis, and one of them said, now the Russians are getting
in to our country we will have to go to our country we will have to
go back to Berlin to defend it and we will have to leave you French

people to defend yourselves as best you can against the English. The servants just listened and then when another German came in then the one who was crying got the same brutal expression on his face as the others, oh said the servants the miserable assassins. We heard firing all this afternoon and the rumor is the maquis had mined the road they went over and caught them, anyway that is the last we saw of them and that was only yesterday. All the same said the mayor they are not quite what they were, they threatened to shoot the mayor of the next village because he had not notified the Germans that the maquis were there, but how could I said the poor mayor when they imprisoned me and, said our mayor, four months ago they would not have listened to him but now they did and let him go. The rumor to-night is that they are all quitting the country and they should go the ill-omened birds that they are, say the country people. So far we none of us have seen any maquis, nor the Canadians that are supposed to be with them, but we will they all say we will. Everybody is worried and a little confused in their minds except about the Germans that they will go, that they will only go, where does not interest anybody.

And now the unhappy description of how a very small percentage of the French population feel, I just had a violent quarrel with our nearest neighbors and I will try to tell just how they do feel.

I forget to say that when these Germans came they came in trucks big trucks pulled by horses, gasoline they have none.

There was a story written about the war the American civil war called The Crisis by Winston Churchill and it was about Saint Louis and there was the north and there was a southerner and there was a northerner and they had been friends for years but when there was a threat of civil war they said can we meet can we keep off the subjects and of course they could not. The French are like that now they are violently divided and they cannot keep off the subject. Then in the last war there was a funny story. A friend of ours Louise Hayden had been all through the war in one way and another and later when she went home to Seattle a friend said to her, my dear Louise you do not know anything about the real hardships of war, over there you were in it you were busy every minute in the midst of it but over here we had the real nervousness and anxiety of war we were not in it we could only suffer about it. Well this time the French have been like that, they could only suffer the nervousness and anxiety of wars, they were not in it, that is to say of course now they are in it but from '40 to '43 well really into the beginning of '44 they were not in it, they had all the nervousness the anxiety and the suffering and the privations of war but they were not in it, and when I first heard that story I thought it was only funny but now that I have been with a nation suffering like that I understand the point of view of the woman in Seattle.

The French not fighting had plenty of time to worry and to talk and to listen to propaganda, and they have gotten so that they do not know what they believe in but they do pretty well know what they do not believe in, I laughed the other day when I met Doctor Lenormant because he surpassed most of the Frenchmen, he was anti-Russian he was anti Anglo-American he was anti-German, he was anti-De Gaulle he was anti-Vichy he was anti-Petain he was anti-maquis he was anti-persecutions he was anti-collabo, he was anti-bombardments he was anti-militia he was anti-monarchy he was anti-communist he was anti-everything. It is very complicated, the majority of the middle classes are anti-Russian that is to say anti-communist so they are anti-Anglo-American because they are allies of Russia, they hate the Germans but they admire them because they are so disciplined and the French are not, nobody in France wants to be disciplined but they cannot help admiring anybody who is and the Germans certainly are, and then there is always the real feeling that in spite of the German being so disciplined and so powerful you can always get rid of them but can you get rid of Russians and Anglo-Americans. In the small towns like this we live in the mutual hatreds of course are much stronger than in the big cities where they do not see each other every day, and they get so bitter that is the anti-Germans that they say to the pro-Germans I wish nothing more than that your son or your husband or your brother should disappear in that Germany you love so, but I hate the Germans the other answers and I hate you and then they hate the maquis because after the maquis have been the Germans come and they shoot and burn and destroy and everybody hates everybody and everybody denounces everybody and then the maquis come and they carry off all the property and sometimes the men themselves who have been militiamen and then everybody gets excited and sometimes they get more fanatical and anyway now that Henriot is dead who heated them up all the time to hate each other and the allies are so undoubtedly winning well there are a good many who are changing opinions, they are quite a few that are keeping still and they are quite a few who are manufacturing American and English and French flags for the day of victory and this is the fourteenth of July, and all the farmers are getting ready to join up with the French army and in a little while they will be so busy eating and drinking and discussing politics that they will all be French together. But there have been moments there most certainly have.

To-day is the fourteenth of July, in Belley they made a beautiful V for victory in flowers and they made American and English and French flags and they were up all day, and even at Cezerieu six kilometers from here they did too but here nothing could be done because we still have over a hundred German soldiers, but we all went visiting and told each other how soon how very soon we expected to be free, and we do expect it.

To-day it was a shock when it was announced that the Japanese had executed the American airmen prisoners, one does hear so many awful things that I do not know why that should have been so shocking but it was and there is no doubt about it one's country is one's country and that kind of harm seems to be so far away from our country. It is queer the world is so small and so knocked about. To-night we expected to have Germans come into the house again but they did not, they came in and out and about and they are exactly like an ants nest if you put a foreign substance in it, the Germans run around just like that. The only thing that is human about them is that they like to eat pork, that is the only human thing about them.

That was yesterday.

I was sitting with the wife of the mayor and in front of us was the main road from everywhere to Culoz. There were quite a few motor cycles rushing up and down with German soldiers and then there was a lull and then there came along hundreds of German soldiers walking, it was a terribly hot day and in the mountains heat is even hotter than below, and these soldiers were children none older than sixteen and some looking not more than fourteen, as they came and I have never seen anything like it since I saw the last lap of the walking marathon in Chicago. Our friend Elena Genin who lives near Belley and who is a Mexican, told us that she had seen the German troops going into Belley and she said I said to Joan, her daughter, this is not a German army this is a Mexican army when I was a little girl, and I did not quite understand but now I understand, these childish faces and the worn bodies and the tired feet and the shoulders of aged men and an occasional mule carrying a gun heavier than the boys could carry and then covered wagons like those that crossed the plains only in small and country wagons with a covering over them and later we were told in them were the sick and wounded, and they were being dragged by mules, it was unbelievable, and about a hundred of them more on women's bicycles that they had evidently taken as they went along, it was unbelievable, the motorised army of Germany of 1940 being reduced to this, to an old fashioned Mexican army, it seemed to be more ancient than pictures of the moving army of the the American civil war. I suppose said Madame Ray the wife of the mayor that they choose them young like that, because children can set fire to homes and burn and destroy without knowing what they are doing, while grown men even the worst of them draw the line somewhere. It was a sorry sight in every way they had been in the mountains to fight the mountain boys who of course got away from them and killed and wounded quite a few of them and so they revenged themselves upon the civil population who were unarmed shooting them and burning their houses and driving away their cattle, they had cows and calves with them dangling along on a string, it was absolutely unbelievable that in July 1944 that the German army could look like that, it was unbelievable, one could not believe one's eyes, and then I came home having put my dog on the leash and when I got home there were about a hundred of these Germans in the garden in the house all over the place, poor Basket the dog was so horrified that he could not even bark, I took him up to my bedroom and he just sat and shivered he did not believe it could be true. They left the next morning and Basket has hardly barked since and I heard to-day that they shot a dog of one of the homes in the village because they said he barked, a big black dog that its owner adored, perhaps Basket will never bark again, I am trying to induce him to bark again, it is not right that a dog should be silent.

The German troops are pretty well out of all this region, the trains are stopped by the French the roads defended by the French as always somewhere in their length they go through gorges and now the only Germans left in the region are the sixty odd here in the town of Culoz in which we are living, the railway was still open between here and Chambery but yesterday it was cut, and to-day the Germans killed their last three pigs and their cow so everybody thinks that they will leave too, they are getting so polite, one woman told me that a German soldier came to her to buy a chicken, she said she could not sell because her husband was not home, but he said you know German soldiers love the French, oh yes said the woman, and said he all French people like German soldiers, oh yes said the woman and then he went away, they know they are caught in a trap and cannot get away, so when they are not demanding something they are very cajoling, the French population are naturally disgusted, the French took their defeat with their heads held well up, and they thought the Germans were strong but now when they behave like that in defeat, they are disgusted. In the last war they were out of the country before they were defeated so the French have never seen them abject in defeat as they are now, and the French the few French who really admired them when they were strong now have nothing to say for them, French people do not like people who are abject in defeat, no they do not.

As for food we are pretty well off, as alas no food goes to the big cities and the Germans are not here to take it away, and so everything that is here, remains and so we have plenty of everything except fruit, this is not a fruit country, and once or twice trucks have gone to Lyon to get fruit and now the last truck has been captured by the mountain boys and the Germans have taken the others so we have no fruit, but as we have lots of butter cheese meat fish vegetables and potatoes and now bread we cannot be said to be suffering, not much sugar but plenty of honey.

Day before yesterday we were told that the Germans we had here were all leaving, then we were told at any rate we knew that they had had butchered their three remaining pigs and their cow and their goats. That was true, and then we were told that they were leaving and actually I did see them along the road with all their cars and a mitrailleuse set up and pointing down the road, the little boys in the villages all play at that, they make their guns out of wood and very lifelike they are and they set them up on the road, I suppose some of the guns I see are what they called tommy guns in gangster stories, there seem to be quite a variety of them, anyway the hundred odd soldiers that were in the village did leave to-day leaving behind some German railroad workers and station masters. They went to say good-bye to the mayor and his wife, the mayor and his wife told me to-day, the interpreter and the captain, made some polite remarks to them and the interpreter and the captain both saying that they expected to come back to Culoz a few months after the war was over, extraordinary people they think that although they are defeated they can come back as tourists as they like, the interpreter went on to say that he supposed the war would be over by the first of September, the only thing he said necessary to do now is to kill two men. We did not know the two he meant did he mean Hitler and Mussolini, or did he mean Churchill and Roosevelt, naturally we did not ask him, in the meantime, the village was much troubled because the soldiers had told them that they were going away but that they were going to be succeeded by really bad men killers, and indeed those who had been here had been quiet and peaceful enough, and with this village on the border of the maquis land it was terribly upsetting it makes everybody feel kind of queer. Naturally enough. This enemy the new lot has not come yet but there has been a rumor that the last lot were killed before they got far, but that is very likely not so. Anyway, after the other soldiers left when I was walking up the road where they had been, I found paper covers, they had covers of German tobacco and French candles and then there was this. Half pound weight Swifts yellow American farmers cheese, distributed by Bright and Company Chicago Ill. and underneath it it said, buy war bonds and stamps regularly and then it said a natural source of vitamins and riboflavin, now what that is naturally we do not know, it seems to have come on since we knew about what they needed to have in America, but where oh where did the German army get this cheese, and it is a far cry to have them leave it here in our garden, I suppose they stole it from Red Cross supplies, what else well anyway.

And now it is coming on to the end of July and things are very mixed up, just at present there are no Germans in Culoz except a few at the station but they say there are a thousand of them just across the river, are they, we do not know but everybody says so and it is a little puzzling just a little, and in the meantime the maquis are moving around the country requisitioning cars bicycles and trucks and between the Germans and the maquis everybody is scared, over at Belley they have been carrying on very livelily there are no Germans there but there are real and false maquis and everybody is frightened, quite a bit, and of course what is the worst is that the maquis come into a village have a clash with the Germans then go back to their mountains and the Germans burn and kill the village and so everybody is frightened when they see the maquis and they are frightened when they see the Germans, in the back country just now everybody is frightened, and with cause, they are no longer frightened of bombardments, because as no trains go there is no use in bombarding, there is no doubt about it, there is always plenty to scare one, to scare every one. In the meantime the mayor is trying to find flour for bread, but naturally the trucks that are to bring it never get here, that is natural enough and in the meantime everybody in the country is ready to sell you flour, it is very confusing, very.

And just now the banker has told us that the department of the Ain that is ours and the two Savoys are going to be almost at once evacuated by the Germans, and he usually knows, in fact now that the communications are cut here to Italy to Lyon to the north and to Grenoble there really does not seem any point in keeping a lot of German troops here when they seem to need them so badly elsewhere, except of course it will give a chance for the French army of the interior to organise itself. Well we must be patient. So we all tell each other.

Our two chickens are laying two eggs a day, which is a pleasure to all concerned, the two baby chickens particularly the cock is growing apace, he is weighed every day and the cook says he is destined for the first dinner party of the first American general who comes this way. To-day I took a long walk and going through a village a woman asked me to come in as she wanted to ask me a question. When I got in she showed me a package, she said her husband had just found it in a field what was it. It was a package of malted milk tablets and I told her and she said is it good and I said yes for children have you some and she said yes she had two, well I said eat one yourself and if it is good give it to them it will do them good, I suggested that she try it first, because I thought it might be something bad that the Germans had put out to discourage the people with gifts from America, but she said, you know so many strange things happen now, yes I will try it. It was strange I walked for several hours over all the roads where one always used to meet Germans and there were none, none at all, not one, they are across the river and just now ten o'clock in the evening we and the dog Basket II jumped because there were two big explosions probably blowing up more bridges. There is another funny thing.

The Germans are not paying any more. They used to hire men in town to watch the railroad cars, the empties and they used to pay the men for this, and now the last few months they have not paid, they do not pay any more, they used to be very regular about paying, for lodgings for breakages for everything and now they do not. Is it that they want to keep what French money they have, the German authorities, is it that the French government is not paying them any more, or is it that they know now that they are not going to continue to possess France and so why pay any one since they are going away.

It is different, last night, we noticed it the most, we kept our shutters open as long as we liked and then later I went out with Basket and I called him all these days I could not go out in the garden after ten at night and I could not call Basket because naturally one did not want to attract attention to oneself, and then later about at midnight I heard a man going down the street whistling, what a sense of freedom to hear some one at midnight go down the street whistling. It is a weight off, the weight is not all off because they are still there across the river and they might come back the Germans might come back but with all the allied victories going on it is not very likely, no not very likely, about eleven o'clock last night there was a loud explosion and this afternoon there was cannonading, all across the river, where there still are a couple of hundred Germans.

To-day the banker from Belley who comes here once a week to do business gave me a copy of a photograph of the monument for the soldiers fallen in 1914-1918 the flags of America and England were made by the young girls of the town and on the 14th of July 1944 they decorated it and the people made a pilgrimage to it all day long and in spite of Germans and police it stayed there till noon.

Everybody is much excited now what between Germans and maquis, or maquisans as they call what is known as the false maquis. There is naturally a certain amount of lawlessness there are bands who steal, under the name of maquis and now the forces

of the interior that is the regular maquis are beginning to police
the country in order to keep order but even they requisition what
they need, cars, bicycles, motor bicycles, tires, and there are of
course exaggerated stories, to be sure anybody connected with the
militia fares badly, and the girls who mixed up with the Germans
fare badly, as badly as is told this we do not know, and then the
German soldiers are escaping from the discipline of the army and
they come along to get bread and provision to which they are
entitled, but as the mayor says as each lot point a tommy gun at you
you naturally give them what they want, in the meantime every day
the airplanes come not to bombard but to provision the forces of
the interior and we are all expecting a considerable battle now in
this region, they say to take the airpark at Amberieu. People turn
up from Paris who have bicycled down, they say the morale is good
but food completely lacking, if they cannot find a bicycle they walk
but French people have to move around they just cannot stay put,
the roads are always full of every kind of progression.

As I was walking along this afternoon I talked to an old man
and he said there were a lot of airplanes this afternoon and they
were all American taking material to the maquis, and they tell us
to stay in the houses but not at all we were all out with spy glasses
looking for the stars and stripes, yes said he reflectively leaning on
his farming implement and I leaning on my cane, yes he said, we
depend on America to pick us up out of our troubles, we have
always been friends we helped them when they needed us and they
helped us when we needed them, the English are all right but it is
America that we count on to take care of us to see we keep our
colonies, to be sure they will want naval stations and of course we
will be pleased to have them have them. The only thing that worries us is that our towns which have been bombarded will they
help us to build them up, there is Chambery it was a nice town and
the people are such good republicans, yes said I and such ardent
patriots, yes he said, we always admire them the Savoyards are like
that and Chambery was their capital and now it is destroyed or at
least a good part of it, they should have hit the station but not the

town, I know I said but there are the unfortunate accidents of war, I know he said but he said the Americans should rebuild Chambery, and say they do and in a year or two it would be rebuilt by them and then when it is all ready and Mr. Roosevelt would be still living he would come over to see it and that would be nice. Perhaps he will I said and then we each went on our way.

To-day we were over in Belley the third of August, nineteen forty-four, and I looked anxiously to see a maquis. We still have Germans here so up to now we have had no maquis. But Belley which is maquis headquarters was unfortunately empty they had gone away to fight and I only saw one at a distance in an nice khaki suit, that is shirt and trousers, with a red cord over his shoulders so we came home satisfied we had seen a maquis, in Belley they asked us with some astonishment and do you still have Germans, we still have forty odd who are railroad men and guard the station but we were very apologetic about them, we are here in Culoz the only ones in the region who still have Germans, so naturally we are apologetic, and add they are railway workers who have nothing to do they are not soldiers. Things do happen quickly, three months ago Belley was a garrison for thousands of German soldiers and now there are none and the people of Belley talk as if they never had had any as if they only had had maquis, and we in Culoz still have them which is a disgrace.

They are funny the Germans, now when the Americans are chasing across Brittany and there is no air defence, they are flying airplanes over this back water here and bombing little villages, in an attempt to stop the maquis from receiving supplies from the parachutists but of course they do not hit either supplies or maquis only the poor little village, that has nothing to do with it, but why should they not use those airplanes where they certainly seem to need them more. I suppose it is because when the orders were given it was different and now communications being so interrupted they were not able to get new orders. Our Germans here are leaving a few at a time, now there are less than a hundred in the whole region, but the airplanes go over our heads and there is a sound of distant guns or blowing up of communications any day and every day and soon very soon they will all have gone away. And now this is a spy story, there is no answer to it, but it is a spy story.

When we had the couple of hundred Germans here, there was with them an interpreter a tall dark man who wore eye-glasses. One day he came here to arrange to have the German soldiers come here when there was an alerte. I was not here and he had a long conversation with Alice Toklas. He talked very good French without any definite accent. He said that as the lower gate was closed he had entered as a brigand over the wall, and could we give him a key to the gate. Alice Toklas said the mairie had one he could get it there, no he said he wanted one to have in his own pocket so she gave him one, and after a little gay conversation he went away. He never came back. We used to see him around the town but the soldiers never came here when there was an alerte and we never had the key back. When I came home Alice Toklas told me about the conversation and said she was puzzled, he was not like a German neither his manners, nor his French nor his looks, later on we were told in the village that he used to keep a hotel in Paris and that his wife was still there keeping it and that is the reason he spoke French so well even though he was only a simple soldier.

From time to time the mayor's wife mentioned him as asking for this or asking for that for the Germans and when German troops passed through the town they never had anything to do with those who were here permanently. Mrs. Mayor said that he was always polite and helpful the interpreter and did what he could to make everybody comfortable, and that he had allowed a taxi to help get some friends of theirs to their home, these friends had come down from Normandy just after the beginning of the fighting there. And then the Germans here left and the interpreter and the captain came to say good-bye to the mayor and his wife and the captain who could not talk much French just said a few words politely and the interpreter said, after all the war is going to be over soon it will only mean killing two men and then it is finished, and said he three months after the war I will come back here to call on you.

Then they went away and a few days after Madame the mayoress told me this story, that was only yesterday.

She said what was your impression of the interpreter and I told her what Alice Toklas said about him that he was not very German and seemed a gentleman which was strange as he was a common soldier. Yes she said it is strange he was a common soldier, and he took his turn at guard like any of them, I do not know whether he slept and ate with them but otherwise he acted like a common soldier, excepting when he was with the captain and then it was very evident that it was the interpreter who was in command, he did not go when he was sent for by the captain until it suited him and anyway there were thousands of little signs that showed that he was the superior in rank. I told you she said about how he arranged for a taxi for our friends who came from Normandy but I never told you what happened. I was with the husband and wife and children and mother at the mairie waiting for my husband to come in and he came with the interpreter, the husband looked startled when he saw the interpreter and the interpreter hesitated a moment and then came in, ah said my friend I am not mistaken we have met in Normandy, oh yes said the interpreter and you were Doctor Fisch and were in command, oh yes said the interpreter and said my friend it was I who succeeded in arranging about your having chocolate, from the chocolate factory there, oh yes said the interpreter politely and there the conversation ended, and the interpreter went and got a taxi for them and I have never seen them again.

The interpreter came to see us on business very often but after this he always stayed and talked, he never referred to the conversation but he became more intimate. He once said that he knew who the members of the maquis in the town were and the captain had wanted to seize them but said the interpreter he would not allow it they are the kind of men I admire patriots and fathers of families. Then one day he asked the mayor if he would do him a personal favor, the mayor said yes of course, he said he would like him in his capacity of mayor to write to two towns in Normandy and ask for information about a certain lady, he said she is my wife, she is a Frenchwoman and she is my wife that is to say we are not married but she is my wife. The mayor did so and as yet had no answer. When the interpreter with the other Germans left he said to the mayor if you should ever get an answer, give it to the German station master and I will get it. Naturally enough there has been no answer. He also mentioned several times that he was a Luxembourgeois, he also said that he had bred and trained horses for the race track in Paris, he never said anything to them about a hotel in Paris, and as I say when he left he said he was coming back three months after the war, and he said there need only to be two killed to put an end to the war.

After the wife of the mayor was all through telling me the story, she said you know I think he was an Englishman, sometimes his French reminded me of yours, it seemed to be you speaking, but of course we will never know, and this is a true story.

There was a young woman in a village near here and of course we were all of us very envious and she had made herself a blouse out of parachute cloth that had been sent down with supplies, now we all want parachute cloth, I would love to have a shirt waist made of parachute cloth from an American airplane, a friend of ours told us that the other day he was out on his bicycle and he was stopped by the maquis who patrol all the roads that the Germans do not patrol. These boys were in a truck and they had an American flag on it, and they said we are not like the other maquis, we are American maquis, and under the direct orders of General Eisenhower, you see even in these days the French have to get gay.

It is very funny really funny, when the mayor went to Bourg to try and get some flour for bread, in order to have the truck of flour pass first you have to get permission for it to come from the Germans and then you get permission for it to pass from the maquis, we all laughed and said the only people who do not have to give permission are the people of Vichy, the prefet and sous-prefet have all fled, there is nobody left except the mayors the maquis and the Germans, it is really very funny, the mayor on his way to Bourg saw the armored train that we had seen at Culoz lying peacefully in a mountain stream at the side of the rails, naturally it never did get to Lyon.

It is wonderful the Americans just chasing around France, everybody used to say, if they only would hurry if they only would hurry, but now they all laugh and they all say but they are hurrying you bet your life they are hurrying up. And Saint Odile, she did say that when Rome fell it would not be the end but the beginning of the end and then she said that the Mohammedan sickle moon and the Christian cross would shine together in peace and look at Turkey, well well, as the Englishman who does the propaganda in English from Berlin always says, well well.

It is nice that the forces of the interior the French are helping things along so well, it makes all the French people content that they are taking part and everybody is happy and gay.

When bread is the staff of life then we eat bread and butter yes we do eat bread and butter.

I remember when I was young and in a book we had with illustrations there was one where the Goths and the Vandals threw around and broke all the works of art in Italy, and I remember being terribly worried about all this destruction and then one day when I felt very worried about it all about the destruction of even more ancient monuments in buried cities I suddenly said to myself well after all there are miles more of works of art that even people who are really interested in them can see in their life time so why worry. But now with Florence being destroyed and Normandy and marching on Paris they are near Chartres to-day the Americans and it does kind of make one feel funny really feel funny it seemed endless this occupation of France and now there they are the American tanks near Chartres, dear me oh dear me it does make one feel funny.

Here we are so excited and rather querulous with waiting except that our minds are pretty well taken off our troubles by our

own local excitements, we still have our fifty odd Germans in the
region but they are frightened and they stay where they are they
were in a village near by to buy some wine and the maquis heard
they were there and they came along and shot dead an officer and
two soldiers and now well naturally the village is frightened the
maquis go away but the Germans well they are afraid to come back
but now they have an evil habit of sending over five or six airplanes
from Amberieu near Bourg and they drop bombs on a village,
three days ago they did this completely wiping out a village and
killing most of the population and almost every day these six odd
German airplanes come over our heads, and what will they do, this
we do not know, but something horrible that is certain.

Besides all this and which is really most exciting are the Robin
Hood activities of the maquis. Night before last they came into the
town, and they visited three of the principal shops whose owners
aided and abetted the Germans and from one they took his car and
fifty thousand francs from another they took all his hidden provisions quantities of macaroni and oil and twenty-five thousand
francs and now all the rest who have either profited or been for the
Germans are naturally most nervous. The maquis are using this
money to help the villagers whose homes have been burnt by the
Germans. They say the friends of the Germans should pay for the
victims of the Germans. And then there are the shop keepers who
are on the border land between friend and enemy and they are
frightened, and then there are the type of old grumblers who
always find everything the young generation do frightful and
naturally they have talked too much against the maquis and they
are worried and then there are the decayed aristocrats, who are
always hoping that a new regime will give them a chance and they
are the most furious of all against the defeat of the Germans they
and the decayed bourgeoisie, who feel sure that everybody but
themselves should be disciplined, I had a row with one of them on
the street last night and my parting word in a loud voice was that
she should be more charitable, using it in the American sense of
charitable in thought, and the whole population laughed because

she is notoriously not in deed, and everybody thought naturally I
meant that but of course I did not. Then there is a very funny
thing about the church bigots, they are all for the Germans, the
clergy in general in France not, distinctly not, but all the old men
and women who are known in France as the frogs in holy water or
the mice of the sacristy they strangely enough considering how the
Germans have treated the catholics in Germany are all for the
Germans. It is like in the last war all the pacifists were for Germany. I used not to understand but I am beginning to now. The
feeling is that all that makes for liberty and liveliness is against
those that either by weakness or by strength want to suppress the
others and so the Germans who are the Germans who are the arch-
disciplinarians because both of their weakness and their strength
they want to stop liberty so those others who want liberty suppressed because liberty is a criticism of them are pro-German.

It is funny really funny, the maquis have taken charge of Culoz,
they have put up notices under the heading of the fourth republic
telling the population what to do and all the time there are twenty-
five German soldiers at the station as frightened as rabbits, they
stay out only long enough to buy their provisions and retire back
to their station, across the river there are still fifty to two hundred
but nobody does seem to pay any attention, the maquis do not even
take the trouble to gather them in, but they will so they say and
put them to work. I like their calling it the fourth republic, the
French dearly love a new form of government, they do love a
change, they might have thought that the third republic was just
going on but not at all there was an in between, the dictatorship or
the oligarchy of Vichy so you just could not have it the third
republic it has to be a fourth republic. There have been so many
these last hundred and forty years, I think I have counted them
once already in this book, three different varieties of monarchy,
two empires three republics, one commune one oligarchy and dictatorship, and now here we are at a fourth republic and everybody
is pleased. It makes them feel gay and cheerful. The German captain who left with the hundred and fifty soldiers was driven to

Lyon by one of the taxis from Culoz, the taxi man came back and he said the German captain cried when he said good-bye, he said he had been so happy in Culoz and had hoped to once more see his wife and children but now he was ordered to Normandy and of course he cried and expected the French chauffeur to sympathise with him. They certainly are a funny people they certainly are.

Alice Toklas has just commenced typewriting this book, as long as there were Germans around we left it in manuscript as my handwriting is so bad it was not likely that any German would be able to read it, but now well if they are not gone they are so to speak not here, we can leave our windows open and the light burning, dear me such little things but they do amount to a lot, and it is so. They have left Florence, that is something to the good and everybody cheers up, they are now expecting it to be all over by the fifteenth of August. The French like to set a date it cheers them, but it does seem rather soon, they all also say that in this region there is an English colonel and fifteen Canadian officers, but are they, sometimes we believe it and sometimes we do not. If they are here it would be nice to see them.

There are the Germans still here some forty odd but we never see them in the village the way we used to, why not, I asked the mayor, he twinkled he said they sleep all day, because they mount guard all night, they are afraid I said like rabbits he said. Everybody is so pleased that the overbearing Germans are afraid like rabbits, everybody is pleased.

Even though the Germans are still here the maquis have taken over the victualing of our town as they have done in all the region, they are distributing lots more butter and cheese than there was. They take all that was being prepared in the dairies for the Germans. Look said the cook excitedly, it is butter done up in tinfoil, oh it was prepared for those dirty Boches for the evil birds and now we have it come quick Madame and taste it. She is keeping the tinfoil as a sacred souvenir, the first spoil from the enemy. Ah she said they made us cry since forty and now they cry. Naturally it is difficult to get medicines, even the Germans have not much of that so

the maquis cannot take it from them so everybody is going back to
old herb remedies. The old people are always being consulted to
remember what they did when they were young, for bruises you use
wild verbena pounded and for disinfecting and reducing swelling
application of the petals of the Easter lily preserved in eau de vie
and foot baths of boiled ivy.

Just how I do not know but the French workers in Germany
commence to come back. How they get away they do not say but in
the last few days three of them have come back. And they describe
Germany as she is.

And just to-day we are most awfully excited because the allies
have just made a landing in the south of France and we will be on
their way up and it is most exciting. One woman just told me that
she had two spare rooms and although it was Assumption and a
holiday she was immediately starting to fix them up for the first
American soldiers, and the whole population wants to learn English and quickly.

As I was saying some forced workers in Germany have made
their way back, you never do know how the French do it but they
always keep wandering back and apparently without very much
difficulty, they decide that they want to come home and they come.

As I say their descriptions of Germany are funny. They say the
civilian population still stupidly believes in victory, they have not
changed but that the army is completely discouraged, and besides
they are comforting themselves by shooting their officers, it would
seem that Hitler has ordered that any soldier should shoot any
officer or soldier whom he heard talking against the government,
and say the French naturally any soldier who has a grievance has
nothing to do but shoot up the man against whom he has it and
say it was because he spoke against the government and then instead of being punished he is congratulated. And moreover the
German army is beginning to mutiny, so these French boys say, but
as long as the civilians still believe in victory Germany will not
give in. The thing that fills all the French in Germany with horror
is the way the Germans treat the Russians, women as well as men,

the Germans fear them so that they go quite crazy with brutality, that is the French explanation of the situation.

All this reminds me that one day in Paris, we had a lot of people for dinner it was about '35 and they were talking Nazi and Hitler and I said it was Hitler's intention to destroy Germany, and that was because he was an Austrian and an Austrian in his heart has a hatred of Germany so great even if unconscious that if he could he would destroy Germany and Hitler can and will. They all thought that I was only trying to be bright but not at all it is true, if Hitler had been a German he could not destroy Germans the way he does, it is like Napoleon who was an Italian and naturally was indifferent as to how many Frenchmen were killed. It is the judgment of Solomon over again, there is the call of the blood, but funnily enough the foreign monster has a glamor for the nation he is destroying that a home grown monster could not have. And so Hitler is quite comfortably waiting for the last battalion to fight and win or be killed, presumably killed but he has made them all feel like that because he is a foreigner and not a German, it is the other way to of a prophet not being recognised in his own country.

Oh well these days nobody minds death from fear of heaven or hell but there is there always is with death the cessation of life and life is interesting, and certainly it is for Hitler so why stop.

The little groups of Germans all over are still all over, ours just left yesterday, they were as inoffensive as Germans can be, but then they were really not soldiers they were mostly railroad workers and the few soldiers they had with them as guards were rather miserable specimens victims of Russian rheumatism, as they call it, and now they are gone to join up with the others across the river and the five hundred at Aix-les-Bains left to go away, but to the distress of the Aix population they have come back, the maquis have cut off all the means of communication and they are back again. The maquis say they are going to mop them up and I suppose they will. We see the maquis now, they have big trucks and all camouflaged, I saw one like that to-day the first one at a little town where I occasionally buy cake, and when I saw that truck I had a shock,

have the Germans come back but no there was a little tricolor
cheerfully waving from the front, and everywhere the cross of
Lorraine and the tricolor painted, and it was all gay and cheerful
not German at all. I heard to-day that Captain Bouvet is the chief
of this region, he was a nice man, he and I in the darkest days of
the war used to have long conversations on the cold winter days
between Belley and Billignin, being cheered by the battle of London being cheered by the Russian entrance being cheered by being
cheerful, and of course I did not know he was mixed up with the
maquis, until just before the Germans left Belley they tried to
catch him and his son-in-law but they managed to hide away not
too difficult there in the mountains, and the Germans did not get
them, he was a retired army officer who had specialised in the
chemical side of explosives so naturally he has been wonderful in
stopping all railroads and destroying bridges, and now everybody
can know that he is he and it is a pleasure.

But really you can understand how the Germans could never
have had colonies, when you see these isolated pieces of the German army get to be like hunted rabbits as soon as they are not
winning, they are always frightened even when they are winning
the most and you really had to be in a country occupied by them to
realise it and if you are always about to be frightened you naturally
cannot impose yourself upon primitive races. Unless there were a
lot of Germans about they never moved without a gun on their
back and that was before there were maquis. And this is undoubtedly true, how could they ever be a dominant race, just how could
they. Everybody is so cheerful now, they are all making their little
flags for the allies everybody the farmers even in the midst of the
harvest, the wives are taking time to make flags. Very nice, oh so
very nice, we can have our windows open, and everybody is cheerful. The poor people of Aix-les-Bains with their five hundred
Germans back again, it is too bad, but it is better and the Aixois
know that, that they were unable to get away, even if they have
for a little while to have them back again. All the men young and
old want to be in it they are all for being up and at them, they are

very envious of those who already joined up are in it, and the French troops landed in the south and now oh how they all want to be with them.

This morning just before dawn we were all awakened by the rattle of tommy guns and magazine rifles, but they did not last, it seems that the two forces of the maquis did not connect and so the coup did not come off, but all through the Savoy the Germans are giving themselves up and those across the river said that they would like to perhaps they will and then we can be peaceful with the maquis until the Americans come, then that will finish the book the first American tank and surely it will be coming along, one week or two weeks the pessimists say three weeks nobody expects it to take a month, and they are thirty kilometers from Paris it is an anxious moment, dear Paris, we saw it escape the Germans in fourteen and now forty-four.

To-day we were for the first time in company with a real live maquis, we were in a taxi and he came along to go to Culoz, and we were delighted, he had the tricolor on his shoulder and looked bronzed and capable, we are Americans we said, yes we know he said, and we solemnly shook hands and congratulated each other, he was a captain in the maquis, and he had been a prisoner in Germany, had escaped two years ago and went back to his job in the water-ways and bridges and joined the maquis and has been working with them ever since, we were all pleased, but everybody is pleased these days, one can hardly realise how strange it seems to see everybody smiling and everybody is smiling.

The maquis were pretty wonderful of course now they are armed and more or less superior in numbers to the Germans they attack and besides they are sure of victory but when they first began to block the German transport system, they were practically unarmed, they were inferior in numbers, they were often betrayed by their compatriots and still they managed to cut railroad lines block tunnels blow up bridges, and besides all their other troubles they had to receive the material sent them by airplane and get away with it and hide and manufacture it and use it all in the face of a heavily occupied country with enemy guards all along, and the poor maquis many of them hungry and cold and not too favorably regarded by many of their countrymen, it was a kind of a Valley Forge with no General Washington but each little band had to supply itself with its own food its own plans and its own morale. We who lived in the midst of you salute you.

While I was walking yesterday evening as I passed through a village little voices came out of the dark saying are not you afraid of the curfew Madame.

On the other hand the little boys who have been playing at being maquis in odd corners and in secret now play it in the open streets, with red white and blue on their shoulders their fathers' war helmets on their heads and their wooden mitraillettes in their hands, when some one asked them what would you do if the Germans came back. No Germans can come back.

Everybody is waiting, they say it goes so fast it makes them feel as if they were at a cinema. They have completely forgotten that they used to moan and say if they would only hurry. And besides they are so very much better fed, not in the big cities alas, but here in the small towns, the maquis, are doing all the policing, they have announced formally that the Vichy government does not any longer function and that they are the government, and with the assistance of the mayor they are going to feed and police the population. Already we have had supplementary butter wine and cheese, and now they are here the people are talking wildly of supplementary white bread and sardines but that is decidedly premature, anyway the maquis are now in command it puts its notices up on the mairie it sends the town crier around with his trumpet to announce what we are all to do and everybody is pleased because it is French and easy, and conversational and all who want can gather together and talk it over. I was coming up the street I heard a man saying yes before the war of fourteen, well yes they can go back to talk about before the war of fourteen it has come now the middle of August to be as peaceable as that.

It is nice to be free my gracious yes and now we have had our

little battle and it was this way. The Germans had left Culoz and
they had all gathered together across the river at Vions there were
then between two hundred and three hundred of them. About a
week ago the maquis decided to take the bridge away from them
and get them on the move but there was some difficulty about the
signals, they all have to come down from their mountains and
there was some mistake. Two Germans were killed on the bridge
but they were still there. Yesterday in broad daylight they got a
gun up on the hill and attacked the bridge, they first had to warn
away the little boys who were bathing in the pools of the Rhone
and two women who came along after were wounded a little bit,
and then the maquis rushed the bridge and it was most exciting, six
maquis attacked eight Germans killed two and the others ran away,
in the meantime eight German airplanes came along from Lyon
but they did not help their comrades in distress they just went on
their way to Germany and we have not been seen again. Just a little
while and the Germans got away as fast as they could. The maquis
put the flag on the bridge and sent round to the mayor to tell the
town crier that the bridge was in the hands of the maquis and
nobody should cross it, then came the night, the maquis gathered
from all sides attacked the fleeing Germans and killed anywhere
from fifty to eighty of them in the marshes, the nephew of our
baker killed five and the butcher boy killed four, the Germans were
trying to escape toward Aix-les-Bains, but there others of the
maquis pushed them back and it became a regular rabbit drive,
the weather was hot and the Germans were in a bad way there in
the marshes, some tried to surrender but others of the group fired
and the maquis killed them all, every one, and then they came
back, and everybody was happy and they said everybody must put
up flags so we all rushed around trying to get flags, and our general
store who had been a well-known collabo unearthed from his stores
a quantity of French, English and American flags we got one nice
one and in the meantime the maquis had given the mayor a nice
big American flag and it and the French flag were hung up in
front of the mairie and we were very moved and Mrs. Mayor was

teaching all the children to salute the flag to say vive la France et honneur aux maquis. It is rather wonderful when you think that a quantity of little children had never seen a flag never, the Germans never had flags and of course there were no French ones allowed, and the little children go up and touch it timidly, they never have seen a flag. What a town everybody is out on the streets all the time, and in between time they sing the Marseillaise, everybody feels so easy, it is impossible to make anybody realise what occupation by Germans is who has not had it, here in Culoz it was as easy as it was possible for it to be as most of the population are railroad employees and the Germans did not want to irritate them, but it was like a suffocating cloud under which you could not breathe right, we had lots of food, and no interference on the part of the Germans but there it was a weight that was always there and now everybody feels natural, they feel good and they feel bad but they feel natural, and that was our battle, the maquis are all down there at the bridge they do not think the Germans can come back, but they are watchful, there was firing just now but it did not last, so it was probably a false alarm, we like the maquis, honneur aux maquis.

They say that six of the wounded and killed Germans escaped into the mountain and they look for them from time to time but as they have not found them they take it for granted that they are dead and gone. It is wonderful to pass the railroad station and see the block house that the Germans had built to defend themselves already gone the barbed wire already gone and the children playing around where the Boches had so solemnly been standing with their guns all ready to shoot any one. The employees of the railroad are very busy, they are getting everything ready so that the railroad track can be all mended and that trains will be able to go as soon as France is free, well it is free but not completely free, in Lyons and Chambery the two chief towns the maquis are still fighting the Germans, but soon yes soon now we can say soon.

Everybody is so pleased with the maquis taking Vichy, it is a good joke une bonne blague à la Française, no it was not an allied army but the maquis who took Vichy, everybody is so pleased with the joke that they have pretty well forgotten their rancor against the government, the French certainly are sans rancune, they cannot remember their hatreds very long it is at once their weakness and their strength, but it is nice, a good joke like the maquis taking Vichy and all the government running away makes everybody gay. It is hot and dry most awfully hot and dry but as everybody knows it is good for the fighting armies to have dry weather they put up with it contentedly, even if the vegetables are drying up, tant pis they say, what of it, if we are free. And now there is more distribution of wine and butter and cheese, so why worry.

And now they have just announced on the radio that the Americans are at Grenoble and that is only eighty kilometers away and no opposition in between, oh if they would only come by here. We must see them. There is no way of getting there.

And now at half past twelve to-day on the radio a voice said attention attention attention and the Frenchman's voice cracked with excitement and he said Paris is free. Glory hallelujah Paris is free, imagine it less than three months since the landing and Paris is free. All these days I did not dare to mention the prediction of Saint Odile, she said Paris would not be burned the devotion of her people would save Paris and it has vive la France. I cant tell you how excited we all are and now if I can only see the Americans come to Culoz I think all this about war will be finished yes I do.

To-night it was just like fourth of July in my youth in the San Joaquin valley, it was just as hot and we all went to-day that Paris was freed to put flowers on the soldiers monument, it had already been draped with flags and the maquis marched down the main street of Culoz, and then everybody stood at attention and sang the Marseillaise, it was interesting to see who out of the population of Culoz were members of the fighting maquis, and then there were another lot of affiliated but not fighting maquis. I like to call them maquis, that was what they were, when every moment was a danger, they had to receive arms they had to transport them and they had to hide them and they had to do sabotage and all the time a very

considerable part of their countrymen did not at all believe in
them, and there they were workmen, station masters, civil servants,
tailors, barbers, anything, nobody knew but they naturally, and
some of them looked pretty tired but my everybody was happy,
everybody had the flag on their shoulders and some of the girls
heaven only knows how had achieved a whole dress made of tricolor ribbons sewn together, Paris was taken at noon and by eight
o'clock all France was putting wreaths on their soldiers monument
because of course every village has that, honneur aux maquis, and
they say that Americans are at Aix-les-Bains only twenty-five kilometers away how we want to see them even a little more than the
rest of the population which is saying a great deal. We found some
American flag ribbon in the local country store, and we gave it to
all the little boys, just as we did in the 1914-1918 war when
America came into the war, we rather wondered whether it was
not some left over of the same ribbon, after all there was no particular reason in this little village that the local country store
should otherwise have had it, vive la France vive l'Amerique vive
les allies vive Paris, and after this most exciting day. Oh I forgot, I
naturally wanted my dog Basket to participate and so I took him
down to the local barber and I said wont you shave him and make
him elegant, it is not right when the Americans come along and
when Paris is free that the only French poodle in Culoz and owned
by Americans should not be elegant, so perspiring freely all of us
including Basket, he had his paws shaved and his muzzle shaved
and he was elegant and as such he took part in the evening's celebration and all the little children, said Basket Basket come here
Basket, they do say it beautifully and then there was a blare of
trumpets and naturally he was frightened and tried to run away,
so I tied him with a handkerchief and the effort was not so elegant
but we were all proud of ourselves just the same.

We are all exhausted to-day the next day, we were so excited we
are so happy we are all exhausted, we just go around shaking hands
and being exhausted.

And that is the way it is after all of us being so happy yesterday, to-day they are once more fighting in the streets of Paris, dear Paris and dear dear Paris, but Saint Odile did say it would be all right and although worried well anyway to distract our minds just now while I was in my bath, bang and the house shook I got out of my bath and another big bang, and the house shook, and there down in the valley were volumes of smoke, they were trying to hit the bridges over the Rhone, the cook was screaming and the people flocking into the grounds, and we could see the railroad bridge and it seemed to be intact, but the maquis who were guarding it, well now everybody says nobody was hurt, and it was the Boches flying home because they could not any longer stay in France in venge-ance dropped bombs, we saw two lots of airplanes in the air and now they are gone I was afraid they were Americans dropping bombs but nobody believes anything bad of Americans, and per-haps not, anyway we are not as happy as yesterday but to-day is to-day and that is all there is to say.

And now to-day that Paris is really free, this is what Saint Odile did say.

Saint Odile said that the world would go on and there would come the worst war of all and the fire would be thrown down from the heavens and there would be freezing and heating and rivers running with blood and at last there would be winning by the enemy and everybody would say and how can they be so strong, and everybody would say and give us peace and then little by little there would come the battle of the mountain and that was certainly Moscow, because even in the time of Saint Odile because of its many religious houses was called the Holy Mountain and indeed it was there that the enemy received its first check, and then she said, much later there would be fighting in the streets of the eternal city, and Rome taken it was not the end but the beginning of the end (which indeed was so) and that Paris which was in the greatest danger would be saved because of the holiness of its holy women, Sainte Genevieve and now it has been saved owing to the valor of its men and its women and we are all so happy, honneur aux maquis.

It is wonderful to go down to the village square on Sunday evening and to see it full of maquis in their nice shorts and khaki shirts with the tricolor on their shoulders talking to the girls everybody smiling and only ten days ago everybody was staying in the house and the Germans were in the square, only ten days ago, what a week, and nobody is really used to it, and yet it is hard to believe that it was not always so, we have one hundred and fifty maquis stationed in our town and it is a pleasure.

Yesterday I was out on the road and there was a tremendous thunderstorm and I went into a roadside café, there were two men sitting at a table with F. F. I. on their breasts and I said how do you do and Basket and I were very wet, and they said how do you do but not quite like Frenchmen, we talked a little more and then I knew from their accent they were Spaniards, I said I was American and we solemnly shook hands and we began to talk, one of them was the typical Barcelona intellectual he reminded me of Picasso's friend Sabatez, he and his comrade with two hundred and fifty other Spanish refugees have been with the maquis for two years now, since said they we cannot fight for freedom in our own country we fight for freedom wherever we can, they have been at it for ten years now, they know about Hemingway and when I told them that I knew Picasso they stood up and solemnly shook hands, all over again. Then I asked where they had come from and they said Annecy and I said you must have seen my compatriots and they said yes and a woman journalist interviewed them and said to them what are you Spaniards doing here, and when they told her she said she was glad to meet them and that they were heroes. They were going to Artemare to see their wives who were refugeed there and then they were going back to Annecy. If said I you see the journalist again tell her that I want to see her, and I told them my name but they wont remember but anyway it was a pleasure to send word. It is very tantalising Americans all over the place sometimes only twenty kilometers away and we do not see them, how we want to see them and send word to America and have news from them. To-night I was all bitten by mosquitoes trying to get more news of them. I went down to the Pont de la Lois which is the only bridge left over the Rhone, it strangely enough was not destroyed in '40 and now again it has not been destroyed. It was near there that our little battle was fought and it was near there that the bombs were dropped the other day or was it only yesterday. Well anyway I was talking to the maquis that were guarding the bridge, among them a boy I knew in Cezerieu and they told me that a car with American officers had passed over the bridge, when I told Alice Toklas about it tonight she said she would take her typewriting down there and await them but when I told her about mosquitoes she weakened, well anyway, one of the train hands who was also there said that they had received orders to repair the train tracks between Chambery and Culoz and that it had to be done in three days, because he said the Americans want to use it and he promised me that when the first train carrying Americans was signaled, night or day, he would leave all and come up and let me know. Dear Americans how we do want to see them.

It's wonderful in the evening hearing the voices of the children playing, for such a long time they played quietly they were afraid to play in the streets or on the sidewalk but now they are let loose and the elders smile indulgently and all of a sudden you hear a childish voice cry pomm pomm pomm, pomm pomm pomm, pomm pomm pomm that's that, of course that is a mitraillette killing the Boches, everybody calls them Boches now, and everybody is easy very easy in their minds, except of course those who made money off the Germans, and there are some, and naturally they are nervous. The maquis of course do revenge themselves a little the French are not naturally a revengeful people but the Germans did commit such awful atrocities in the mountain regions that when the mountain boys caught the S.S. troops in Annecy naturally enough they made them parade the town with their hands in the air and then took them up into the hills and there nobody knows what did happen to them, and naturally the young ones who had seen farms burned with men women and children inside them as well as the beasts, when they take a German prisoner they cannot help giving him a kick in the behind. But the French are not a vengeful people and they will soon now that they feel their strength they will not feel revengeful.

Our friend Monsieur Godet came yesterday and said he was going to try to get through to Switzerland, he has business there, and so we are hoping that he will be able to cable to America for us and tell all our friends that we are all right, he left on his bicycle with a permit from the F. F. I. and once he gets to Saint Julien, the way we always used to drive into Switzerland, he thinks he will have no trouble. It will be nice when he comes back and brings us news of the Americans. We have asked him to bring back with him a newspaper man or a newspaper woman, or two of them, if he did that would be nice. There are American cars and officers that pass so they say from time to time but I have not seen them and of course seeing is believing, because with the population, the wish is so much the father of the thought, but they will come, bless them.

I met to-day Monsieur Burtin whose daughter is at the University of Grenoble and who kept telling him when he worried about her student activities but my dear father you do not understand, this is our war not your war, and now that the F. F. I. have covered themselves with glory she said to her father, you see we were right, to be sure people of your age are less credulous than people of our age, but this time we were right in persisting in our credulity, look at the results, they are magnificent said the father, yes said the daughter you can understand it was no work for veterans.

A little later I was talking to a young fellow who is now in Culoz but whom I had often seen in Belley where he was in the first battalion of Chasseurs before they were demobilised when the Southern zone no longer existed. I had not seen him since those days. So naturally I asked him if he had been in the movement. He said because of his health, his lungs are not very strong he had not been able to be but actually all his comrades in the battalion were in the movement, not the officers, he said, this was not an officers movement, regular army officers did not in general have the kind of intelligence that makes a maquis. No I said, all the army officers that I know who were patriots, all managed somehow to get to Africa and join the regular army, yes he said they did not have the kind of quality that makes maquis, the non-commissioned officers yes lots of them were in the movement, it was said he marvelously secret, you do not know perhaps he said that one of the leaders of the Paris F. F. I. was hidden for three months in Culoz, no I said did you know at the time, oh no he said, I knew his sister very intimately but she never mentioned it, how old is he, I said, oh about twenty-four and the Germans got on his track two of the crowd were taken by the Germans but the rest of the leaders escaped, and the two who were captured in spite of frightful tortures did not give their comrades away, after three months they heard that the Germans had lost trace of them so they all went back, and continued their work, now that it is all over his sister told me all about it. And where said I did all the arms come from that the Parisians seem to have had, oh he laughed most of those have been hidden since '40, not possibly I said, yes he said I do assure you. Well honneur aux maquis, one cannot say it too often, it is nice to have two countries to be proud of that belong to you, mine of course are America and France.

To-day the village is excited terribly excited because they are shaving the heads of the girls who kept company with the Germans during the occupation, it is called the coiffure of 1944, and naturally it is terrible because the shaving is done publicly, it is being done to-day. It is as I have often said, life in the middle ages, it certainly is most interesting and logical it certainly is.

Speaking of all this there is this about a Jewish woman, a Parisienne, well known in the Paris world. She and her family took refuge in Chambery when the persecutions against the Jews began in Paris. And then later, when there was no southern zone, all the Jews were supposed to have the fact put on their carte d'identité and their food card, she went to the prefecture to do so and the official whom she saw looked at her severely Madame he said, have you any proof with you that you are a Jewess, why no she said, well he said if you have no actual proof that you are a Jewess, why do you come and bother me, why she said I beg your pardon, no he said I am not interested unless you can prove you are a Jewess, good day he said and she left. It was she who told the story. Most of the French officials were like that really like that.

And now everybody says all the time that American officers are passing through Culoz, you can tell them they all say because of their large hats. Do American officers wear large hats, oh yes they say. Do they, I wonder, or is it only a sort of cowboy idea that the population have. Perhaps the American do wear large hats, we are so eagerly waiting to see.

What a day what a day of days, I always did say that I would end this book with the first American that came to Culoz, and to-day oh happy day yesterday and to-day, the first of September 1944. There have been six of them in the house, two of them stayed the night and then three were there besides the first three not here at Culoz but at Belley. Oh happy day, that is all that I can say oh happy day.

This is the way it happened. We go to Belley about once a month to go shopping and the bank and things like that and yesterday Thursday was the day, so we went over in a taxi, and when we got to Belley as I got out of the taxi several people said to me, Americans are here. I had heard that so often that I had pretty well given up hope and I said oh nonsense but yes they said, and then the son of the watchmaker who had been the most steadfast and violent pro-ally even in the darkest days came up to me and said the Americans are here. Really I said yes he said well I said lead me to them, all right he said they are at the hotel so we went on just as fast as we could and when we got to the hotel they tried to stop me but we said no and went in. I saw the proprietor of the hotel and I said is it true there are Americans, yes he said come on, and I followed and there we were Alice Toklas panting behind and Basket very excited and we went into a room filled with maquis and the mayor of Belley and I said in a loud voice are there any Americans here and three men stood up and they were Americans God bless them and were we pleased. We held each other's hands and we patted each other and we sat down together and I told them who we were, and they knew, I always take it for granted that people will know who I am and at the same time at the last moment I kind of doubt, but they knew of course they knew, they were lieutenant Walter E. Oleson 120th Engineers and private Edward Landry and Walter Hartze, and they belonged to the Thunderbirds and how we talked and how we patted each other in the good American way, and I had to know where they came from and where they were going and where they were born. In the last war we had come across our first American soldiers and it had been nice but nothing like this, after almost two years of not a word with America, there they were, all three of them. Then we went to look at their car the jeep, and I had expected it to be much smaller but it was quite big and they said did I want a ride and I said you bet I wanted a ride and we all climbed in and there I was riding in an American army car driven by an American soldier. Everybody was so excited.

Then we all said good-bye and we did hope to see them again, and then we went on with our shopping, then suddenly everybody got excited army trucks filled with soldiers were coming along but not Americans, this was the French army in American cars and they were happy and we were happy and tired and happy and then we saw two who looked like Americans in a car standing alone and I went over and said are you Americans and they said sure, and by that time I was confident and I said I was Gertrude Stein and did they want to come back with us and spend the night. They said well yes they thought that the war could get along without them for a few hours so they came, Alice Toklas got into the car with the driver and the colonel came with me, oh a joyous moment and we all drove home and the village was wild with excitement and they all wanted to shake the colonel's hand and at last we got into the house, and were we excited. Here were the first Americans actually in the house with us, impossible to believe that only three weeks before the Germans had been in the village still and feeling themselves masters, it was wonderful. Lieutenant Colonel William O. Perry Headquarters 47th Infantry Division and private John Schmaltz, wonderful that is all I can say about it wonderful, and I said you are going to sleep in beds where German officers slept six weeks ago, wonderful my gracious perfectly wonderful.

How we talked that night, they just brought all America to us every bit of it, they came from Colorado, lovely Colorado, I do not know Colorado but that is the way I felt about it lovely Colorado and then everybody was tired out and they gave us nice American specialties and my were we happy, we were, completely and truly happy and completely and entirely worn out with emotion. The next morning while they breakfasted we talked some more and we patted each other and then kissed each other and then they went away. Just as we were sitting down to lunch, in came four more Americans this time war correspondents, our emotions were not yet exhausted nor our capacity to talk, how we talked and talked and where they were born was music to the ears Baltimore and Washington D. C. and Detroit and Chicago, it is all music to the ears so long long long away from the names of the places where they were born. Well they have asked me to go with them to Voiron to broadcast with them to America next Sunday and I am going and the war is over and this certainly this is the last war to remember.

EPILOGUE

Write about us they all said a little sadly, and write about them
I will. They all said good-bye Gerty as the train pulled out and
then they said, well we will see you in America, and then they
said we will stop on our way back, and then they said we will see
you in California and then one said, you got to get to New York
first.

It is pretty wonderful and pretty awful to have been intimate
and friendly and proud of two American armies in France apart
only by twenty-seven years. It is wonderful and if I could live
twenty-seven more years could I see them here again. No I do not
think so, maybe in other places but not here.

In the beginning when the Americans were here we had officers
and their companion drivers. They were companion drivers, companions and drivers drivers and companions. The French revolution said, liberty brotherhood and equality, well they said it and
we are it, bless us.

Of course the driver is a little prouder when it is a colonel than
when it is a lieutenant or captain, well just a little. The first one
was Lieutenant-Colonel Peary of Colorado, he came with me in the
taxi from Belley and Miss Toklas went with Jake in the jeep, his
name was not Jake but the colonel called him Jake because he
used, while sitting in the jeep waiting, to sign his name as autograph for the French who crowded around him and wanted it, just
like a film star, so the colonel called him Jake.

Well Miss Toklas asked him if the other one was a soldier like
himself, they were our first Americans and we did not know how
to tell one from the other as on the outside they all look alike
particularly when their outside jacket is buttoned up, Miss Toklas

asked him and he said with contentment oh he is a lieutenant colonel.

After that we had lots of officers and finally I met three majors in Aix-les-Bains. I said well it's all right, but now we have had everything from a second lieutenant to a full colonel and indeed several specimens of each now I want a general. The majors at least one of them said I think I can get you one. Would you like General Patch. Would I, I said, well I guess I would. If, said he, you write him a note I am sure he would come. He gave me an old card, I had already given him my autograph on a piece of French paper money, it is hard to write on French paper money but I finally did get the habit, so I wrote the note to General Patch and of course we thought it all a joke but not at all. About ten days later, came the personal secretary of General Patch with a nice driver from Arkansas who said modestly he always drove the general, and they brought me a charming letter from the general saying he would be coming along very soon, to eat the chicken dinner I had offered him. The secretary said that the general would be coming along in about two weeks. When that time came heavy fighting began in the Vosges mountains, the general's headquarters moved away from our region, and now we are still waiting, but he surely will come, he said he would and he will.

Gradually as the joy and excitement of really having Americans here really having them here began to settle a little I began to realise that Americans converse much more than they did, American men in those other days, the days before these days did not converse. How well I remember in the last war seeing four or five of them at a table at a hotel and one man would sort of drone along monologuing about what he had or had not done and the others solemnly and quietly eating and drinking and never saying a word. And seeing the soldiers stand at a corner or be seated somewhere and there they were and minutes hours passed and they never said a word, and then one would get up and leave and the others got up and left and that was that. No this army was not like that, this army conversed, it talked it listened, and each one of them had something to say no this army was not like that other army. People do not change no they don't, when I was in America after almost thirty years of absence they asked me if I did not find Americans changed and I said no what could they change to except to be American and anyway I could have gone to school with any of them they were just like the ones I went to school with and now they are still American but they can converse and they are interesting when they talk. The older Americans always told stories that was about all there was to their talking but these don't tell stories they converse and what they say is interesting and what they hear interests them and that does make them different not really different God bless them but just the same they are not quite the same.

We did not talk about that then. We had too much to tell and they had too much to tell to spend any time conversing about conversation. What we always wanted to know was the state they came from and what they did before they came over here. One said that he was born on a race track and worked in a night club. Another was the golf champion of Mississippi, but what we wanted most was to hear them say the name of the state in which they were born and the names of the other states where they had lived.

After every war, there have only been two like that but I do not think that just to say after the other war makes it feel as it does, no I do mean after every war, it feels like that, after every war when I talk and listen to all our army, it feels like that too, the thing I like most are the names of all the states of the United States. They make music and they are poetry, you do not have to recite them all but you just say any one two three four or five of them and you will see they make music and they make poetry.

After the last war I wanted to write a long book or a poem, I never did either but I wanted to, about how Kansas differed from Iowa and Iowa from Illinois and Illinois from Ohio, and Mississippi from Louisiana and Louisiana from Tennessee and Tennessee from Kentucky, and all the rest from all the rest, it would be most exciting, because each one of them does so completely differ from all the rest including their neighbors. And when you think how ruled the lines are of the states, no natural boundaries of mountains or rivers but just ruled out with a ruler to make lines and angles and all the same each one of the states has its own character, its own accent, just like provinces in France which are so ancient. It does not take long to make one state different from another state not so very long, they are all just as American as that but they are all so different one from the other Dakota and Wyoming and Texas and Oklahoma. Well any one you like. I like them all.

After all every one is as their land is, as the climate is, as the mountains and the rivers or their oceans are as the wind and rain and snow and ice and heat and moisture is, they just are and that makes them have their way to eat their way to drink their way to act their way to think and their way to be subtle, and even if the lines of demarcation are only made with a ruler after all what is inside those right angles is different from those on the outside of those right angles, any American knows that.

It is just that, I do not know why but Arkansas touched me particularly, anything touches me particularly now that is American. There is something in this native land business and you cannot get away from it, in peace time you do not seem to notice it much particularly when you live in foreign parts but when there is a war and you are all alone and completely cut off from knowing about your country well then there it is, your native land is your native land, it certainly is.

After all the excitement of all the jeeps and all the officers and all the drivers was over we were quiet a little while and we wondered are they all gone will we not see them again, and then Culoz which is a small town but a railroad center began to have them and we began to have them.

Troop trains began to pass through the station on their way to the front.

I was coming home from a walk and an F. F. I. said to me there is a train of your compatriots standing at a siding just below, I imagine it would please you to see them, thank you I said it will and I went quickly. There they were strolling along and standing about and I said Hello to the first group and they said Hello and I said I am an American and they laughed and said so were they and how did I happen to get caught here and I told them how I had passed the war here, and they wanted to know if there was snow on the mountains in winter and there was a large group of them and I told them who I was thinking some one of them might have heard of me but lots of them had and they crowded around and we talked and we talked. It was the first time I had been with a real lot of honest to God infantry and they said they were just that. We began to talk states and they wanted to know about our life under the Germans and I told them and they were interested, and they told me about where they had been and what they thought of the people they had seen and then they wanted autographs and they gave me pieces of money to write on, and one Pole who was the most extravagant gave me a hundred franc bill to sign for him, funny that a Pole should have been the most wasteful of his money, perhaps he was only going to spend it anyway, and one of them told me that they knew about me because they study my poems along with other American poetry in the public schools and that did please me immensely it most certainly did and then I left and they left.

I came away meditating yes they were American boys but they had a poise and completely lacked the provincialism which did characterise the last American army, they talked and they listened and they had a sureness, they were quite certain of themselves, they had no doubts or uncertainties and they had not to make any explanations. The last army was rather given to explaining, oh just anything, they were given to explaining, these did not explain, they were just conversational.

Then more troop trains came along and we took apples down to them and we talked to them and they talked to us and I was getting more impressed with their being different, they knew where they were and what they were and why they were, yes they did, they had poise and not any of them was ever drunk, not a bit, it was most exciting that they were like that.

The last American army used to ask questions, why do the French people put walls around their houses what are they afraid of what do they want to hide. Why do they want to stay and work this ground when there is so much better land to find. This army does not ask questions like that, they consider that people have their habits and their ways of living, some you can get along with and others you can't, but they all are perfectly reasonable for the people who use them. That is the great change in the Americans, they are interested, they are observant, they are accustomed to various types of people and ways of being, they have plenty of curiosity, but not any criticism, that is the new army. It was all very exciting.

Then one day down at the station, it was raining, I saw three American soldiers standing, I said hello what are you doing, why we just came here, they said, to stay a few days. I laughed. Is it A. W. O. L. I said or do you call it something else now, well no they said we still call it that. And said I what are you going to do, just stay a few days they said. Come along I said, even if you are A. W. O. L. you will have to be given some tea and cake so come along. They came. One from Detroit, one little one from Tennessee, one big young one from New Jersey. We talked, it seemed somehow more like that old army, their being A. W. O. L. and deciding to stay here a few days. They came back with me, and we talked. They were interested, Tennessee said honestly he was tired of ten inch shells, he just had had enough of ten inch shells. The other two seemed to be just tired, they were not particular what they were tired of, they were just tired. We talked and then in talking to them I began to realise that men from the South seemed to be quite often men who had been orphans since they were children, the men from Tennessee and from Arkansas seemed to tend to be orphans from very young, they were members of large families and the large family once having been made, they promptly became orphans, I also began to realise that there were lots of pure American families where there were lots of brothers and sisters. The last army seven to eleven in a family was rare, but now it seemed to be quite common. Not emigrant families but pure American families. I was very much interested. And now the difference between the old army and the new began to be so real to me that I began to ask the American army about it. In the meanwhile the three A. W. O. L.s after moving into the village and then moving out and then moving in again did finally move out. They came to see us before they left, they did not say where they were going and they said it had been a pleasure to know us.

In the meanwhile, five M. P.s had come to stay in the station to watch the stuff on the trains and see that it did not get stolen, and with these we got to be very good friends, and they were the first ones with whom I began to talk about the difference between the last army and this army. Why is it, I said.

They said, yes we know we are different, and I said and how did you find it out. From what we heard about the other army, that made us know we were very different, I said there is no doubt about that, you don't drink much I said, no we don't and we save our money they said, we don't want to go home and when we get there not have any money, we want to have a thousand dollars or so at least to be able to look around and to find out what we really want to do. (Even the three A. W. O. L.s felt like that about money.) Well I explained what one used to complain of about American men was that as they grew older they did not grow more interesting, they grew duller. When I made that lecture tour in '35 to the American universities I used to say to them, now all sorts of things interest you but what will happen to you five years hence when you are working at some job will things interest you or will you just get dull. Yes said one of the soldiers yes but you see the depression made them know that a job was not all there was to it as mostly there was no job, and if there was it was any kind of job not the kind of job they had expected it to be, you would see a college man digging on the road doing anything and so we all came to find out you might just as well be interested in anything

since anyway your job might not be a job and if it was well then
it was not the kind of a job it might have been. Yes that did a lot,
they all said, it certainly did do a lot.

Yes said one of the younger ones even if you were only kids
during the depression you got to feel that way about it. Anyway
they all agreed the depression had a lot to do with it.

There is one thing in which this army is not different from that
other army that is in being generous and sweet and particularly
kind to children.

They are sweet and kind and considerate all of them, how they
do think about what you need and what will please you, they did
then that other army and they do now this army.

When our M. P.s had got settled completely in their box car I
used to go down to see them, and one day one of the mothers in the
town told me that her nine year old daughter had been praying
every single day that she might see an American soldier and she
never had and now the mother was beginning to be afraid that the
child would lose faith in prayer. I said I would take her down to see
the American soldiers and we went. Naturally they were sweet and
each one of them thought of something to give her, candies chewing gum, one of them gave her one of the U. S. badges they wear
on their caps and one gave her a medal that the Pope had blessed
in Rome and given to the American soldiers. And she was so happy,
she sang them all the old French songs, Claire de la Lune, The
Good King Dagobert and On the Bridge of Avignon.

Then as we were going home I said to her, about that chewing
gum you must chew it but be careful not to swallow it. Oh yes I
know she said. How do you know that I asked oh she said because
when there was the last war my mother was a little girl and the
American soldiers gave her chewing gum and all through this war
my mother used to tell us about it, and she gave a rapturous sigh
and said and now I have it.

More Americans came to stay at Culoz station, this time railroad workers and it became natural to have them there, natural
for them and natural for us. They used all of them to want to know

how we managed to escape the Germans and gradually with their asking and with the news that in the month of August the Gestapo had been in my apartment in Paris to look at everything, naturally I began to have what you might call a posthumous fear. I was quite frightened. All the time the Germans were here we were so busy trying to live through each day that except once in a while when something happened you did not know about being frightened, but now somehow with the American soldiers questions and hearing what had been happening to others, of course one knew it but now one had time to feel it and so I was quite frightened, now that there was nothing dangerous and the whole American army between us and danger. One is like that.

As I say we were getting used to having Americans here and they were getting used to being here.

In the early days when the American army was first passing by, in jeeps and trucks the Americans used to say to me but they do not seem to get used to us, we have been right here over a week and they get just as excited when they see us as if they had never seen us before. You do not understand, I said to them you see every time they see you it makes them know it is not a dream that it is true that the Germans are gone and that you are here that you are here and that the Germans are gone. Every time they see you it is a new proof, a new proof that it is all true really true that the Germans are really truly completely and entirely gone, gone gone.

Yes even now when it has become so natural to see them here there are moments when it is hard to believe it. Yes of course they are really here.

Just this evening I saw a nun who had come over from Aix-les-Bains to see some sisters here, she had been in a convent in Connecticut. She said to me you know I just saw some American soldiers in the square and I just had to speak to them I just had to.

That is the way we all were we just had to.

So there were more Americans here and naturally we talked a lot, and one day one of them Ernest Humphrey from Tennessee was here and a French friend was here, he had known the American army of '17 and he too was struck with the poise and the conversation of this army. He asked him lots of questions, about what Americans feel about France about the French country and about French girls and about American men, and said my friend after Humphrey left, they are different now, they are so easy to converse with, the last army was easy to get along with but this army is easy to converse with and as French people do believe that conversation is the finest part of civilisation, naturally what he said meant a great deal.

Is it, said the Frenchman, the cinema that has taught them to be such men of the world, to be sure it has not much effect on our young men he added.

I asked so many of them about it, we had long talks about it, they all agreed that the depression had a lot to do with it, it made people stay at home because they had no money to go out with, all the same said some of them that military service that they did before we came into the war had something to do with it, it kind of sobered everybody up, kind of made them feel what it was to get ready. Some of them said the radio had a lot to do with it, they got the habit of listening to information, and then the quizzes that the radio used to give kind of made them feel that it was no use just being ignorant, and then some of them said crossword puzzles had a lot to do with it.

The conclusion that one came to was that it had happened the American men had at last come to be interested and to be interesting and conversational, and it was mighty interesting to see and hear it. Naturally we exchanged books a lot, I have all kinds here and they gave me what they had, two I enjoyed immensely, Ernie Pyle, Here Is Your War, and Helen McInnes, Assignment in Brittany, some of the boys passing through on the train gave me the one and the railroad boys at Chambery gave me the other, the house here is filled with English books that I have been buying as I could through the war and other odds and ends, I was interested that they were a bit tired of detectives, I like them as much as ever but that is because I am so much older and they do like

Westerns and then they like adventures, and any longish American novel. They do not care for English ones, they say they can't seem to get into them. They also gave me a book on Head Hunters in the Solomon Islands which they all read. Well of course they did in the last war give me The Trail of the Lonesome Pine, they did not read much not those we knew. Undoubtedly the depression had a lot to do with that, a lot.

They asked me in Lyon to go and speak to the French on the radio. When I was there I saw lots of Americans on the streets but as I was in cars I could not speak to them but one evening I wandered out on foot and in a school near by I found a number of them. Naturally well just so naturally we talked, they were glad to see me and I was glad to see them, there were about thirty of them and we told each other a lot. One who had been a school-teacher in North Carolina walked home with me and we interested each other very much. He said I was quite right about the difference between the two armies, he said he had noticed it before he had left home but now he was sure. We said we would meet again but in a war it is always difficult to meet again, very often not possible. I do hope that we will meet again.

Of course one has to remember that many in fact most of these soldiers have not been home for almost two years. It is a long time a very long time.

When I got back from Lyon the Americans here in Culoz wanted to know what I had talked about in Lyon, I said I had been telling French people what Americans are and they said what are they, and I said this is what I told them and so I told them. They were interested.

I said that I had begun by saying that after all to-day, America was the oldest country in the world and the reason why was that she was the first country to enter into the twentieth century. She had her birthday of the twentieth century when the other countries were still all either in the nineteenth century or still further back in other centuries, now all the countries except Germany, are trying to be in the twentieth century, so that considering the world as twentieth century America is the oldest as she came into the twentieth century in the eighties before any other country had any idea what the twentieth century was going to be. And now what is the twentieth century that America discovered. The twentieth century is a century that found out that the cheapest articles should be made of the very best material. The nineteenth century believed that the best material should be only used in expensive objects and that cheap things should be made of cheap material. The Americans knew that if you wanted to make a lot of things that is things that will sell cheap you had to make them of the best material otherwise you could not turn them out fast enough, that is series manufacture because cheap material could not stand the strain. So America began to live in the twentieth century in the eighties with the Ford car and all the other series manufacturing.

And so America is at the present moment the oldest country in the world because she had her twentieth century birthday in the eighteen eighties, long before any other country had their twentieth century birthday.

There is one thing one has to remember about America, it had a certain difficulty in proving itself American which no other nation has ever had.

After all anybody is as their land and air is. Anybody is as the sky is low or high. Anybody is as there is wind or no wind there. That is what makes a people, makes their kind of looks, their kind of thinking, their subtlety and their stupidity, and their eating and their drinking and their language.

I was much taken with what one American soldier said when he was in England. He said we did not get along at all with the English until they finally did get it into their heads that we were not cousins, but foreigners, once they really got that, there was no more trouble.

The trouble of course is or was that by the time America became itself everybody or very nearly everybody could read and write and so the language which would naturally have changed as Latin languages changed to suit each country, French, Italian and

Spanish, Saxon countries England and Germany, Slav countries etcetera, America as everybody knew how to read and write the language instead of changing as it did in countries where nobody knew how to read and write while the language was being formed, the American language instead of changing remained English, long after the Americans in their nature their habits their feelings their pleasures and their pains had nothing to do with England.

So the only way the Americans could change their language was by choosing words which they liked better than other words, by putting words next to each other in a different way than the English way, by shoving the language around until at last now the job is done, we use the same words as the English do but the words say an entirely different thing.

Yes in that sense Americans have changed, I think of the Americans of the last war, they had their language but they were not yet in possession of it, and the children of the depression as that generation called itself it was beginning to possess its language but it was still struggling but now the job is done, the G. I. Joes have this language that is theirs, they do not have to worry about it, they dominate their language and in dominating their language which is now all theirs they have ceased to be adolescents and have become men.

When I was in America in '34 they asked me if I did not find Americans changed. I said no what could they change to, just to become more American. No I said I could have gone to school with any of them.

But all the same yes that is what they have changed to they have become more American all American, and the G. I. Joes show it and know it, God bless them.

...made, upon Danube, Ireland and Germany, but perhaps
... know how to read and write the
... in the language, and either to much
... language, not of changing. Indeed English
... America, in their minds their tongue,
... same place, and the results had nothing to do with their land,
... the old inhabitants. As a nation, and change the whole tongue
by reason only which they liked better than only, just to
by reason which is no explanation, in a different way, that the
Indian ways. For the last year the language around, but I do not know the
... have the use the same words as the English do but the words
are in entirely different thing.

Yes. In a sense the idioms have changed. I think of the first,
when, in the first a... they had their language but they were not yet
in possession of it, and the children of the depression, as that
generation called itself, it was beginning to possess its language,
but it was still struggling but now the job is done, the G. I.'s just
have this language that is theirs, they do not have to worry about
it; they dominate their language, and in dominating, they feel,
... just as which is now all theirs they has ceased to be anxious
and they become men.

When I was in America, so they asked me, so I did not know,
... more or less. I said no what could they change to, just as
... more American. So I said I could have gone to a more
... them of them.

That all the time is that is what they have changed to, they have
become more American, all American, and the G. I. does know
and now it, God bless them.